Society 3.0

Mastering the Global Transition on Our Way to
Society 3.0

Ronald van den Hoff

Published by Society 3.0 Foundation
www.society30.com

ISBN 9781496007230

Mastering the Global Transition on Our Way to

Society
3.0

PREFACE

When Ronald asked me to write this preface, I didn't give it a second thought! Ronald is, and has been, my business-associate for many years, so it's more than my pleasure to add some words to his book.

Ronald is an extremely analytical man. He is capable of absorbing mountains of information and see the cross connections others don't see. He thinks with lightening speed and is always ahead of the crowd (this makes him impatient every now and then).

I experienced his huge innovation power and his willingness to allow me to explore my own talents to translate our mutual vision into reality, creating perspective for all stakeholders in our value network.

May I take you back a couple of years? We were active in the world of meetings, conventions, and trainings by offering physical locations. However the years of economic abundance and growth are over. We see the change of our society, contaminating our markets. Ronald and I experience powerlessness from our traditional clients. They are lost and if we, as an organization, wouldn't be careful we could have been sucked into their downfall. We like the old Chinese saying "When the winds of change are blowing, some people are building shelters and others are building windmills".

So we chose the windmill option!

Our holding company is called CDEF, an abbreviation of the Spanish 'Cada Dia Es una Fiesta': everyday should be a celebration! This credo requires an attitude to start everyday with a healthy dose of playful curiosity. This, in turn, gives our stakeholders and us the opportunity to do the things we enjoy doing. And working with pleasure means following your passion and creating space for innovation.

We are looking ahead into the future on a daily basis, and discuss all development we see with our stakeholders. We analyze our mistakes openly. As a result, our 'markets' do not surprise us often. A society in transformation, failing government and politicians, and techno-logical developments result in the increasing virtual connectivity of our stakeholders. These are developments we saw already years ago. We have to look ahead; we have to offer sustainable products and services needed by the market tomorrow. The present transition of our society becomes visible by the crises we are going through. For us, however, it is a time of major opportunities.

We see people organizing themselves without organizations, get-ting stuff from each other, and creating value every day. Often, we use reciprocity as a currency. The Web has made us 'social'; people are connected locally and globally. Mobility has become a reality. Many traditional organizations run into trouble, stuck with their old strategies of cost cutting to achieve more efficiency and only grow by (often too expensive) takeovers. Traditional employees lose their security and trust in these corporations and many decide to become a self-enterprising professional or knowmad. Step by step, we see a growing demand for what we call 'coworking,' flexible office- and meeting space locations.

In 2007, we saw an opportunity for a disruptive innovation of the traditional 'corporate meeting market.' In one of the suburbs of the Dutch city of Utrecht, we startted a (silent) pilot with clients who are eager to change. We call this formula Seats2meet.com, a strong brand name as it proves by now. Good and creative thinking, Ronald!

After the pilot, it was time for the serious stuff. In the fall of 2008 we were able to get office space within walking distance of the larg-est central station in The Netherlands, above the Hoog Catharijne shopping mall. We stripped the entire place. And, we rebuilt it form scratch.

Our concept?

We created THE meeting point, the starting point, the incubation space, and the inspirational atmosphere for off- and on-line value creation. In the offline mode, the central 'lobby' is the heart of the location. We offer FREE coworking and also offer free coffee, tea and lunch. Around the corner from the lobby, we offer meeting rooms and shared office spaces. We offer our stakeholders a sophisticated online reservation system, including a property management- and yield management system through which we achieve an optimal occupancy in the right balance at an optimal 'price.' We offer freedom for clients to book, but also to cancel their space reservation with no penalties. Vitally important to us are the social connections and new value creation between people, not so much the offering of hardware (spaces). We offer the software to third parties, which made us grow within years to become the leading organization in The Netherlands in this field. We are on the brink of an international breakthrough, and we are already open (or will be shortly) in Japan, Belgium, Egypt, Spain, The UK, Germany, India, and the USA.

We think that by creating abundance by opening up the organization, seeking stakeholder connection and engagement, and by offering a serendipitous stage for new value creation by transforming stakeholders to become a 'better' professional, we have created, what we like to call, a Society 3.0 Ecosystem. The founder of this vision, Ronald, will explain and elaborate on the topic in this book.

I am convinced that this book *Society 3.0* will inspire you, as mastering the *Global Transition on our way to Society 3.0* inspires me daily! This book will assist you to achieve open innovation and explore the road to become a Society 3.0 global citizen, creating value with the organization 3.0. The book puts all development into the right context and perspective, and makes the daily dynamics of our time understandable. In the end, it makes you a better person looking ahead with confidence into our future. The glorious Society 3.0 is imminent!

Mariëlle Sijgers
Co-founder CDEF Holding BV.
December 2013.

INDEX

Genetic transfer
Stories, experiences
Life is eternal

1
A REVOLUTION IS ALWAYS THE CONCLUSION OF DECADENCE

You and I live at a juncture. There is no escaping it. The certainties of yesterday are gone. One after another, there is anew crisis. Our financial systems failed and dragged us into an economic recession of unknown proportions. The cogwheels of our society have stopped. Everywhere you look, there are traffic jams. A crisis – or more?

Our technological and social mobility are greater than ever. Our world seems to have shifted into top gear, but why are its wheels not turning? Every right-minded person must agree that our countries are being derailed structurally. Our craving for the faster, bigger, and better has crippled us. This makes me angry – angry that we do not allow ourselves to use new technologies, new ventures, new legislation; and that the political and governmental elite of Europe is redistributing, in a very inefficient way, over 50% of our Gross National Product. This is like they did 100 years ago, and with the approval of the established, larger corporations.

When we look at the European road systems, people tend to smile with pity. Getting around by car has become a contradiction. We are stuck in traffic jams more often, for a longer period of time, and this can happen at any time of day. It is such a shame after all those (alleged) efforts by our governments. The extensive road system serves as a model for the state of our nations. Some stretches of road are wide enough and properly surfaced; while other stretches show the signs of overdue maintenance. Privately owned highways, like in France, are making profits higher than ever on tolls, but going to a highway petrol station means you will have to get in a queue, and it often will cost you over one hour just to get some gas. The plentitude of traffic rules, signs, CCTV, and speed traps have given us the illusion that we have everything under control. And, it has cost us a bundle!

In China, about four thousand miles of highways are constructed annually. In The Netherlands, we reach a mere seventy kilometers. In addition, the European public transport system is not providing the answer either. This sector, which has been in an identity crisis for years between a private company and a government service, will never be able to meet the rising demand of its services. The annual traffic jam length in The Netherlands has been dropping roughly since 2010/2011, and that really worries me. It means that economic activities are slowing down more than we expected.

Looking at The Netherlands as an example, a symbol of the 'richer' Northern European countries, we have to realize that many (semi-public) organizations are no longer capable of doing what we call their 'core-activity'. Take the construction industry for example: property developers, builders, investors, and the government have shamelessly capitalized on this self-created shortage, and they have allowed the average cost for building a home to rise more than 5% each year. Housing corporations are the biggest players in this sector. They were given the task to create affordable housing for everybody. Unfortunately, they have been busy with polishing the silverware and enriching themselves. They bought hotels, residential areas abroad, islands, and cruise liners. Or, they found it necessary to invest public funds in Icelandic banks. They have wasted a lot of money – billions of Euros – and, yet, they are still called 'housing' corporations.

Our schools still educate people in an industrial way. Students are 'end products', however, they are prepared to fill jobs which no longer exist. There is an enormous mismatch. Youth unemployment throughout the European Union is staggering.

What about the healthcare system? There is no movement there either. Players bicker about capacity. They bicker about remuneration, quality, funding, overspending, and about a free market. But what about the patients? They are left totally out of the picture, and the result is waiting lists in hospitals – hospitals that go bankrupt, but are bailed out by the government. Another result can found in European elderly nursing institutions, where annually, hundreds of people die unnecessarily due to bad management and lack of leadership. We are getting older and older. The system costs of elderly care, as well as our health systems, are astronomical.

The resulting indecisiveness of our political leaders has proven to be crippling for the innovative forces of Europe. All in all, our political system has survived itself. The gap between the voter and candidate has never been so wide. First of all, we have the central European government with the European Parliament: a non-transparent, but costly layer. Then, the national government, with beneath that, a layer which is called the province, Bundesland, or county. Finally, you end up in the pit that citizens and entrepreneurs deal with the most: the local municipal government. And, in between, there are all kinds of semi-governmental organizations, or quangos (quasi non governmental organizations). All in all, they are a suffocating blanket of governmental institutions, consuming, costing, and redistributing over 60% of our Gross National Product.

1.1
A decadent society:
the end of Europe as we know it

We are living in the aftermath of the plutocracy of the previous century. We are stuck due to the dynamics around us. We do not oversee our actions throughout our social, economic, and political systems – systems dating back over 200 years. Some European countries are still rich, while others are not. Gradually, there is an awareness that our wealth is gone. There is awareness, especially among younger people, that things can and have to be organized differently. Forced innovation, or 'revolution' by the 'lower caste' is something of all ages. So, be prepared: 'all is quiet' can, under the influence of the modern social media, change in no time.

Robert Adams mentions in his book, *Decadent Societies*, five drivers leading to the decay of rich and influential societies:
- Indecisive leadership
- Extreme taxes
- Social inequality
- Extensive laws and rules
- Smugness and arrogance

Decadence in Europe? Let's do some checking:
Moving the European Assembly every two months between Brussels and Strasbourg is costing us €200 million per year as a result of an old compromise, still stubbornly in place.

The average Dutch European Parliament member earns a monthly salary of €6,000 (after taxes!), has a monthly expense account of €4,000, and is allowed to spend €21,000 on staff each month. 'Staff' may be his/her partner, child or any other broadly-permitted designee. Members have access to Mercedes limousine transportation in Strasbourg and Brussels, making an average of €1,000 per trip to their home country. On top of that, there is a royal pension arrangement the likes of which we 'paupers' can only dream of obtaining.

Construction of an 'office' (headquarters) for the European bank in Frankfurt, Germany cost €1.2 billion in 2013.

In spite of the fact that in The Netherlands there are over 1 million square meters of empty office space, the European Patent Organization is building a new office near The Hague. 'One of the largest building sites in this country, over 80,000 square meters'. For me, this tower-shaped building is giving a symbolic 'middle finger' to the European taxpayer.

In Europe, we redistribute only € 140 billion annually. That amount has to increase, crisis or not: the two European self-appointed leaders (President of the European Council and President of the European Commission) have asked for a European budget for the coming years (2014-2020) of a staggering €1 trillion(!).

Nevertheless, the European Commission (EC) annually spends more than the budget and the European countries (taxpayers) can afford: an additional € 7 billion in 2013!

According to a 'secret' investigation of the European Audit Committee, a meeting of the Euro Agency EFSA board costs taxpayers €92,000. This agency is one of the 30 European Agencies, each having between 30 and 80 board members. Together, they spend € 1.5 billion per year, and nobody has a clue how, and how appropriately, this is done.

One market? When it suits us – otherwise, forget it!

Germany is blocking any European equalization on European cross-border trucking, as the lobby of Deutsche Bahn (German railway company) is against any improvements to road transportation. And, in The Netherlands, the Secretary of State is an errand boy (or girl, in this case) for Nederlandse Spoorwegen (primary Netherlands railway operator). In 2013, she fought the introduction of foreign train companies on the Dutch infrastructure all the way to the European courts. In the UK, the postal service, Royal Mail, even after going public, doesn't have to pay the 20% VAT, a luxury commercial postal services don't have. Germany is blocking of new CO_2 regulations for cars, as its automotive industry has problems coping with these new rules. But, they are quick when they want to impose a highway tax for non-German cars

On a country level: the soccer club Real Madrid of Spain buys, in 2013, a soccer player for €100 million, despite having a debt of €600 million. The deal is financed through a Spanish Bank, which, in turn, has recently been saved by the European taxpayer for an amount of

€18 billion. And then, they 'fix' their matches, so the European tax-payer is screwed twice. In total, all Spanish soccer clubs have a debt with the banks and government tax offices of almost €5 billion. In this way, 'sport' is obviously not healthy.

France is planning to impose, unilaterally to other Europeans, an 'air tax', while Germany and Austria want a 'transit road tax'. And the Germans can't even finish building a new Berlin airport. Even after spending €5 billion (double the budget), nobody in 2013 dares to predict when it will be open. Opening a Seats2meet.com location in Greece leads to warnings from Greek entrepreneurs 'not to establish a corporation in Greece itself, because the cost are diffused, and the bureaucracy is killing any entrepreneurial initiatives'.

The smallest legal stupidity: VAT ('value added tax' or 'sales tax') on rabbit food is 6%, but for guinea pig food, the VAT is 21%. A rabbit can be eaten, where in Europe, a guinea pig is a luxury pet. Bird seed is 6%, but 'sing-bird-seed', you guessed it right, is 21%. And if you want to produce a meatball, you'd better check Commission Regulation (EC) No 1162/2009 of 30 November 2009, 'laying down transitional measures for the implementation of Regulations (EC) No 853/2004, (EC) No 854/2004 and (EC) No 882/2004 of the European Parliament and of the Council' in order to comply with this 'One European Market.'

Is any of this recognizable?

A whole generation has lost its way. And, with it, are its corporate and governmental organizations. Our Europe is showing all Adams' symptoms. The future is unstable, as politicians focus on fragmentation, damage control, and polarization.

On a European, national, and local levels there are no longer big majority governments, so real decisions are no longer taken. The traditional corporate, governmental, and political establishment does not see the reality of the changing society. They refuse to abrogate their institutions, so in order to finance this old system, taxes will go up in the coming years, decreasing the buying power of the taxpayers, thus leaving the economy in its zombie state. Greece is already forced to sell its assets, so if you want harbors, trains, and other infrastructural stuff, you know where to go.

We still refuse to realize that our growth of the past decades was based on creating debt, and that this game of debt creation is still a reality today. We also forgot that economics is a social science and not a mathematical prediction machine.

Let there be no doubt about it: I am in favor of Europe as a network of smart, collaborative, Society 3.0 citizens. That is why I am against any further development of Europe! In spite of the good intentions in the 1950s, when the European Community for Coal and Steel was founded in order to prevent future wars between Germany and France, this construct cannot be maintained in its present state.

In the coming decade, I foresee a split within Europe: countries will leave the system and form smaller cooperatives with each other, like a Scandinavian or a German-Dutch-Belgium-Luxemburg combination. Or, they could remain part of the Euro as a currency, but leave the rest of the European Community.

1.2
Europe: the zombie shopping mall

The Austrian architect Victor Gruen invented the shopping mall. The design of such a mega shopping center is aimed at disorienting visitors when they enter the complex, make them lose sight of time and reality, and this causes them to buy completely different things than they came for.

Our society is like a shopping mall, a zombie economy. It is a society of the living dead, in which all sight of reality has been lost. A society that is like an almost bankrupt store with empty or scarcely-filled shelves, with highly overpriced, inferior products and long queues in front of the tills. It is a shop with customers who are forced to drift about and is manned by impolite and indifferent staff. Naturally, it has an actual management who drive around in big cars, who live plush lives, and who drive from one old boy's network to another to compare each other's bonuses: 'We are doing so well!' Because once the economy bounces back, it is business as usual, right?

So let me ask you: do you really think that our banks are capable of repaying the 'emergency loans' our 'financial governmental leaders' lent to them? Loans with a value in Europe of over €1.6 trillion!

"Ronald, what are you worrying about?" people often ask me. "You can't change the situation." Our brains are indeed conditioned to maintain the status quo. We are comfortable in familiar lifestyles and we have learned to amble about it. We are only prepared to change if we really have to, and if there is no other option – in times of crisis, for example.

Yet, there is a crisis now!

We find ourselves in a crisis of unprecedented proportions. It is much larger than the visible financial crisis. According to the economist Tomáš Sedláček in his 2009 book *Economics of Good and Evil* we made the economic system following instead of leading the system, and we created more debt, which we mistook for economic growth.

We are at a turning point in our society, which is not obvious to everyone, but at point in which we will all go through. This juncture reminds me of Copernicus. Around the year 1500, he posited that the planets revolved around the Sun in his heliocentric theory. In doing so, he contradicted mainstay public opinion that the Earth was at the center of the Universe. But Copernicus struggled with his theory, because it undermined the fundamental values of religion, science, and the political and royal powers.

My human-centric theory revolves around the human being. In particular, the organizations revolve around the human being. This means there is a new spotlight, a new frame of reference, which means that manufacturers, service providers, or society as a whole, no longer have a leading role in the events that shape the world.

It is time to change. It is time to make a U-turn. It is time to take responsibility.

This is natural for me. I have never believed that 'nothing can be done about it'. This is why I became an entrepreneur: it is possible to do something about it! And, that goes for everybody. You can always take action and take responsibility. You have to have self-confidence, and faith in the process because it is always impossible to know what changes will lead to. Call it a chaos theory, which does not make it easy for us. We cannot predict the outcome of our changes, because each step leads to an increasingly uncertain outcome, which means that the solutions or views we are heading to are quite unpredictable. Change scares people; we prefer to hold on to (apparent) certainties, even though our social- and economic system has collapsed like a house of cards.

1.3
Stuck? Move your a..!

During a gathering at Nijenrode University in 2009, C.K. Prahalad, an unequaled management thinker in my book, showed a YouTube advertisement video, which is still popular today. Not due to the company behind the video, but due to the story told: two people are riding an escalator. The escalator suddenly stops. The two stranded people do not know what to do, except call for help and reassure each other that help is on the way.

It is an excellent metaphor for our times: it goes without saying that the economy will grow. We believe we can hitch a ride on the road well-travelled and take credit for it. We think that everything will right itself, but not essentially contribute to a responsible economic and social addition to value. In the YouTube video, the main characters first complain about others. They complain about overdue maintenance on the escalator, and that there should have been a lot more escalators. They look at each other helplessly, but do not want to admit they are powerless or wonder, 'what should we do now that the escalator is stuck?' The solution is, of course, painfully obvious. If the escalator is stuck, you start walking, you take matters into your own hands, and you mobilize yourself! Yes, change can be scary, especially if you have gotten hold of a comfortable, plush spot. Change can be painful; in particular, if you only focus on what you can lose, and don't look at what you can gain. And, there is so much to gain.

I like to look forward, and focus on this view in this book. Can tomorrow be different from today? In fact, we have to do things differently tomorrow, because if we continue in this way, The Netherlands and Europe will globally fall behind even more. What can we do, or do we have to do, to change, and how can we do that? And why is it also fun and easy to make significant changes? I speak to audiences about this on stage on a regular basis, and I thought it was time to write it down. Our world is already changing significantly, and a lot of good things are already taking place. But, if we want these efforts to blossom in the future, we will have to do some serious pruning in other areas.

Which areas are growing? If you look around you, you can see a growing group of people who are living and working differently than usual. A new world has arisen parallel to our current conventional economic reality, which is creating sustainable value every day. This added value does not always go hand in hand with monetary reward. I'm talking about a world where people work together in coalitions of opportunity and temporary collaborations. And, these people share, share, and share. In this world, it is understood that sharing is equal to multiplying. A revolution in thinking has taken place in this world. One that seems to be very profitable: in value and especially in happiness. Where can you find this world? Everywhere. The easiest road is found on the Internet. I am talking about the world of (virtual) social networks. Many think it is a strange and especially fast-paced world that flies past like a bullet train, but this is not the case for the people who have already jumped onboard...

If you watch a train drive by, it's travelling very fast, but if you are on board that train, it doesn't feel like you are travelling that swiftly. The train even seems like a haven. It is a place to reflect. A place to meet other people, start up a conversation, and listen to other people's stories.

Virtual and social networks are places on the Internet where like-minded people find each other. Outsiders often do not understand this, and thus underestimate the strength behind them. A new world literally opens up for members of these networks; there's an abun- dance of ideas, knowledge, and lots of amazing people. Money is not necessarily the leading motive here. There are almost natural universal ethics, and an unwritten constructive code of conduct is upheld. Many discussions take place in and about this world while – a very important factor for me – a lot of responsibility is shown. Social networks are popping out of the woodwork. And, like any good network, their powers are growing exponentially. After they connect, they begin to share. They share knowledge and experiences about all kinds of products and services. Ultimately, people start making stuff themselves. Or, they 'co-create' stuff with organizations they like. Publishing, access to knowledge, actually making or producing stuff, thanks to 3D printers, is not for the happy few anymore. Marx would be delighted!

Outsiders and established market players fail to notice this and are in danger of missing the boat. There are endless forms of collaboration. There are project groups and knowledge-based groups, but there are also groups with a commercial goal, who, as a group, buy or sell their (group) services. Informal social networks of connected people are our future powerhouses, or rather, power sources. Some already are! As a government, entrepreneur, service provider, or manufacturer, it is paramount to enter into this world. In principle, it's never too late, but remember that developments in social networks move faster than you are used to.

1.4
Our mission:
access is more important than possession;
the personal is global

Let's connect the world of the old system, at least the salvageable parts, with these new power centers. I think the key to new added value (that will help us recover from this crisis) lies here. We are growing in spurts into an interdependent economy, in which the old economy's scarcity is transformed into collective abundance. We need a new democratic model for this, one in which we work together in a different manner. Nouveau work. And, we accomplish this within open and non-hierarchical organizational structures.

We all join network organizations that are in harmony with their environment, which results in sustainable operational processes. New social software will make this all possible. Individuals present and organize themselves on the Internet, and, in this manner, they get in touch with like-minded people. Naturally, their communication is multilingual because the Internet can translate (literally). Groups can work together, grow organizationally, and merge. All the social software is accessible through the Internet, and is largely free of charge. No more investing in hardware and software; instead, using subscriptions in which one only pays for services used.

In this way, access becomes more important than possession, which is illustrative for society as a whole.

The people of today and tomorrow, and the more classic people of yesterday and today, depend on each other to create sustainable value. In this way, the social virtual network acts as the mobile cement of this new creation of value. People from Society 3.0 still want to work with you and each other, but no longer under the terms of employment. They work in different teams for different clients simultaneously. One moment they consult as an expert, the other they experience the role of a customer.

The added value of tomorrow arises from the mobility of people, knowledge, and energy. It arises from people who strive for the same goal from within their social network structures. The knowledge that is shared results in new knowledge, and thus, new added value. The energy and interpretation that is involved with this turns 'the plush human being' into a valued member of the new tribe again, and the tribe is part of a society that is a nice place in which to live – for everyone, anywhere in the world, at home, and far away. The personal is global. As far as I am concerned, this is the new perspective. It is a beckoning perspective.

On average, we are not that mobile anymore. On the road to that beautiful interdependent Society 3.0, you and I will have to learn to walk again. By trial and error, we will have to think about the necessary, fundamental changes in our society. We must learn to view our social problems in a new light. Generally, we will have to learn to treat each other, live together, and share together in new ways. How will you learn to love that new mobility if you remain stationary? I think that is the main question we need to ask ourselves now, at the start of the 21st century. The right answer will bring us a new Golden Age, but this one will include everybody.

1.5
Note from the author

This book is a snapshot. As we speak, or while reading this book, new social and technical developments are born. This book has an end, but the ideas of a Society 3.0 do not stop here. Recent developments, discussions, and meetings take place on the book's website:

www.Society30.com. On this platform, the content of this book is evaluated, contradicted, deepened, and extended. You will also find apps, games, and general information, in addition to the lists of all resources consulted.

To my readers, I have to apologize up front: I am aware that, in certain cultures, it is inappropriate to criticize publicly your country, government, organizations, and people. However, being Dutch, I have a tendency to be very direct, as you may have noticed while reading the first pages of this book. And, too many institutions and their people have lost their credit in my eyes, so please forgive my inclination to 'call a spade a spade'.

In a sense, this book is the result of a value network. In our Seats-2meet.com ecosystem, there are many active innovators who develop new ideas on a daily basis, and the incubation of projects and new companies prosper due to many actors, some of whom I know through social media and their stories. Actually, these people are my co-creators: their books, blog stories, and tweets inspired me. Their questions and reactions to my blog postings kept me sharp. Many experts, like Joseph Pine, John Moravec, Sebastian Olma, Cees Hoogendijk, and Marco Derksen have been interviewed by me or acted as verbal sparring partners. A production team of knowmads (or independent professionals) assisted me in the basics of publishing a book. Thank you Vincent, Elise, Anne-Kee, Ferhaan, and Albertine. And Cees Hoogendijk for the (un)grateful task of coaching me and editing the initial Dutch version of this book and Chloe Taipale with John Moravec for being our English editors.

The production team used many software products from our Cyberdigma Lab, where specialists like Wouter, Dennis, Peter and Nancy, complemented by a team of independent professionals like Eric, Horst, Jurjen, and many others, make great stuff every day.

All in all, there are many people who have added something vital to this Society 3.0 value network – too many to mention them all. There are my daily sources of inspiration: my colleagues from the Seats2meet.com organization (operating under the inspiring leadership of Linda and Marloes) and all its stakeholders, whom I meet daily, in real life, and virtually on the Web. I give special thanks to

29

my business associate, Mrs. Marielle Sijgers, with whom I have had the pleasure of a successful collaboration for more than 15 years. Finally, there is my wife, with whom I try to coach three adolescents who are permanently gaming, Facebook-ing, and What's App-ing, on their way to Society 3.0.

I wish you, my readers, inspiration, wisdom, health, and hope while reading this book!

Ronald van den Hoff @ rvandenhoff
The Netherlands,
Spring 2014.

This book was first published in Dutch in 2011. This international version was translated, updated, and partially rewritten in the summer and fall of 2013.

A revolution is always the conclusion of decadence

A picture, a thought
Sun, spirituality
Reflections of life

2
THE ZOMBIE STATE
OF OUR SOCIETY

The economy has become a zombie economy. 20th Century business is unable to grapple with the challenges of the 21st Century. Vast swathes of the economy are paralyzed and crippled: inhabited only by zombie companies. They are the economic living dead: unable to create authentic value.

– Umair Haque in his Harvard blog, 2010

The economist and Nobel Prize winner Friedrich Hayek warned us in 1941, after the Wall Street crisis of 1929 and the resulting Great Depression:

"The past instability of the market economy is the consequence of the exclusion of the most important regulator of the market mechanism, money, from itself being regulated by the market process."

Hayek thought that central bankers could never have the proper information to 'manage and control' the financial system. The world market, according to Hayek, was too complex for that. Again, that was in 1941!

In the classical economic theory, the market is always on the move to its equilibrium, the market balance. Billionaire George Soros introduces, in his 1987 book *The Alchemy of Finance*, 'reflexivity'. In this theory, Soros argues that markets are, by definition, unstable due to intangible influences not calculated in the existing economic models. By this, he means national financial supervisors are missing the real picture on the playing field of subjectively-formed bank credit ratings. These ratings, and other intangibles, have a huge impact on the behavior of other players in the economy, and cause an unpredictable imbalance.

When we realize that the global stock markets between 2002 and 2008 grew from $35 trillion to $115 trillion (a growth of over 230%), but that the expansion of the real economy only was about 50%, we see some of that 'imbalance'. Value creation by using money to make more money always has been a fundamental weakness of our financial systems. When politicians than mentally forget that this growth is not growth, but in fact more debt creation, the result is a financial system holding us collectively hostage.

Many commercial and governmental organizations thankfully used this instability, almost invisibly due the lack of transparency, to divert huge money streams and presented us, with joy, all kinds of superfluous products and services. And, we, as consumers, consumed all there was to be consumed!

In 1999, the US left the Glass-Steagall doctrine. The 'wall' between classic savings banks (earning money on the savings of people) and commercial banks (making money with money) was torn down. It was the staircase to the financial downfall. We saw money institutions become bigger and bigger. It was no longer clear who owned the money, nor where the ownership (and thus, responsibility for the debts) fell. On top of that, the Federal Reserve Bank of the US kept the interest rate low to stimulate the economy after the Internet bubble collapsed in 2002. The mountain of cheap money was supplemented by even more money from the Far East and Europe. Simply making money by putting surplus funds into a savings account wasn't earning enough interest. So, in the meantime, besides the consumer, the European pension funds, local municipalities, and other semi-governmental institutions also got access to this pile of cheap money. They also started making money with money. The casino was open!

Profits were high and losing money was only a 'theoretical' possibility for pessimists. The craving for more and more, stimulated by the well-known bonus systems, created all kinds of new financial products and new terminologies entering the boardrooms: derivatives, securitizations, leverages, off balance products, and collateralized debt obligations (called by insiders 'Chernobyl Death Obligations'). And, if there were no buyers, they were made. People could get mortgages based on their (in many cases nonexistent) income, which they could not afford: NINJA loans – no income, no jobs, and no assets.

In his book, *Liar's Poker*, former bonds salesman Michael Lewis portrays less-than-scrupulous people on Wall Street taking advantage of others' ignorance, and thus growing extremely wealthy. The insight reveals terms such as 'Big Swinging Dicks' for traders making millions, and 'blowing up a customer', or convincing a customer to purchase an investment product which ends up declining rapidly in value, so the client has to leave the marketplace.

Pine and Gilmore state strikingly in their document, *Economic Sense*, that:
"The growth of services in the past two decades has largely been in financial services. And this growth in financial services has largely come from artificially propping up a world of goods (beginning with automobiles and housing, and extending to mall development and other commercial ventures) with ever-more desperate attempts to devise financial instruments that more highly leveraged old wealth (in the form of protected classes of existing assets). Incessant as it had been, all this intangible activity created precious little tangible value. And so, eventually the bubble burst."

2.1
All good things end. Or is it business as usual?

All good things come to an end. The result of this whole financial-casino-zombie-world is that only 5% of our global volume of money is used for its original purpose: facilitation of bartering goods & services. The financial system, thus, is holding us hostage. No real growth, but a financial fiction, expressed in terms like 'Gross National Product' and other theoretical financial parameters.

"Making money and working with interest, so making money with money, without work and actually producing something tangible has been a sin throughout the ages and forbidden by law. In ancient times, misbehavior in this field was rewarded with capital punishment. You paid for it with your life. Aristotle, the Greek philosopher, warns us in his book *Politica,* which introduces the concept of 'oikonomia' that, 'usury (use of interest) as value creation is not the purpose for which money was invented... Interest is money from money, and as such, the most unnatural kind of value creation there is'. Only in the Islamic world, the idea of interest, or 'riba', is forbidden in a number of countries, although one country may be more strict than others. In short, making something out of nothing, without making a tangible product or naturally grown crop, never has been considered a good idea. According to Aristotle, it even touched the borders of the 'actual existence of mankind'."

In June 2007, the U.S. bank, Bear Stearns, reported that two of its hedge funds are in trouble. This meant the start of a complete lost of trust by everybody in the financial system. Nobody trusted anybody anymore – banks did not trust other banks, and the entire financial world ground to a halt. Companies no longer had access to credit, so they shrunk and started to lay off employees. Consumers' trust was down, so they stopped spending money. That is the endgame in a nutshell. The financial crisis leads to a global economical crisis.

According to *The Economist magazine*, this mash-up was a combination of factors. Looking back from 2013:

"With half a decade's hindsight, it is clear the crisis had multiple causes. The most obvious is the financiers themselves—especially the irrationally exuberant Anglo-Saxon sort, who claimed to have found a way to banish risk when in fact they had simply lost track of it. Central bankers and other regulators also bear blame, for it was they who tolerated this folly. The macroeconomic backdrop was important, too. The 'Great Moderation' – years of low inflation and stable growth – fostered complacency and risk-taking. A 'savings glut' in Asia pushed down global interest rates. Some research also implicates European banks, which borrowed greedily in American money markets before the crisis and used the funds to buy dodgy securities. All these factors came together to foster a surge of debt in what seemed to have become a less risky world."

In the meantime, our money is gone, and so are most of our natural resources. People are angry and blame politicians, bankers, and others who have organized this 'consumption system'. So, on one hand, people ask for more control and legislation, which is happily provided by vote-addicted politicians; on the other hand, we see bankers and other administrators saying 'trust us, we can self-regulate and make it up with you', without showing any real remorse. Amazingly, no U.S. or European bankers have been prosecuted for the roles in the economic collapse.

We have recently seen the Libor and Euribor scams, and reoccurring articles in newspapers about banks, like: "The Royal Bank of Scotland, which is owned by taxpayers and forecast to lose several billion pounds, is expected to pay its bankers an estimated £500m in bonuses this year (2013)."

No real change, but there are still lessons to be learned here!

Just take a look at some financial data, randomly chosen: during the last rescue round of European banks, The Netherlands funded €26 billion. How often can we do that? Our financial limits are in sight. Our 'national guarantees' to the IMF, the European Central Bank, and the European Emergency Fund have risen to over €200 billion. That is almost 50% of our GDP. The total European bonding is over €700 billion, mostly lent to Italy and Spain. In 2013, the European Central Bank is still buying European government bonds to keep the system afloat. By doing this, the bank gives away its political independence, as it is supporting governments who are rumbling with their national debts and inter-European financial agreements. It is clear that countries like Italy and Spain cannot pay back the short terms loans they've received from the European Central Bank in the past years. Portugal and Greece will not be able to execute all the economical reforms they promised, and, in the next couple of years, they will need more European funding. This way, the liability for national governments, and thus the European taxpayer, remains unclear. It does not show itself on the national budgets.

The 40 largest European banks still need €70 billion in funding to comply with the new Basel 3 standard. The remaining 125 midsize banks, however, still need €225 billion.

In 2013, the Fed still takes (by buying mortgage-backed loans and state bonds) $85 billion out of the market monthly in the US. The Fed's total balance has gone up 3.5 times since the beginning of the financial crisis, and is now, in the fall of 2013, $3.5 trillion. The total national debt of the United States in the fall of 2013 is already more than $16.7 trillion! However, downsizing this federal buying program creates an immediate increase in the US interest rate, causing, in turn, a dollar flow from emerging markets to the US. That drives local currencies to go down in value, making exporting to the US cheaper, thus destroying U.S. jobs. A 'Catch-22' is what they call that in American slang: no matter what you do, it is always wrong. The 2013 government shutdown and the recurring struggle concerning the debt ceiling may have tremendous consequences for the global economy in the years to come. There is no guarantee whatsoever that we will not see the meltdown of the U.S. dollar (or the Euro) in the near future.

Another example: Japan, with a national debt of over 200% of the GNP, sees its financial institutions lending over $150 billion to countries like Brazil instead of keeping the money in the domestic economy. Solitarily, from a company's point of view, this is understandable, but somewhere, this chain of money streams and expanding debts has to be broken.

The global monetary system is holding us hostage, even 5 years after the outbreak of the financial global crisis, and will be doing so for the next decade... there seems to be no way out. It is amazing that our social, financial, and political leaders still can sleep at night! The money used to pay the interest on the national debts, squeezed out of the taxpayer in order to release pressure on the banks, is destroying our economies.

The question arises: 'What do we do about it?'

I think we have to regain our civil power. First in our own countries, then on a European level. By doing so, we will have to fight the established political and economic regimes. We have to be aware that these regents are still around. Somehow, the establishment still has enough money. Write off the debts and let the shareholders of the banks bleed. Make the system less important by allowing local alternative currencies. Support local credit unions. Take away the monopolies of all the quangos, as well as the power of monopoly to create money by the national banks. I will elaborate on these topics later in this book.

On top of that, we see countries like Brazil, India, China, Turkey, and Russia claiming a larger role on the global political and economical stage, so we also have to deal with, via acceptance, a global power shift.

Look at it from the bright side: in the Chinese language, the word 'crisis' does not exist. The term is formed by a combination of two other terms: 'danger' and 'opportunity'.

危机

So, obviously, we also live in an era of opportunity. Or, as I would like to say, we are at the end of the lifecycle of the industrial era, and on the brink of something new: Society 3.0.

The road we have to take will not be an easy one. Our lives will change for a couple of decades, so we have time to adjust ourselves, but also, we do not have time to sit back and relax.

Let's have a closer look at this development.

2.2
Industrial Revolution: reinvention of society

The invention of the steam engine by Thomas Newcomen and John Calley in 1705, followed by the improved steam engine by James Watt in 1764, caused a period of turmoil throughout the world. Many processes could be done differently, and we had to rethink all known economic models. We had to reinvent society. So, we reinvented the political and governmental structures of our countries, financial structures, educational systems, and value creation processes with organizational management thinking. Money as a barter converter – a facilitator – always played a role throughout the ages, but during the Industrial Revolution, the modest use of money was thrown overboard. The establishment needed lots of money fast to industrialize the world. Afterwards, this period was called a 'revolution': the Industrial Revolution. This was a period of time in history comparable to the turmoil we experience Today. However, we invented two steam engines: the Web and the 3D printer.

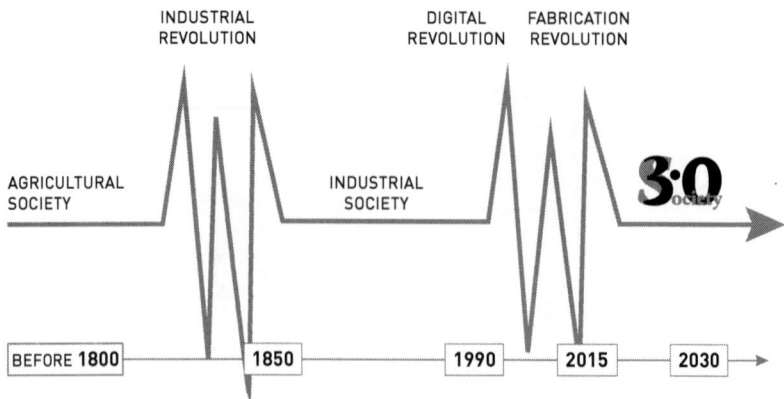

Industrialization has brought us plenty of good stuff. We reinvented society. By giving money a larger role in the process of bartering products and services, economic value could be up- scaled. Education, institutionalized as an industrial process, gave more people access to learning, and thus encouraged prosperity. By using steam engines in an efficient way, organizational management was introduced. Economic science entered a new stage. Organizational knowledge divided organizations into compartments, like human resources, sales and marketing, and purchasing, and new jobs and disciplines were developed. In Western Europe, political structures for better democracies were introduced. Unions, suffragettes claiming women's emancipation (and thus, voting rights), and political parties: they all demanded a portion of the prosperity cake.

This whole process didn't go flawlessly. Industrialization also created the possibility to fight mechanized global wars with millions of casualties, and created economic bubbles – and financial crises, as well. The Amercian Wall Street crash of 1929, also known as Black Tuesday, was a financial crisis like never seen before, and created a 10-year depression throughout the Western world. It was only concluded when the economy transformed into a war industry, with World War II as its 'marketplace'.

We are presently in the middle of our own revolution. Society is transferring to a new era, which I have called Society 3.0. So, it is up the global Society 3.0 citizen to reinvent our social and economic systems. That is where the opportunity lies – an opportunity to get us out of this turmoil. It is not an easy journey, as the establishment is resisting; however, their inability to show us the way out and guide us to this new era shows that the industrial system, with its political and economic components, is really at its end.

Every now and then, you hear politicians say, 'in two years things will be better!' Or, 'I already see some bright spot on the horizon!' Don't be fooled; this transition period will last at least another 15 to 20 years, if not more.

We will have to face more crises. More civil wars. More social unrest. People feel the fear of the establishment, and people feel the impotence of our 'leaders'. As hard as China is struggling to keep its rising middle class happy in order to avoid a collision between 'old and new', in Europe, the threat is there, too: do you think that in countries where youth unemployment is over 50%, this young generation of desperate people will stay at home because some politician saw 'the light at the end of the tunnel?' No way – they will start a fight for their share in the declining, but still remaining, prosperity, and they will refuse to pay for all the financial mishaps of our time.

In the next stories, I will look at the foundations of the value creation elements of industrial society, after which we can have a look how these basic principles will have to change in order to grab the opportunities presented by Society 3.0.

2.3
An organization is a simple pyramid

Organizations always consist of people making or doing something other people wish to pay for because paying is simpler than making or doing it yourself. Or, it is impossible to make it yourself, due to a lack of certain production tools.

Organizations organize processes, coordinate the people and means, and communicate to make those products and services, otherwise they do not work. Organizations always have a structure and hierarchy. There is a boss or a manager. A manager knows more than his workers, or has more capabilities than someone else. That is the theory. Becoming a boss is also possible when you know people higher up in the hierarchy, or have lots of money, and thus claim ownership.

In the early days of our industrial society, all those economic value creation activities took place at one physical location. Work was done at the factory in its offices. Learning was done at school or at the university. That was efficient 'efficient' being the key word of the industrial era), as machines, buildings, workers, managers, and teachers were close to each other. The board could thus keep an eye on them.

Every organization knows limitations in time, people, and means: knowledge, money, factory size, production capacity, commodities, and so on. The knowledge of these limitations: scarcity connected with decision-making has become the foundation for our economic science, however, many people nowadays wonder whether 'science' is the right term.

Nobel laureate Ronald Coase, who recently passed away at the age of 102 years old, wrote about the limitations of industrial organizational structures in his 1937 book, *The Nature of the Firm*. The term 'Coase Ceiling' is named after him: the moment at which the organization collapses under its own weight. Put differently, it is the point at which a new employee adds less value than the work his presence creates for other employees (are you thinking yet of all these overhead corporate offices? I am!). Reaching a Coase Ceiling means that additional organizational growth is costing more than the value added, causing the organization to grow itself to death.

2.4
Grow to grow, until you no longer fit reality! But who really cares?

It may sound strange, but growth was, for many organizations, a way of life. Managers fought to postpone the reaching of their Coase Ceiling, or to avoid necessary changes. We even created a word for this unlimited growth: 'globalization'. It was, often, not natural growth, but growth from 'buying' market shares. The newly-bought corporations were quickly integrated in the existing organizations, and the hunt for new takeovers started all over again, with, as a management mantra, 'the takeover is justified by the advantages of the increased efficiency, with a higher profit potential as a result'.

It works alright...
If the transaction is done from the existing cashflow.
If the integration is a smooth proces.
If the synergy advantages are a reality and not wishful thinking.
If the Super Mario leader, the loner at the top, the Wizard of Oz,
can keep the whole under control.
If the markets keeps on growing.

But, if the takeovers are financed with borrowed money, the integration is less simple than assumed, and the short-term shareholder thinking, stimulated by big management bonuses, prevails, and the Coase Ceiling arrives soon!

Organizations start to produce 'commodities', where all goods or services look alike, added value disappears quickly, and creativity and innovation are killed. Marketers stumble upon each other with slogans like 'new' or 'improved', and have no other option than to start competing on the price.

Organizations have become so big that operational costs are out of control, which signals the entrance for more controllers, hatched managers, reorganizations, and lay offs. Corporation headquarters are far away from the battle zone, and they create their own bureaucracies.

"Organizations no longer fit reality," states the management thinker Peter Drucker in his *Theory of the Business* (1994) to describe organizations going through a Coase Ceiling. One could say that shareholders, seeing this happening, should or could intervene. However, over the past decades, the role of these commercial organizational owners, has changed. As a result, the roles of the board of directors and management of these organizations also has changed.

In the old days, shareholders, often being the management or direct representatives of the owner-families, may have been dictatorial or autocratic, but they had a direct relationship with the company. Think about the beer brewery Heineken, in which the family still plays an active role. If a company like this went under, these people would lose their assets, money, and social respect. In short, they are playing a game with their own future at stake. That deserves a premium, like a decent dividend.

Over the past decades, however, the distance between the shareholder and the organization has increased enormously. Shareholders play with the stock market, and put their money into index portfolios. When a company in Pakistan, China, or Vietnam goes under or is closed down, the shareholder, or better known as the investor, does not even notice. His shares are in exotic funds, like 'Far East Accelerator Futures of The Global Green Speedy Growth Fund'. As investors, the shareholders keep a safe distance from the organization, itself, and delegate all responsibilities to portfolio managers, business banks, supervisors, and management.

But this investor wants an ever-increasing, short-term return on investment, with less risk and involvement. But wait – that is what portfolio managers, business banks, supervisors, and management also want, although these individual interests may conflict with the interest of other stakeholders, like the employees.

Also, a smaller investor can be a nuisance. Organizations have created all kind of barriers to deny these investors any influence. There are shares without votes, and shares getting more profit than others. Some shares are placed at more 'friendly' administrative offices than others. All in all, the distance between the average shareholder and organization has become greater and greater.

2.5
Quangos

Besides commercial organizations, the industrial era has rewarded us with another group of organizations. They are part of the governmental structure, although they are not always 'managed' by that government.

While we're groaning under the strain of powerless governments and politicians, there are a number of 'independent official bodies with administrative duties' operating in the twilight zone between the democratically elected and appointed government, its politicians, and society.

These bodies operate inefficiently in a government-created position of monopoly, and they don't have to justify their actions, except to their peers. In The Netherlands alone, there are 3,000 of those dim and non-transparent organizations: pension funds, housing corporations, power companies, telecommunications businesses, trading organizations, commodity boards, chambers of commerce, boards of public works, employers' organizations, trade unions, the Social Economic Counsel, cable companies (infrastructure for television and Internet) as well as many supervisory and 'levying organizations', such as the Bureau of Musical Copyright.

These organizations, known as Quangos (quasi-autonomous non-governmental organizations) are good at one thing: raising the price of 'servic' when they have a budget deficit. The consumer will, naturally, pay for it – he has no choice, and he should not dare complain!
Every country has its own system of quangos. These organizations are filled to the brim with regents, who shamelessly protect their own

position and mainly enrich themselves. The system is completely in-effective.

They behave as casino capitalists, losing other people's money, but most of them are still there. Quangos block off every social innovation. They have the money, the legislation, and the politicians on their side.

Within Europe, there is only one way out of the crisis: get rid of all these superfluous organizations. The organizational costs of these quangos run up to 10% to 15% of our GDP, so eliminating them would give us a European economic financial nudge, by rough estimation, of €1 trillion per year!

2.6
A society in transition:
disruptions, our Armageddon, or...?
We don't live in an era of changes, we are living in a changing era.
　　　　　　　　　　　　　　　　– Professor Jan Rotmans.

The Golden Age has long since passed. Globally, Europe doesn't play the big role we think we do. But the establishment, with its limited power for self-reflection, still thinks it's doing a great job! This complacency, typical for the decadence in Europe, is one of the main reasons for our social and economic decline.

According to thought leader and social economist Carlota Perez in a 2013 interview, should our governments remain stuck in old fashioned, neo-liberal thinking, which is blocking a quick transition, "it will become even more painful; all kinds of capabilities are superfluous; whole regions will be destroyed economically; unemployment rises quickly; and, in general terms, the rich get richer and the poor get poorer."

We are stuck, hostages within our traditional systems. It is the transition phase, our own could-be-revolution, which creates uncertainty. The big question is, are we collaborating on our way to Society 3.0, or are we creating our temporary Armageddon, where the Old fights the New?

I see themes like royalties and loopholes in the laws, power hungry executives, and the new generation of Internet users starting mercilessly to get in each other's way. This is going sour very, very quickly. This is great and a pity at the same time; we only learn what our new boundaries are when we cross them.

In the meantime – the 'inter(net)bellum' period – one can really slam into these old walls. In the US, people are mercilessly prosecuted if their children have downloaded a song, which is for sale on an eight-dollar CD. The punitive claims range from $8,000 to $30,000. In The Netherlands, these amounts, so far, are limited from €250 to a mere €1,500. Who are the victims of this issue? Naïve music fans who scour the Internet. Or worse, the chronically ill who publish 'copyrighted material' about their disease. Debt collectors and other obscure firms blow their own trumpet in the hopes of a quick settlement. In fact, they are playing detective, prosecutor, and judge at the same time.

Keep the cultural differences in mind. While we are worrying about copyright in the West, a different wind is blowing through China. In China, copyright means 'the right to copy', and it is done on a large scale. It is seen as a mark of respect to 'copy the masters!' It is leading to renewed business models there. The traditional Chinese music and movie industry simply gives everything away for nothing and earns money through Google ads. What is not (yet) possible in the West is being done in China. Many performances are sponsored by companies that want to reach consumers via free concert tickets. In other words, the artist lives off the sponsorship deals.

The rise of the disruptive low cost carriers like Blue Air, Southwest Airlines, Ryanair, and EasyJet has turned the airline industry upside down. With a 40% market share on internal European flights, they have become sizable players. The entire sales system of these parties runs through the Web, leaving the traditional middlemen, such as travel agents, on the sidelines. Holding meetings at locations such as Seats2meet.com will be the deathblow for the conference rooms in hotels. In addition, hotels have formidable competition from couch surfing: staying over, free of charge, at the home of somebody you have met via the social Web. Through Couchsurfing.com, there are over 20,000 free beds available in The Netherlands alone. Couchsurfing is presently the largest hotelchain in the world without owning and/or operating one single hotel. Via the site Airbnb.com, you can even rent apartments, floors, and suites, with prices ranging from $50 to $500 per night.

Our legislators don't know what to make of it – are they commercial bed and breakfast and camping ventures, or aren't they not? The establishment complains and government officials start fining expeditions. Useless. There is a complete lack of oversight, and that's all right with me. It is an unstoppable market development. In fact, there is an ever-widening road opening up to Society 3.0!

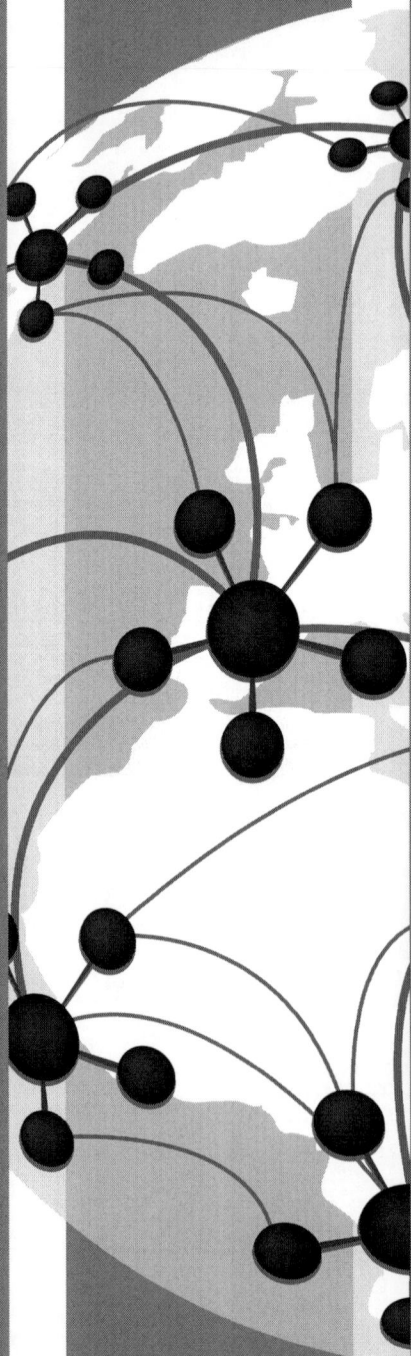

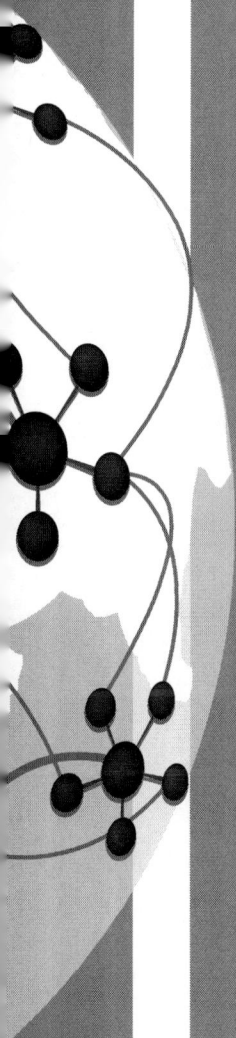

Coral is the color of personal mastery: authentic, autonomous and connected to many. The color of a value network. The value system of a global citizen. The color of Society 3.0.

3
A REVOLUTION IS BORN

In the past you were what you owned. Now you are what you share.
— Charles Leadbeater

After my first experience on the Internet, I saw the enormous opportunities it had to offer. I developed an unremitting fascination with this new world. The Internet granted me access to unexpected sources of information. After growing up with the telephone and fax, I already found email to be brilliant. We set up one of the first Dutch companies with its own webmaster, a college dropout who did not learn much at school, but all the more with us. He stuck around after his traineeship with us, and he is now known as one of the leading Web developers in his league.

I literally subscribe to all developments of the Internet. I scan a couple of hundred weblogs daily; am active on Twitter and several other social networks, like Google+, Facebook, and LinkedIn; but also use YouTube, SlideShare, Netvibes, and more. I met my current wife through a dating site. As an Internet entrepreneur and trend strategist, I gradually became a much sought-after speaker, and I do consulting work for the government and private sectors. We integrated the Internet into our business processes in such a way that we shielded ourselves from the current economic crisis and never stopped growing. Thus, it helped us to make (always difficult) decisions when saying goodbye to old formulas and business units.

Our growth is invariably the strongest in the formulas wherein the Internet is optimally connected to the physical world. A prime example is how our new meeting and coworking concept, Seats2meet.com, has shown excellent growth due to a practical and inexpensive social media strategy. It has caused a change in our business scheme: we have become, rather than a provider of physical meeting spaces, a global player in offering serendipitous software systems that connect places and people.

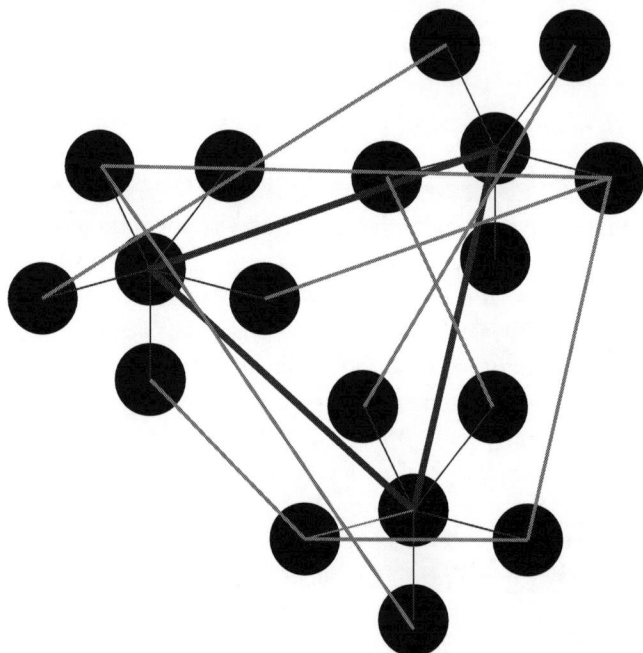

The Internet has changed my life dramatically – and not just mine. One and a half billion people are active on the Web every day. That is a quarter of the world's population. Second only to Canada, The Netherlands has the highest Internet user density in the world. After printing, the music industry, movies, radio, and television, the Internet has become a real mass medium. The main difference from its predecessors is that it really is a medium for the masses. The Internet has brought about a social upheaval. The circumstances are evident: huge technological developments on one hand, and a financial-economic crisis of confidence on the other. The Web connects our computers together, and thus, also our information. In addition, it connects people anywhere in the world. Certainly, now that it is becoming more mobile, the Internet is paving the way to Society 3.0.

3.1
The start: Web 1.0

The human being is a social animal. For our wellbeing, we need other people. Otherwise, we become lonely and die. As human beings, we are also rational animals. We are aware of our own identity and of our own ego. Being social and developing an ego can conflict. Do your own needs take precedence, or do you serve your fellow man first? And, does your own group then go first? If they do something you do not agree with, do you leave the group, or do you go with the flow? Politically, this is an interesting question, too. What do you stand for? These are questions we (should) ask ourselves every day, and they always lead to alternative issues.

In the previous century, you were a part of a group and a part of its sectional interests. It was not always pleasant, or a place in which you could get something off your mind, but there was a basic principle, a framework, and therefore, there was a reference. The paradigm was clear. We knew many groups. We called this 'pillarization' (or compartmentalization along socio-political lines). You belonged to a certain religion or philosophy of life. The social network this was a part of determined where you lived, where you went to school, where you played sports, where you went to church, which broadcasting corporation you watched, which newspapers you read, which political parties you were expected to adhere to, where you went to work, do your shopping, and even whom you married. In the 1960s, we started to remove these traditional religious and socio-political barriers. Our increasing prosperity gave us the emancipated consumer on one hand, and the start of the search for a new identity on the other. 'Who am I?' and 'What do I want from this life?' were the questions that presented themselves more strongly than before. Recently, these questions have been supplemented with concerns for the future of our society, because it has become quite clear that politicians, the government, and the business community, as systems, are not the omniscient and reliable partners we had hoped for, even though we are connected to these systems in one way or another.

This process of awakening has been going on for some time, but gained momentum due to of the Internet. The Internet democratizes. To me, 'WWW' does not only stand for World Wide Web, but it is also an acronym for Where to buy, What & When. The consumer is emancipating him- or herself and is taken for less of a ride by sellers. More and more people are reading fewer newspapers and watching less television; they surf the Internet a lot more (especially on tablets). So, in order to stay in touch with the consumer, organizations (and also private citizens) started to post information on the Web, statically, like a digital sign. These signs grew at such a rate that we needed search engines to help find what we were looking for. Is there anyone who has never heard of Google? The posting and retrieving of information is defined as Web 1.0, the information-based Web.

3.2
Web 1.0 becomes Web 2.0, the social Web

Very quickly, and almost invisibly, a new world emerged. And, by this, I mean a virtual world. It was partly due to increasing bandwidth (speed) and new software applications, and that more people were using the Internet to do things together, such as talk to each other and engage in something together. Interaction and conversations are brought about between like-minded people, and between organizations and stakeholders. This is more of an interactive Internet, which we call Web 2.0, or the social Web. In mid-2013, three quarters of the European population is active, in some manner, in social media. Organizations are starting to dangle their feet in it. It's funny to notice that people who meet virtually end up meeting in person as well. People seek each other out at all kinds of meetups, Tweetups, Twitterazzi pow-wows, open coffees, and other similar offline events. We see new companies who have responded to this by lending support to the proposition that wonders if these meetings might lead to profound relationships. That is quite different from the meat inspections on current dating sites.

Knowmads, the self-enterprising professionals, in particular have an above average need to meet others in person; distances are not so great in Europe. These meetups are taking place on a massive scale. In this way, some of the Knowmads will feel like 'colleagues' in the large network-organizations. On our Seats2meet.com events platform in The Netherlands alone, more than 10,000 physical meetings, attended by over half a million people, are being organized annually. Meetings are shared live with the outside world by usage of what we call 'second screens', dashboards that offer live streaming of events on the Web, curate Twitter streams on particular event topics, and more. We call these meetings '3rd Space Events', and often there are more people from all over the world following these events from a distance than there are actual physical audience numbers inside the meeting room or convention hall.

So, **Web 2.0** is mainly about being social, doing things together, with the Internet serving as the connecting information and communication structure.

Being and working together in this way helps us address the questions, "what do I stand for, and what is my place in this world?" This is how the Internet facilitated a new social playing field parallel to the economic crisis. Is this the new paradigm? I prefer to call it cyberdigm, a dynamic paradigm that appeals to people as self-managing and meaningful beings.

3.3
Communicative self-steering

A paradigm is a line-up of convictions, values, and policies that are shared by members of a group or society: the playing field that we – our customers, suppliers, co-workers, and ourselves – move around in. 'Paradigm' is becoming an old-fashioned word. We tend to use it negatively most of the time, like in the context of a 'management paradigm'. In a paradigm, the players on the playing field, wittingly and unwittingly, self-impose limitations. These limitations characterize our old, Western economic thought processes.

Arnold Cornelis introduced the concept of the cyberdigm in his book, *Feelings Logic*. In this book, he says, "A human being finds happiness to the extent in which he directs his own learning processes, while listening to his feelings. Every person will find the question to what gives meaning at the final destination of the development of the life program."

According to Cornelis, as a society, we are ready to leave the social regulation system and are on our way towards a new level of stability in 'communicative self-management'. Communication has opened up a world with new, unprecedented possibilities. The people of the social regulation system – a certain paradigm – are discovering that they need each other, depend on each other, and are willing to learn, gain new insights, and create new value. I visualize the cyberdigm as a three-dimensional cluster of paradigms, containing all sorts of players at different times on many playing fields. There are no boundaries; once the game comes to a halt on the one field, the players step onto another field with (perhaps) different parties, rules, and procedures. The players regulate themselves. The paradigm shift is their second nature. The Internet, and Web 2.0, in particular, offer opportunities to live and work from within the new cyberdigm, and in doing so, accelerate the process towards communicative self-steering.

"The principal idea in the creation of this human cyberdigm is the accessibility and the growing use of social media, where information and knowledge is made available, that can be easily accessed by everybody – free from time and space. This is one movement. A second movement is when people create personal knowledge, add to it, and make it available by sharing their experiences, stories for others. Often free of charge," says Gonnie Joosten (Joosten Consultants), a senior coach in the Seats2meet.com ecosystem.

The cyberdigm contains an unprecedented level of transparency; everybody is fully visible. One can easily assume a social or professional brand experience. However, users will unmask this experience when the offered knowledge, skills, and integrity of the actual business transaction do not meet the image of what they believe should be offered. Every statement you make about yourself will result in dozens being made by others through logical connections between pieces of information. In principle, information is verified very well in this manner because the opinions of many are used instead of one expert, which is why authenticity is one of the most important values when operating within social media. I find this to be a nice side effect.

In his book, *Civilizing Process*, Norbert Elias describes the increasing complexity of our society and the appeal that this complexity makes to people. Elias published his theories in the Interbellum (the period between the end of World War I and the beginning of World War II), a turbulent era. He believed there is a parallel between the increasing complexity of society and the increase in and condensing of networks in which people belong. He states that networks will interweave emphatically, both nationally and internationally. And, these networks will connect between themselves, too. Elias calls this 'figuration', and these groups have an external, as well as internal, dynamic. Elias named the external dynamic the socio-genesis: an increasing number of connected networks create a greater cohesion of everything with everything. The internal dynamic, the psycho-genesis, concerns self-analysis and self-knowledge, and refers to the place in a network in which one is assigned.

Suppose you invite someone to enter a community you belong to personally, like Seats2meet.com or Twitter. The unique value that person will add, such as knowledge, authenticity, skills, or a membership to other networks or communities, for example, will give that person and you a (new) position in that network.

Taking part in these configurations requires the individual learning capacity to occupy a place from within. This person requires adaptability, creativity, and self-knowledge. Self-knowledge leads to development of one's own autonomy, and this leads to self-management. This is when people follow the road to authenticity: the capacity to freely chose from within what information, or which community, to connect with (or not).
(From: W. Veenbaas/P. Weisfelt: *Personal Leadership*)

Consciously and unconsciously, we are a part of a decision-making process, the area of tension between being alone and being together, the individual and the group, and something existential as 'wanting to belong, but not wanting to go into'. Autonomy development in particular – increasing discovery from within of what we stand for – gives people relative freedom again in their restraints within the configurations, and, with that, their choice of group to connect with for a short or long period of time.

All of this has at least two big consequences:
1. The value of information will change according to the global availability of it, and the growth of the population that is accessing it. It is that availability and accessibility of information that offers everyone the opportunity to tell their own story, through a variety of sources. By sharing a story on the Web, the dialogue with like-minded people is advanced, resulting in the continuing increase of joint knowledge and information. This cyberdigm is not limited to the local sources and people who experience it. Imagine I am looking for someone who has

specific knowledge about a topic or theme. The possibilities offered by Web 2.0 are not bound to the restraints of space and time. This changes the value of my knowledge, and it becomes easier to access information from somebody else. I can share knowledge, organize, and mobilize across borders. In other words, knowledge acquired locally is no longer cheaper than knowledge that is acquired remotely. The question is whether we need to pay much for knowledge at all.

2. The notion of the consumer does not fulfill its definition any more. Consumption implies passivity. Every stakeholder of a product or service is challenged to be more proactive. The possibility of unlimited sharing of knowledge is the catalyst that changes the needs and demands of consumers. After all, we can pore over the service experiences of previous consumers and decide if we want different or better future experiences. In fact, every consumer is able to pose his unique question or demand, and is able to keep searching until a supplier is found that can meet these demands. And, what do the suppliers who missed out do? The business-to-business and business-to-consumer concepts will be a thing of the past. We are moving towards the concept of business-to-user. All this co-creation will turn the consumer into a producing consumer: a prosumer.

3.4
Organizing without organizations and the introduction of social capital

Sharing work, creating value with each other, undertaking endeavors together, helping others through social networks on the Internet: We are more than capable of organizing and self-managing these things without the help from a traditional organization. This idea has taken such flight that organizations who do not adapt and make sure they are connected properly will loose their right to existence and will disappear.

In his book, *Here Comes Everybody*, Clay Shirky identifies various stages of 'organizing without organizations'. He explains that every next step represents a more intense form of working together:
1. Sharing
2. Exchanging experiences
3. Co-creating and collective action

Collaboration is a form of mutual reward. Money is hardly (or even not at all) an issue in these new forms of collaboration. And, that is quite special – working together, organizing together, and creating value together without money changing hands. The old body of thought would call this 'free of charge'. I call it reciprocity. People help each other in exchange for recognition, status, welfare, or just for the fun of it. Call it non-tangible value, intangibles, or social capital.

Clay Shirky talks about "Cognitive Surplus: The Great Spare-Time Revolution": instead of wasting time on one-sided consumerist activities like watching television, people prefer to spend their time providing significant contributions to their (virtual) social tribe.

Traditional organizations are only able to give things away, and then they're literally gone. In a connected society, or with a connected individual, something that is given is always returned. Only you do not know exactly where, when, or in what shape. This is asynchronous reciprocity. I believe social capital is the essential new element in our economic thinking about creating value in Society 3.0.

3.5
(Web) collaboration

Sharing has become a common phenomenon that has long surpassed the 'nerd' stage.

Web content is shared in a way and with a volume we have never seen before. Our grandparents watch YouTube or Vimeo videos as much as we do. We share photographs on Flickr, important news items on Digg, and interesting websites on Diigo. With just a few mouse clicks, we place our stuff in an endless display.

As said, this sharing is being done on an enormous scale: more than 1 billion unique users visit YouTube each month, and daily, close to 1.5 million photographs are uploaded to Flickr. Do you think that is a lot? Instagram claims they have over 40 million photo uploads per day!

Blog sites – hundreds of millions of them – tell personal stories, share experiences, or express opinions of their bloggers. Corporate blogs, weblogs where companies post their stories, have become an indispensable element in the branding of a company or organization.

"Word of mouth is now a public conversation carried in blog comments and customer reviews... "

– Chris Anderson

We also have become very busy in exchanging experiences. Review sites for customers invite the 'hands-on' experts; they review a wide range of products, services, and the organizations that provide them. In the travel sector, Tripadvisor is one of the larger ones. With over 100 million reviews, you can safely say there is no touristic destination, hotel, or attraction in the world that has not yet been reviewed. In this way, the range of holidays offered is incredibly transparent. In fact, you can have a customized travel guide made for your holiday, containing tips from like-minded travelers about interesting locations, exhibitions, and other events. The sales brochure of a hotel is no longer decisive for making a booking, but the experiences of previous guests are – especially if those travelers are a little bit like yourself: peers.

These review sites, along with the so-called comparison sites, will ensure that every product, service, company, organization, or independent professional will have an essential review. We learned that sharing experiences is good for a thorough decision-making process.

On the next level of cooperation, we construct new knowledge and information. We share this, often for free, with the rest of the world. Wikipedia is a prime example of this: a huge source of knowledge on millions of topics. To date, the quality is quite good, because usually, a group of diverse users conscientiously enrich the wiki pages. There are people who are writing Twitter novels together. And, think of software like Google Docs, which enables people to create documents, spreadsheets, or presentations together. Organizations are building their own wikis. In this way, their own knowledge is literally 'up in the air', and can be used by colleagues wherever they are. This is how organizations can become increasingly self-developed.

When knowledge and information are shared, there arises a new sort of 'power to the people'.

On sites like the Chinese Teambuy.com, or myfab.com in Europe, you can order goods collectively. The group has so much buying power that they make deals with manufacturers directly, thus ignoring the entire intermediate layer of the old value chain. In the US, there is 1bog.org for the purchasing of solar panels. Sites like this offer discounts of up to 70%. Groupon.com works slightly differently. In its network, Groupon has so many members in a city or region that they can almost guarantee sales to a manufacturer or retailer, if said manufacturer or store makes a great offer. In 2011, Groupon turned down a $6 billion acquisition bid by Google, because the company simply believes it is worth a lot more. Well, in the new world, lifecycles are short, and a valuation like this disappeared quickly, as the concept was easily copied.

Connecting with other people is always the first step for sharing, collective buying, and collaboration. Connectivity creates a collective intelligence, according to professor Henri Jenkins. And, connected we are! In the fall of 2013, Facebook had over 1.1 billion registered users. In other countries, you will find Orkut (in Brazil) or RenRen (in China). Who doesn't know LinkedIn, Twitter, or Google+? These major properties have taken over many 'smaller' and more specialized social network services, like YouTube (for video sharing) or Flickr (for photo sharing).

People are sharing their lives with each other by posting photographs, movies, stories, and all their personal preferences. And, in the process, they find new friends with similar tastes. These friends become small networks, and networks become constellations.

By using the Web these groups are starting to share their abundance (of physical goods, time, spaces) in order to create new economic value; we see the emergence of the interdependent economy, also called the "sharing" or "collaborative" economy, as the base of the economic order in Society 3.0.

So, now that we know how it all started, let's see where it will lead us.

3.6
Social cohesion, the Web, and 3D printing contribute to a groundswell

It seems as if the essence of the terms paradigm and the new cyberdigm lies in the human need for belonging. The Internet accommodates an ever-increasing number of online communities, and this has very large consequences. As it happens, this does not limit itself to 'belonging'; in all these virtual social networks, more people are doing business with each other in their own way.

In other words, we are organizing without formal organizations. For me, this is the real revolution. By saying this, I also imply that this revolution means the end of the organization as we know it. Most of the organizations will become superfluous.

The American market research company Forrester Research calls this phenomena a groundswell: "A groundswell is a social trend in which people use technologies to get the things they need from each other, rather than from traditional institutions like corporations and/ or government..."

On the surface of the sea, everything seems calm, but many miles offshore, out of sight, and at the bottom of the sea, there are huge rumblings. Big shifts are taking place. Of course, you may think that it will not come to that, or that it will sort itself out, that Web 2.0 and Web 3.0 are more hype, but nothing could be further from the truth. The simple fact that the Internet enables people to organize without organizations, and that people are actually doing that, will turn out to be the final blow for our traditional economic and the ruling establishment's organizational thinking, based on 1920's industrial psychology..

The job as we know it will be gone. The way we've educated people means that most traditional employees will not be ready for Society 3.0-type organizations. Many jobs are going to the dustbin.

Dear manager: your self-managing stakeholders no longer require your organization to get what they want. People can and will use a disruptive bypass around your institution. This is thanks to the virtual social networks, the tribes of the Internet. We can belong to a tribe again, find like-minded people, create collective intelligence in a fast changing environment, and start sharing the abundance. Communicating digitally is fast and accessible. We are bound 24/7; we find ourselves in a state of permanent connectivity.

Thinking about 3D printing, we only need designs for everything from cups to houses, and the costs of having these products printed on site will be cheaper than your current supply-chain. 3D printing is becoming readily available to people with no equipment of their own. Service providers that print objects on demand, such as Shapeways, show there will be a new breed of companies on the horizon.

However, having many digital friends, connections, and a 3D printer does not equal having a lot of value automatically...

3.7
From network connections to value networks

Social networking starts with people connecting with others, the process of which I have labeled 'scoring friends'. Also, if possible, people connect with like-minded people. The Dutch network 'Ambtenaar 2.0', consisting of thousands of civil servants, is such a network. In this case, we talk about communities of interest.

When information and experiences are shared between people in the broadest sense of the term, like within the social network LinkedIn and its many groups, it is a matter of developing communities of practice.

These networks are especially useful for outsiders - if I'm looking for an HR manager, I'll find about 15,000 of them in LinkedIn groups. There will have to be a suitable candidate among them! This congeniality also often limits these groups. Because members 'stick around', there is not enough renewal, and the community does not evolve.

Yet, this development is the prelude to a new form of creating economic value: some call this a community of purpose if, besides creating value with social capital, something is actually produced that represents 'old money' value.

The old industrial society and the new Society 3.0 can find each other in the next phase of these communities of purpose if they grow in serious numbers and form new value networks, which, in turn, will form a new economic playing field.

We see swarms of people, with a collective intelligence, where the power of the network is stronger than the sum of the parts. The development of these networks will have a natural turnover: people will enter it and will leave as well. Yet, this value network is intrinsically stable. In fact, it evolves – a natural condition for the survival of a species. You can read more on this in the next chapter.

The Dutch social media expert Marco Derksen of Marketingfacts. nl visualizes and describes this social-economical development as:

"The rise of digital media (that is increasingly connected to each other via the Internet) makes the distance between institutes and individuals continually smaller. We come from the 1.0-era where institutes spread their message through traditional media to their audience (send), in which case the power lies with the institutes. In the 2.0-era individuals have more options to share their own message with their environment (dialogue) as a result of which the influence of the individual increases. In our vision, this leads to the 3.0-era, where the hierarchical relations between institutes and individuals disappear, and where there is increasingly more equal communication and cooperation. We define this as the participating customer, citizen, or patient. Social media and other technological developments contribute to the communication and cooperation going off more intelligently and smoother, while customizing products and services to personal situations."

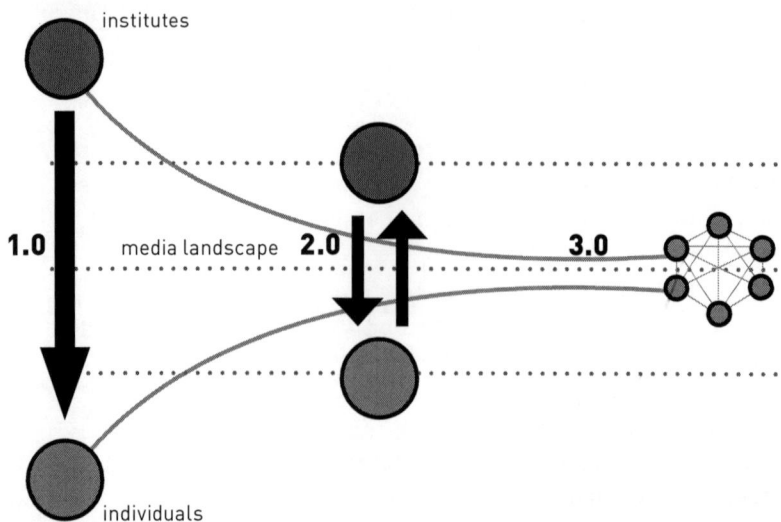

Source: Marco Derksen, Upstream

So, organizations have to rethink all of their strategies. The traditional client is long gone, and, in the literature, you see new groups popping up with names like 'Millennials'. Basically, there is a new generation of clients who want to be involved in the value creation process. A generation of people with a different mindset, but also different communication and information needs. They are tough to identify. You need a strong brand, have to connect with them on social networks, align yourself with a cause, have an open culture, and include their opinions as you build new products. If you want them to work with you, you need to invest in their careers, mentor them, and feed their entrepreneurial ambitions.

3.8
Valuable leadership

Communities, the virtual tribes of connected people, generally have a somewhat self-appointed tribal leader. The seeking human follows him or her and waits. You will, therefore, see the phenomena in communities of interest where too many kindred spirits wait for the leader to say or do something; the members are not yet taking enough responsibility. The goal, and the way it can be reached, is not always clear.

A social network with sheer non-tangible results is granted only a short life. It will fail under its own one-sidedness. The like-minded members indeed show their connection, dedication, and involvement, but they miss a link to the 'outside', which means that non-members will not be able to adopt the combined ideals that are produced in the network. Virtual communities of purpose, with only kindred spirits who exclusively live off the social capital, have proven to be ineffective. At the same time, the economic and financial crisis has shown us that we are also not sustainable if we only focus on financial aspects when working together.

In the introduction, I pictured a train, moving quickly through the landscape. Looking out of the window of the bullet train between Shanghai Pudong Airport and the city of Shanghai, our eyes are having trouble getting a clear picture. It is almost a blurred reality out there. However, inside your own compartment, there is the 'real life', or at least your perception of it. The same thing, again, is our present. The world around us is changing so fast, and we are confronted

67

with new technologies every day. The amount of available data and information streams are so huge that our picture tends to blur, and we are desperately sticking to the world as we know it (knew it?) in order to keep our sanity. I take my time digesting a selected number of sources, and try to picture (a very big picture, though!) if, and if so, how, these events will influence my life, my company (with all its products and services), and even my world. I see a future. Or, at least, a direction in which my future (commercial) life is taking me.

So, I know what train to take.

Then, inside my compartment, I start exchanging notes with my follow travellers. Almost on a informal and daily basis, innovative ideas come up – some more sustainable to what we are doing, and others are more disruptive. We start prototyping, a nice word for 'trial and error' product development. And, we learn every day. Of course, you need people around you with different talents to get the best results. Some are daredevils, and some act from within an internal vision, almost intuitively. Others are more mathematical, and some are, frankly, boring.

Having some 'boring' people around you is handy. Boring people form the stability a company needs. They keep the day-to-day stuff going, and make sure things like accounting, tax returns, and conversations with your financial stakeholders are moving along at the right pace and on the right paths. They may have an innovative idea sometimes, but it better be for the sustainability of the organization. A disruptively thinking banker, accountant, or bookkeeper is not my cup of tea. That is a cup of tea I'd rather drink at the casino, or with the cups and balls players in the streets. Then I know upfront I am being screwed.

So, I have become, over the past years, what I call a trend strategist, or trendwatcher (in Dutch, we like to mash words together). I trendslate trends into pieces of information, or business models, and help my stakeholders to stay 'on board', mentally and physically, with the things we are doing. Of course, I am being assisted by other stakeholders doing this. My Web guys and girls watch and report what's going on in their world, and others help me, like a mirror, to put my thoughts in order. So, who are your trendwatchers and trendcoaches on the team?

Some people are talented at making connections with the more traditional organizations. Sustainable economical value creation needs connections between the old world of financial capital and the new world of social capital. The established organizations, which are doomed because of their disastrous course, need so-called 'new leaders' to be reinvigorated. This has to become a continuous effort within new Society 3.0 organizations. The author Kim Korn calls this, on his blog, *Create Advantage*, 'regenerative management'. The independent professionals, or knowmads, are natural connectors. When the new leaders and these independent professionals meet each other in new value networks, a sustainable base is created for the development of economic value. Co-creation takes place.

In the end, we need a kind of organizational structure that provides value networks a transparent place, starting points, and a mission. The knowledge to do this is available within many organizations, so if all that knowledge can be put into action in a new way, something beautiful can arise. If organizations work together with knowmads, they will form a kind of construction, which I call a Social Economical Entity (SEE).

This means that the known Internet groups, like LinkedIn and Facebook, indeed form the starting point for new value creation, but that creation will only come into being if the old and the new worlds merge, and cooperation moves away from the traditional value chain to the Society 3.0 value networks.

3.9
New leaders, new organizations

Between those Internet tribes – or 'swarms', as Martijn Aslander labeled them in his book, *Easycratie* – we need daredevils: people who dare to innovatively steer and interpret for traditional organizations. And in such a way that the employees in the established organizations are encouraged to act autonomously, and thus take part in change and organizational renewal.

The Belgian management thinker Jef Staes calls these daredevils 'Red Monkeys'. Thanks to their new leaders, these new employees, the Red Monkeys, will look for the connections with enormous potential of energy and knowledge that are available within the virtual social networks (and within their own organizations). This way, the new leaders and their new employees safeguard the future of their organizations. And, in doing so, they safeguard their own futures as well. New leaders have the capacity at their disposal to prompt a group or organization to move independently. Hierarchy is marginally important. New leaders are able to break through large and small existing structures, disrupt the immobilizing equilibrium, and re-enable innovation.

Stephen Covey describes new leaders as: "people who are taking charge of their lives or are taking matters into their own hands in certain situations, without depriving others. Thinking in terms of synergy. Continuously learning. Communicating openly. Acting from their own vision."

As a matter of fact, all new employees are potential new leaders! With so many new leaders from and in organizations and virtual value networks, we will be able to find a balance between money, alternative value systems, and social capital. This balance is vital for the sustainability of the new value networks. New leaders, new employees, new organizations...

You can learn much more about these Organizations 3.0 in part three of this book.

Social virtual networks have not been solely for private use for a long time. Particularly in companies and organizations, they offer unprecedented possibilities because networking with people externally and internally – thanks to the Internet – can solve the classic Coase Ceiling dilemma. Our self-imposed economic restrictions will thus disappear. We can move from scarcity to abundance. Value creation with (virtual) social networks means that we are no longer bound to traditional economic limitations such as time, place, and means!

The current crisis has made it clear to us that the old ways are no longer sufficient. Contrary to the past, this applies to many more people at the same time. Information is increasingly available and penetrable. We are able to determine more and more what is wrong with it. Technology progresses at a dazzling speed. Obviously, we have to utilize them. It is time we took matters into our own hands and enter the era of communicative self-management. The Internet is our vehicle. The virtual social networks form the movement. Many people are already moving. For others, this shift may still be invisible; they see a calm sea. But, under the surface, a real seaquake is taking place. I find the word 'tsunami' to be the best to use to describe the fundamental social changes that are awaiting us, and heading our way at a blistering pace.

The TrendSpeech group of Trendwatchers state in their 2013 document that 'the biggest challenge humanity presently has is not technology, but adaptation. Are we going to adapt to new technological opportunities from an existing paradigm of consumption and control, or from human measure and balance?'

3.10
The power of social networks: introduction
The free access to a worldwide market of hundreds of millions of people turns the Internet into a liquidity machine.
– Chris Anderson in *Free*, (2009).

Millions of people are connected through social networks. These are formal networks that require a kind of membership, but are also specialized networks. This is being researched on an ongoing basis, which has led to information and theories on network behavior. Obviously, we want to use these networks as effectively as possible. So, we collect their data, the meta and big data. It resembles the search for the Holy Grail: we are looking for something that we cannot yet always define. Data and experiences are hunted out of economic and personal interest. The question remains of what we want to know about this reasonably unpredictable (swarming) dynamic, and whether this knowledge is uniformly applicable. The fact is that there is steadily more insight into ways to develop maximum force from social networks, or rather, out of social networks. I consider myself an above average active network user, and thus draw from my own experience when it comes to the effective use of social networks. In my opinion, this is not just about relational intensity, but also about connective density, strategic construction, relevance, and trust.

3.11
Different networks, different people, different friendships

Not everyone is as active within networks as others, which makes sense. There are givers and takers, people who 'hang', and people who do not participate. Forrester Research has developed the Social Technographics Ladder, which identifies seven different groups within networks.

- **Inactives**, who do nothing on the web.
- **Spectators**, who watch, read and listen within networks.
- **Joiners**, who join networks and create profiles.
- **Collectors**, who organize the content for themselves via RSS feeds or tags.
- **Critics**, who review, comment on blogs or are active on forums.
- **Conversationalists**, who use Twitter.
- **Creators**, who create or enrich content.

You have to be careful not to label people too quickly within these archetypes. The Web is simply a dynamic system; within one network, someone's role can be different than in another network. I am a collector on LinkedIn, a critic on Facebook; a conversationalist on Twitter; and a creator on Society30.com. These network roles give an interesting interpretation, but nothing more.

We all have friends. However, the friends of the industrial age are different from your friends in this digital age.

Friends in social networks are people you are connected to. The word 'friends' was only introduced because Marc Zuckerberg happened to start Facebook as a 'book with the faces of friends'. Obviously, different people define friendship differently.

In the past, our social network was defined by an activity: you had friends at school or at work, at the sports club, within the family, or at your favorite bar. You knew more about a particular friend, and he knew you quite well, so you trusted him more than others. That one friend was literally and figuratively closer to you than other friends. For that matter, you did not call all of them a friend.

There is a completely different picture in your virtual social network(s). In fact, you have nothing but friends. In principle, they are all only a mouse click away...so, instead of friends, I think of them as my connections. You obviously have stronger and weaker links. However, the speed at which you can expand you network of friends in the virtual world is incomparable to that of the past. Some celebrities have hundreds of thousands of friends, but for mere mortals, having a couple of thousand is exceptional. Is this in any way useful to you?

The British anthropologist Robin Dunbar posits in his book, *Dunbar's Law*, that human beings have the capacity to maintain a serious social relationship with about 150 people at the same time. The question that is asked the most is, "why do you need 1,500 'friends' in your network?" This is when the dynamics of the Internet reared its head again. If I am working on, for example, yellow cups in France, then that relates to a part of my network, and when I'm interested in cumin cheese, I could perhaps share this with others. So, for me, the hard number of 150 is right by itself, but there can always be another group of 150 people...

These ex post facto analyses of network roles and friendship intensities are, of course, fun. It is evident that the effectiveness of your network behavior increases as you take a more active or intense role in the network. Relationally, this is actually an open door.

I find it more important to view my network as a whole and, in particular, its:
- **Size:** how many players does the network consist of?
- **Strategic composition:** who does what in my network?
- **Relevance:** which groups around a certain theme of the network members, are important for me?
- **Trust:** which of my network members can I really trust?

3.12
Is mine bigger than yours? Connect!
Metcalfe's Law states that the power of a network increases exponentially as the number of members grows larger. This law is derived from the mathematical graph theory. A graph consists of a collection of vertices (nodes) and edges (that connect pairs of vertices) – what we would call a network. You can calculate with graphs. The so-called 'complete graph' is an interesting one, where every node is connected with every other one.

73

De *volledige graaf* op N knopen (afgekort tot K_N) is de graaf waarin alle punten onderling verbonden zijn.

$$K_N = (V_{K_N}, E_{K_N}) \, met$$

$$V_{K_N} \, een \, verzameling \, knopen \, en \mid V \mid = N$$

$$E_{K_N} = \{\{ v_1, v_2 \} \mid v_1, v_2 \in V_{K_N} \wedge v_1 \neq v_2\}$$

De volgende grafen zijn voorbeelden van volledige grafen:

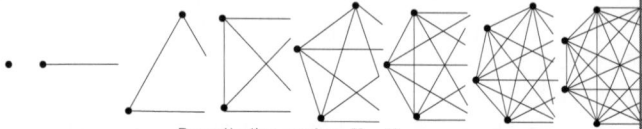

De volledige grafen $K_1 ... K_8$.

Het aantal kanten van K_N is $\dfrac{N \cdot (N-1)}{2}$

If I have a network of 10 vertices, or contacts, then according the formula, there is a possibility of 10 • (10-1) : 2 = 45 edges between the contacts. A network of 100 contacts can hold a maximum of 4,950 interpersonal relations. How can we use this knowledge? There is an enormous difference between having individual relationships with ten contacts on one hand, and knowing that those ten contacts are mutually connected as well on the other! One does not need much imagination to recognize that the communication force is much stronger in the second case than in the first case. In the second case, my contacts can talk about me among themselves, and, together, they form an opinion about me. This scenario is a lot stronger than a system of individual 'lines' (something managers with about ten reporting staff members can think about...).

It is important to realize, with regard to efficiency of networking, that a message (a Tweet for example) sent to ten followers will not always be read by all of them. Too many messages are sent for all of them to be read. I would maintain a 'star network' with those ten people, and leave it at that. But because they are connected to each other as well – and you need to encourage your contacts to do that (divide and rule is certainly not the adage here) – my message can still be picked up through another channel. In other words, the denser my network is (or the more complete the graph is), the greater the effectiveness of my communication is in that network.

I have over 9,000 followers on Twitter. According to Metcalfe, I could have 40,495,500 connections among these followers. This means that there is a big chance that a message I send will actually reach as many of those 9,000 followers as possible. But if you realize that those 9,000 followers have followers who do not follow me (are you still following this?), then every retweet is sent to people who do not follow me. Only one of them has to have a couple of thousand followers like me... does that make sense?

In short, make sure that you not only have enough contacts, but encourage them to connect to each other as well. Be a connector! Managers should take note of this as well: do not build a wall around your own employees with the idea that that is the best way for you to manage them. Instead, ensure that the staff of your team or department connect to employees of other teams or departments.

In 1967, the American academic John Milgram published his Six Degrees of Separation theory. According to this notion, someone can be connected to anyone in the world in an average of six steps, from your own friend, through his friend, etc. It is also called the Small World Theory. After a while, it became evident that Milgram's theory did not work right away, and that certain preconditions were necessary, but the essence of the theory still stands: we are closer to the people we value than we realize. In virtual social networks, we can often approach people we do not know swiftly and directly, without having to be introduced by a mutual friend. Sometimes the social introduction is a retweet or a forward. It is no coincidence that our virtual social networks are called small world networks.

"The significance of weak ties is that they are far more likely to be bridges than are strong ties. It should follow, then, that the occupational groups making the greatest use of weak ties are those whose weak ties do connect to social circles different from one's own."
– Sociologist Mark Granovetter in his paper,
The Strength of the Weak Ties: a Network Theory Revised

According to Granovetter, I do not actually need to maintain a serious social relationship with all my contacts all the time. If my reputation (my personal brand) is sound, people from my network will be inclined to help me if I ask for it, even if I do not know them personally. Such a request for information or help will spontaneously activate a temporary little network out of the larger network – a provisional network. Granovetter writes, "I activate my weak links. The people in question react because they are interested in the subject themselves and want to share their knowledge with me; I have labeled this a resonance network." With these networks, you can mobilize a kind of collective intelligence. Such resonance networks behave like a neutral network. There are people who process information in networks and subsequently pass it on, and a (subconscious) learning element arises.

3.13
The strategic composition of my network

As soon as people start using social networks, they try to 'score numbers'. Which makes sense because a network without any people is not a network. Many social networks help you acquire contacts. They help you to cross-reference your other contact lists or offer suggestions: 'If you know Jack, you may know Jill'. At a later stage, you will start to think about which people are actually useful to you and how you will organize them. Who are the 'right' people in a network, exactly? In other words, who are relevant to me in relation to my activities and preferences?

According to the Quantum Theory of Trust by professor Karin Stephenson, a certain category of contacts in your network is more strategic than another. They are particularly more strategic because they enable you to reach other contacts more efficiently. They are your great connectors.

Stephenson distinguishes hubs, pulsetakers, and gatekeepers.

- **Gatekeepers:** they are the gateways to (new) networks, and are also the corridors between different networks. As this representative role is usually not directly visible – especially not in informal, learning networks – you will have to look for it.

- **Pulsetakers:** they are the people who pick up the posed question intrinsically and interpret it for the network they belong to. The pulsetaker actually does something with your request or question.
- **Hubs:** they are people who have an above average amount of contacts. They have a large network. Once you have ended up in a hub, in principle, you will reach a large audience.

These strategic positions are the outcome of the network behavior of the involved person. Someone is a hub for a reason. So, the strategic position is a measure of someone's reliability. As it happens, this position is ascribed by others in the network; you cannot apply for it.

The roles that Stephenson discerns are dynamic and can change hands in an instant. Finding out how to map these strategic positions, and how to provide insight into the relevance of various members, is akin to searching for the Holy Grail.

3.14
How (real time) relevant are my network friends?

The strategic positions in networks are of a generic nature: a gatekeeper is a gatekeeper to everybody. But that does not mean he has to be relevant to you. And by relevant, I mean in relation to the topic or theme that I'm dealing with. Imagine I am looking for somebody who knows about logistic processes in France. The gateways 'logistics' or 'France' are of greater importance, and thus are more relevant, than the amount of possible connections someone can make for me.

Most networks won't help you further than filter someone's job, position, or trade. I find that totally inadequate. Container concepts like 'marketer' or 'CEO' mean nothing to me. Besides, most self-employed professionals cannot match their qualifications in these pre-defined profile boxes. All information concerning a person, including his or her behavior in the network, should be able to serve as a search option.

Within our Seats2meet.com ecosystem, we operate with a digital DNA structure. For instance, Seats2meet.com visitors, when reserving their work-spaces, use keywords (or tags) to show what they are involved in and which specific knowledge they have to share. This real-time information is part of their social capital payment.

Also, all events have been provided with the same tagging system. Someone's S2M-DNA is just as dynamic as it is current. So, if I want to search through the S2M Serendipity Machine dashboards with the keywords 'logistics' and 'France', the system will present me with all network members whose DNA contain these keywords. That makes it easy to make real-time, relevant connections. This unexpected relevance (serendipity) of meeting the right people at the right time and place becomes leading in the booking-selection of workspaces. So, it is no longer necessary to offer a network of physical locations throughout a geographical area like hotel chains do, for example. People can now be led, if you as a physical location owner, 'have the right people available' to meet their peers.

This unexpected real-time relevance through meeting other people at Seats2meet.com locations is part of our Serendipity Machine, and creates an unbelievably strong competitive advantage.

We share the Serendipity Machine with any physical location where people come together, such as museums, theaters, retail shops, airplanes, events, and more.

3.15
There is still the matter of reliability
As soon as you ask if someone is reliable, his or her trustworthiness has already been a little bit infringed upon. Reliability in network traffic is as important as it is complex. In my opinion, people who are active in my network, and share and give a lot, are more reliable than others who only come to consume. It is all about a feeling of reciprocity. But beware of the principle of 'you scratch my back, I'll scratch yours'. Before you know it, you will be keeping score to see if you have received as much as you have given. This is disastrous network behavior. Real reciprocity is indirect and asynchronous: if I give a lot, my reliability factor will rise within the network because I have shown my willingness to share.

'The willingness to share' shows involvement, responsibility, and autonomy of the players in the network.

And, as I have said earlier, this social capital is an indispensable factor. When you succeed in mapping this, it will create a network of confidants. For the time being, this mapping will rely on your own insight. We can expect the development of more analytical functions, which will make the Holy Grail of the effective network more visible. We are working very hard to achieve this at Seats2meet.com, as is Google. Google is taking more and more notice of your behavior in social media channels, so that your tweets and links will influence your position in natural search results. Retweets of your messages or links from people with lots of followers will become more 'valuable'.

4
SOCIETY 3.0: WHAT WAS AND CAN BE;
the authors intermezzo

In his book, *The World is Flat*, Thomas Friedman claims we've entered the third phase in globalization, which he calls 'Globalization 3.0'.

Friedman describes Globalization 3.0 as "the newfound power of individuals to collaborate and compete globally. With cross-border skills and contacts, immigrants with small businesses are leveraging the Internet and connective technologies to exploit global trade opportunities. This is creating a new wave of small business globalization, and creating broader and deeper economic links across the globe."

If this book were a business plan for Europe, Inc. (which it is), but one of those operation plans consisted of at least forty pages of indecipherable text, then somewhere halfway through this plan – after the elaborate SWOT analyses – we would arrive at the crux of the matter.

The old-establishment business plan author would have called this crux 'The Corporate Strategy', but the observant reader would immediately notice that this chapter would merely contain a large amount of one-dimensional operating results. They are broken down in more detail into sectional results per organizational division, and are complemented with key performance indicators, which are meant to measure if these results can actually be met. More and more copies of these kinds of plans are found with a note in the margin saying, 'had a good read and a good laugh'.

Up to now, I have described the enablers who can help me and you, the reader, to build the interdependent Society 3.0. I have dedicated the entire first part of this book to painting the picture of the current organization of Europe, Inc., which is not a pretty picture, and hopefully this a good reason to change. Then, I described the favorable armamentarium – the Internet and social networks – which will hopefully provide the reader with sufficient starting points to start experimenting with themselves. I believe I have actually contributed to bringing Society 3.0 a step closer. This book could end here, or perhaps a couple of pages back. It is evident that there are results; what kind of results remains the question (as is the case in the old business plans).

At the same time, one would expect to arrive at the crux of this book after having read the extensive preliminary work. The title of this book supports this expectation: "Here it comes, now Ronald is going to tell us what to do, now we can expect the big change strategy." It may have worked this way in the old school business plans, but it does not work that way in the new style business plans.

This connecting chapter is not the crux of the book; at the most, it is a turning point in the treatment of the reader. After all, up to now I have written about things that already exist, issues that give our society a reason to do things differently, and the upcoming issues that will make it possible for us to actually do things differently. Because this chapter is the turning point, this book – the business plan – will continue. It will continue on into the future, as it will unfold. And well, the future is something we simply do not exactly know. What we can do is look at our society with renewed vision, while keeping the new forms of value creation in the back of our minds. We can cherish the 3.0 elements that are slowly unraveling and let them blossom. This outlines the core of my intentions with this book. I would like you look with me through my 'Glasses 3.0' at the important issues of our society, and to the ideas the addition of '3.0' perspectives can deliver.

Once again: do not expect an assignment, task, and certainly not any KPI's, but behold the perspective – my perspective – the rest of this book gives from your own autonomy, and add your own perspective to it. This chapter, Society 3.0, is merely a crossroads between what was and what can be. So, basically, you could skip it...

4.1
A new playing field

There is a new economic reality parallel to our current conventional economic system, where sustainable value is created every day...
                                                    – Ronald van den Hoff

Four value systems symbolize Society 3.0 and its interdependent or sharing economy:

GREEN
There are feelings of solidarity between people that we are on our way. There are desires for personal growth, attention to the environment, and problems concerning our surroundings. In work, one is motivated by human contact and contribution. There is tolerance for, and acceptance of, differences. Being liked is more important than gaining a competitive edge. The primary values are openness, trust, collectivity, humanitarianism, and learning from others.

YELLOW
Thinking in systems. This is the value system in which a quantum leap takes place in the capacity to have different perspectives in life. People are motivated to be self-taught, and are organized in the integration of complex systems. There is an understanding that chaos and change are self-evident. Change is a congenial part of the organizational processes of life. People like challenges. Thinking is characterized by systems thinking – how parts interact to create a whole. Unique talents and idiosyncrasies are seen from the point of view that they can make a contribution to the larger entity.

CORAL
People with some connection to the coral value system discover, in the process of aligning the inner and outer world, the understanding that we are the field: there is no inner versus outer world. Continuing to think that way preserves the discrepancy. Our senses mislead our purest experience of reality: the transcendence of duality.

TURQUOISE
Comprehensive, with a holistic focus on global renewal and 'experience'. There is synergy between all life forms and forces. Work needs to have added value for the complete welfare of life. There are

skills to see and respect different perspectives, and among them are many of the underlying value systems. The importance of being aware of energy fields, Jungian synchronicity, having a need to utilize human intelligence, and having the intelligence to work on large-scale problems without sacrificing individuality are emphasized. Planetary problems transcend limited sectional interests. There is a reorganized world with new meaning and welfare for all. People strive for a balance between their inner world and their outer world in the turquoise value system.

Sources: *Spiral Dynamics*© and *The Cubrix*
Thank you, Marcel van Marrewijk.

Spiral Dynamics is a bio-psycho-social map of living human systems that focuses on natural designs and offers whole new integral solutions that are ecological, systemic, and life-affirming. In effect, the theory describes and makes sense of the enormous complexity of human existence, and then shows how to craft elegant, systems-based problem-solutions that meet people and address situations where they are.

4.2
The interdependent economy

We are ready for a new economic model (and with that, a new social and political model, too). I call this sharing economic model, the domain of value creation within Society 3.0, the 'interdependent economy', an economic system based on:

- Solidarity
- Sustainability
- Reciprocity

Actually, it is a logical next step in the development of our society. History shows us a certain evolutionary order of ranking in different economic systems that, evidently, had limited shelf lives. Every system was suitable for the specific circumstances of that period. Evidently, economic systems are transient, which is caused by changing environmental factors. Because of this, systems no longer connect to social reality at a certain stage.

"After the decline of the classic economies, the first outlines of a market-oriented system arose in the early days of the European Community that emphatically focused its attention on redistribution and brought about solidarity between economic factions. This variant became ultimately known as the Rhineland Model. The interests of different groups in the society were discussed, attuned, and negotiated between their representatives, the social partners. The problem in our current juncture is that representatives have become redundant, because people are in direct contact with the 'end-organizations' thanks to social media. Global warming, supervision of the global banking system, and depletion of our natural resources also can not be coordinated in the Rhineland Model. Redistribution mechanisms simply do not work and so this most recent variant of capitalism has reached its limits and with that clearing the way for a next emerging, yet to be awakened variant.

In contrast with socialist redistribution policies, the Interdependent Economy is trying to create an innovative and visionary solution for today's big challenges. This new ecosystem will, once again, need leadership based on vision and authenticity. The mutual dependency – of time, place, and of social groups – shape the starting point of this system. It requires an intelligent design if we want the problems of these times to be adequately tackled."

– Marcel van Marrewijk, Research to Improve BV,
in an interview in 2010

The interdependent economy will create value by leaving the value chain and adapting our value systems to a sort of continuous productivity system that fosters a seamless integration between consumer and business platforms. Continuous Productivity manifests itself in an environment in which the evolving tools and culture make it possible to innovate more and faster than ever, with significantly improved execution. Continuous productivity shifts our efforts from the start/stop world of episodic work and work products to one that builds on the technologies that start to answer what happens when, in Society 3.0, a generation of free agents has access to the collective knowledge of an entire profession, and experts are easy to find and connect with. And these experts have access to data, knowledge, and analysis, so they develop the ability to time slice, context switch, and proactively deal with situations as they arise.

> "Today, after a long history of regional success, the nation-state is failing us on the global scale. It was a perfect recipe for the liberty and independence of autonomous people and nations. It is utterly unsuited to interdependence. The city, always the human habitat of first resort, has in today's globalizing world once again become democracy's best hope."
>
> Benjamin R. Barber: *If Mayors Ruled The World*

The location of these Society 3.0 citizens and their globally inter-connected networks, will be in cities. Big, big cities – agglomerations of over 20, 30, or even 50 million people. That way, these cities are also globally-connected through their inhabitants and start to act interdependently with other big cities. They even will have their own currencies, like the Calgary Dollar or the Brixton Pound and may even accept corporate and/or virtual currencies, like Amazon Coins or Bitcoins.

Cities will become more influential and more important than the actual countries they are located in, and also more important than the European Union. The economic potential is huge. If we really start collaborating within European cities, and create, for instance, a free-trade zone with a number of U.S. cities, we would have over 1 billion consumers with an income totaling over €26 trillion. And, how about the sharing and collaboration possibilities of all those consumers? A real paradigm shift, to put it mildly...

4.3
The rules of the game in the interdependent and collaborative economy

The interdependent economy shapes our new playing field for value creation. The personal is global. It is a playing field where we will have to mobilize ourselves to find solutions together. Everybody's in-volvement is an absolute condition for this. We are deeply dependent on each other. We can call it a new form of collectivity and solidarity, but it is a solidarity driven by choice, and not imposed by government. It is a playing field where connectivity, sustainability, and reciprocity are the most important rules of play.

Connectivity

People are gathering in social networks. Globally, these networks form an enormous potential for (knowledge) workers. The people in these networks share all kinds of data, information, and knowledge in the cloud and supply context with this information. Technology is striding on, resulting in software solutions, large and small, that work smarter using collaboration software, mostly free of charge. Everything is available, and shareable, in abundance. Wherever we are, we have access to our data, systems, and other people from our networks. Modern, open organizations are actively looking to connect and engage with all these people, their stakeholders. They make clever use of their knowledge, and make this knowledge available again to others. This is how people and organizations strengthen each other. So, there is connectivity between people, information, and knowledge. With that, groups of value networks, or value constellations, replace value chains. We call this group of loosely connected, but engaged, stakeholders who share the abundance and appreciating social capital aside from traditional capital, The Mesh.

Sustainability

Sustainability does not simply mean working 'green' or making 'green' products, but particularly, dealing with each other and our resources in a way that is beneficial to future generations.

A sustainable society:
- Meets the needs of the present generation
- Does not compromise the ability of future generations to meet its own needs
- Provides each individual the opportunity to develop himself in freedom, within a well-balanced society, and in harmony with its surroundings

(Source: Sustainable Society Foundation)

Reciprocity

Value creation conveyed in capital does not just mean money in the interdependent economy. Capital is made up of social capital, the combined transactional value systems (money in the classic sense), and the alternative value systems (or local currency). In this mix of ingredients, reciprocity is much easier, and naturally realized.

4.4
Economic growth & The Mesh
The Interdependent Economy of Society 3.0 has other growth regulators than we are used to:
- It is all about what goes out, and not what comes in. So, you will not hear 'Are we richer today than yesterday?' It's all about people being better off. Why produce more products that nobody wants?
- It is about connections, not transactions. Growing smart is about connecting and co-creating, and not just about trading goods with each other.
- It is about people, not products.
- It is about skills – the commitment and creativity of people.
- It is about openness, fading boundaries, and originality or authenticity. Trusting the processes, trusting each other.

From this point of view, growth can no longer be described with indexes such as GNP (the only reason to show growth in our GNP is to convince the banking dragons that we are able to repay our debts within the agreed upon term). After all, we are able to grow in the indirect tangible affairs mentioned above. This is called social capital.

My question is whether you would want to exactly measure such growth...

The new value networks, the place where the old and the new work together again, are characterized by clear communication and directly doing business, designing, producing, and assessing together.

This is The Mesh, not just a network, but the basic foundation of connected and engaged people that forms the starting point of new value creating social networks. When I explained this 'mesh' concept to the Dutch philosopher Jan Flameling, he immediately mentioned Gilles Deleuze's model for society, a rhizome: a (botanical) organism that, in this case, allows for multiple, non-hierarchical entry and exit points in data representation and interpretation.

A grown-up Mesh is an enormous cluster of value networks. Processes in this chaordic (chaotic and organized) playing field are simplified by the use of social media and technologies: the 'easycracy', as Dutch Management Thinker Martijn Aslander coined it, arises.

Josephine Green, ex-trend-watcher at Philips, calls it the 'pancake society'. Our society will become much flatter, and therefore simpler, because we are better connected with each other through knowledge and through transaction systems.

So, a new economic playing field is arising. The alliance of pro-sumers with the new Organization 3.0 ensures that consumers are participants at an early stage, and in doing so, determine what and how things are being produced. By doing so, all stakeholders in The Mesh of an organization combine social capital and traditional capi-tal, both of which are needed to co-create value. According to Lisa Gansky, author of the book *The Mesh*, "Mesh companies create, share and use social media, wireless networks, and data crunched from every available source to provide people with goods and services at the exact moment they need them, without the burden and expense of owning them outright".

More and more products are being packaged as a service. Many people want to have access to something, but do not necessarily need to own it. In the book *What's Mine is Yours*, the authors Botsman and Rodgers distinguish three systems of what is called 'collaborative consumption' (although I prefer to call consumption collaborative 'prosumption'):
- Product-service systems
- Redistribution markets
- Cooperative lifestyles

With product-service systems, the prosumer wants the pleasures of ownership, but not the burdens. In many large cities in the USA, there is Zipcar, for instance. If I want to rent a car, I can check where the nearest car is via the Internet and book it using an app on my cellular phone. With the help of Google Maps, I'll have no problem finding the vehicle. The car recognizes my phone and enables me to start it. Before I drive off, I rate the cleanliness of the car in the re-view section. This way, a literal self-cleaning capability is built into the system, because if someone routinely leaves a car in a mess, he is simply ejected from the system and can't use the services of Zipcar anymore. Once you check out, the account is settled through your cell phone and the car checks in from its new location. In 2009, Zipcar already reported revenue over $100 million. Their revenue in 2012

89

increased to over $280 million. Avis, a traditional car rental company, 'moved in' to the market in spring 2013.

Obviously, this model can be applied to other services and products. The American company Solarcity rents, installs, and maintains solar panels, and manages the sales contract for the excess of produced electricity with the power company. Why do garden owners have a lawnmower, a leaf blower, hedge-clippers, and other rarely used tools? At Zilok, you can rent garden tools, and much more, from other individuals in your neighborhood.

In redistribution markets, objects that are no longer needed are passed on. At Swaptree.com, you can swap CDs, books, and games with other consumers. As is the case with children's clothing, books, and much more, swapping is better than throwing things away! Google is also entering this market with Google Mine.

Cooperative lifestyles offer products and services to social acquaintances. In the hospitality industry, we see opportunities to sleep over, free of charge, at 'friends' houses, on the couch or in the spare room, via Couchsurfing. There are 16,000 hosts in the Amsterdam area alone. Globally, there are more than 7 million! Couchsurfing has become the largest hotel chain in the world, but it is not a chain at all. It is an Internet platform, connecting people and matching supply and demand of the abundance of a good or service. In this case, it is hotel beds. AirBNB offers apartments and guest rooms for a fee in over 34,000 cities around the world. Of course, the establishment tries to stop these initiatives, calling it 'illegal hospitality'. To me, this resistance is already impossible, due to the large number of adopters. So, traditional hotels better adjust their business models!

4.5
Growth of the economy, but not of the GNP?

We have seen that social capital cannot be expressed as a GNP-type number. On top of that, a collaborative prosumption economical system, as part of The Mesh, is made possible by the solidarity of people, the possibility of 'monitoring' the quality and integrity of the network, the will and the capacity of people to share, and the transparency of the supply. Social media enables us to meet these conditions. Perhaps it may not be visible to everyone immediately, but some of these services are starting to grow out of proportion. Eventually, this development will render the current traditional supplier-chain model useless, and it will deny the present governments of sales and income taxes as their most important financial resource.

During the transition phase towards Society 3.0, this sharing economy is a huge new economic activity apart from some of the more traditional processes. The sharing economy will make the total economy – however, not always the GNP – grow again. It means that money becomes less important. We see this already in the traditional financial statements of our S2M locations: their turnover is lower than in traditional meeting centers, however, the profits are much higher. Higher without even including or trying to measure the social capital being built up at the same time.

According to global business analyst Jeremiah Owyang at the US-based Crowd Companies, "every car sharing vehicle reduces car ownership by 9-13 vehicles, a revenue loss of at least $270,000 to an average auto manufacturer."

"Airbnb, the world's leading marketplace to list, discover and book unique, local accommodations today released a new study highlighting the Airbnb community's positive economic impact in New York City. Conducted by HR&A Advisors, the study found that Airbnb generated $632 million in economic activity in New York in one year and supported 4,580 jobs throughout all five boroughs. The study also found that nearly 90 percent of Airbnb hosts rent out the home they live in – their primary residence – and use the money they earn to help make ends meet, while Airbnb guests spend more time and money in New York than typical tourists."
– Airbnb press release October 2013.

So, every business segment is hit by this development! And so is your government. They will miss an enormous amount of taxes, an amount which I estimate could run up to 50% of their tax-based income. Think about the consequences: what do you think will happen to the financial strength of your country's national budget when this non-taxpaying system forms an equivalent of 50% of your GNP? The cities in your country will definitely become stronger, but your government with its politicians is in deep trouble as their income diminishes. They will lose importance. The mega-cities and its Society 3.0 citizens will simply circumvent them.

Owyang distinguishes 3 segments in this collaborative economy:
- The company as a service (rent your car from the manufacturer instead of buying)
- Motivate the marketplace (resell, co-op, swap)
- Provide a platform (co-sell, co-market, co-fund, co-distribute)

Jeremiah writes on his blog: "These patterns are inevitable: Start-ups, fueled by VCs create new efficient tools and technologies. Customers move, companies follow, and a new industry is born. Then the process repeats itself. It's as inevitable as the tides, Sun and Moon, and rotation of the planets..."

> "People are bypassing companies by sharing goods, services, space, and money with each other in the sharing economy. They're also empowered to build their own goods in the maker movement by crowd funding, tapping global marketplaces, and preparing to accelerate this with 3D printing. The crowd, is starting to become like a company: self-financing, self-designing products, self-manufcaturing, self-selling to each other – bypassing inefficient corporations in the process".
> – Owyang on the Resilient Summit Website.

'Prosumption through collaboration' is the new theme of the collaborative- and sharing elements of the Interdependent Economy. We have to get used to the fact that in this new economic system. 'value' does not always translate into an immediate return on investment that can be measured in real money. Traditional production will, under the influence of robotics and/or 3D printing, go through an enormous change as well. So, we had better get used to new balances: social capital vs. monetary systems, value vs. cost price, and ownership vs. access.

These developments will allow us to wrestle away from the stranglehold of our current financial and production systems. This is the way out of our zombie economy!

4.6
The stars of the interdependent economy: you and me!

Small and medium-sized enterprises (SME's) dominate the European Union's economy, make up 99 percent of businesses, provide two-thirds of private sector jobs and create most new jobs.
    – From *A Green Knowledge Society*, a report written for the European Union by the Ministry of Enterprise, Energy and Communications, Government Offices of Sweden.

The most important players in the interdependent economy are no longer large organizations, but increasingly, small- to medium-sized enterprises, complemented by an army of independent professionals. And, if the attention is turned to social issues, the civilian will have a large role to play. We're talking about a new generation of people who consider virtual social communication to be normal, and find sharing even more of a common good; use of the Internet is common practice to them. The collapse, or even the disappearance, of large traditional organizational entities (as in the present transition happening all over the place) will accelerate this process.

"In this changing ecosystem, collaborative partnerships between big and small firms will be on the rise. Small firms will contribute innovative practices with market agility and customer knowledge that big firms can't easily achieve. Big firms will offer small businesses marketing and distribution power, enabling them to penetrate broader markets more effectively. Small businesses will proliferate in response to increasing niche market opportunities. Large firms will consolidate and get even bigger to compete more effectively in the global economy. The Web and mobile technologies will become the great equalizer of big and small, with customers no longer knowing – or even caring – about the size of the firm that provides their goods and service." - *The 2020 Intuit Report*.

The real power will therefore shift to the consumer, or the Society 3.0 citizen. As it happens, they organize themselves. They want to participate. They want to engage with suppliers. Prosumers want to co-create in order to develop customized products and services of impeccable quality. Transparency, accountability, and authenticity are their core values. The Internet makes these affairs transparent. The prosumer is more educated than ever on what is for sale at what price. The prosumer knows exactly how your organization interprets its social role and responsibility. The prosumer has a whole range of alternative suppliers that can be tapped, provided by his or her social network. The prosumer wants to choose, can choose, and will choose.

> We protect our neighborhood, because photographs and movies made with our phones make up the eyes and ears of the judiciary.
> February 2011: the car of our colleague Vincent is stolen. The police have 'no time' to file a report. Vincent mobilizes his, in those days, 700-person-strong Twitter network. These 700 people start ReTweeting his message. We determined, using special software, that his appeal reached over 80,000 people. Within 14 hours, the car is found and is returned...positive developments!
>
> However, there is always a downside: on the site Spotsquad, people are rewarded for reporting parking violiations. Is this a revival of *The Lives of Others*, a movie about the monitoring of East Berlin civilians by the Stasi, the GDR's secret police, with the (forced) help of other civilians?

Our current politicians and business community have sparsely discovered this force of the organized masses, which I call crowd-forcing. The Move Your Money campaign created by the news website The Huffington Post and other influencers mobilized nearly 10 million Americans to switch from a large bank to a small, local bank. Crowdforcing has certainly played an important role during the Arab Spring. Time and time again, social media proves that it can make the individual more powerful than ever before.

This is all that concerns the turning point in my book. I have handed you my Glasses 3.0. I invite you to look through them together, to look at our living environment, our work, our money, our democracy, our educational system, and our healthcare system. Let us all determine what can be improved and what has a little resemblance to 3.0 in these areas; and let's continue to develop from here on. In part three of this book, we will have a closer look at the Organization 3.0 itself.

5
ENVIRONMENT 3.0

For most European municipalities or Quango organizations, such as the Amsterdam Airport Authority, buying agricultural land, changing the zoning, and then closing in for the financial kill, has been one of the big money makers for these institutions over the past years. All of a sudden, due to the crisis, this money machine has also come to a halt. Municipalities will have to devalue billions of Euros on their municipal land holdings in the next few years.

Due to the focus on the recession, our environmental planning receives very little attention. As residents, we are served quite poorly, because most decisions in this policy area are made in consultation with a limited amount of parties, often only serving their own economic interests.

In countries where there is ample space, we see a tendency for people to move to the larger cities, thus causing the same effect. The future lies in cities. Cities, interconnected with other cities, feeding creative and sustainable value creation. Using their own currency. Where access becomes more important than possesion, the abundance in cites can be used favorable by its citizens.

Neal Gorenflo of the Internet platform Shareable.net has made a list of Policies for Shareable Cities.

Cities where citizens are able to take much more control over their economic destiny. Here are some policies that are expanding choices for city dwellers and taking shareable transportation to the next level:

- **Designated, discounted, or free parking for car sharing:** Easy, plentiful parking is consistently one of the most cited incentives by folks who share cars.

- **Create economic incentives for ridesharing:** To overcome the presupposed inconveniences of the practice, economic incentives could be implemented, including high-occupancy vehicle (HOV) lanes, discounted parking and reduced tolls.
- **Adopt a citywide public bike sharing program:** Quite a few cities have hopped on the bike sharing bandwagon in recent years, and pretty much all of the other cities should, too.
- **Financial incentives to encourage urban agriculture on vacant lots:** In every vacant lot, there is a community garden waiting to grow.
- **Create food-gleaning centers and programs:** The amount of food wasted from farm to grocer to table adds up to about 40 percent of the total.
- **Mobile food vending:** Even though food trucks seem to be taking over some cities, the launching of such a venture is a really big deal.
- **Support the development of cooperative housing:** Housing cooperatives can lower housing costs in a variety of ways including restrictions on profit from resale, self-management, nonprofit status, shared facilities, and subsidies.
- **Encourage the development of small apartments and 'tiny' homes:** Municipal codes often include size restrictions for housing units that prohibit things like micro-apartments, tiny houses, yurts and container homes.
- **Factor sharing into the design review of new developments:** Forward-thinking urban planning is vital to creating a shareable city. Housing that encourages resident interaction and properties that include mixed-use units.
- **Expand allowable home occupations to include sharing economy enterprise:** The zoning codes that separate home life from commercial life — thereby making it illegal for many people to generate income at home — needs to be relaxed intelligently.
- **Use idle commercial spaces for community benefit:** Facilitate the use of empty commercial spaces by startups in order to test products and services without the big upfront costs and long-term commitments associated with commercial real estate.
- **Assist cooperatives through city economic development departments:** Local jobs, local money — that's what cooperatives are all about. Every city should provide support staff and resources to help folks who want to set up a co-op.

It has always surprised me that housing is scarce, and that you cannot buy land to build on anywhere in The Netherlands at a reasonable price. 'Land is scarce' our political and governmental elite always say. Is this true, or are we making land scarce because of our rigid legislation? Or is real estate development only for our politicians and their selected companies?

Most politicians misinterpret the esteemed economist Keynes, since it suits them well:
'Spend money and stimulate the economy' is what they like to remember. That Keynes also said that in good times money had to be saved is consequently forgotten. It seems the ambition of an individual politician has taken precedence over the consequences for many. Megalomaniac projects require a disproportionate portion of public funds, while the damage to our everyday environment is 'inhuman'. We are still taking action with tunnel vision, instead of with a shared vision.

Burning Man is a week-long annual event, described as an experiment in community, art, radical self-expression, and radical self-reliance held in the Black Rock Desert in northern Nevada, in the United States. It takes its name from the ritual burning of a large wooden effigy. The Burning Man event is guided by 10 principles that are meant to evoke the cultural ethos that has emerged from the event. Some of these priciples deal with the Communal Effort (creative cooperation and collaboration) and Radical Inclusion (anyone may be a part and the stranger is welcomed and respected) while other touch topics like Leaving No Trace (leave a places in a better state than it was found).
I think it is a nice showcase of how people can live and create value together in a sustainable way.

On the road to a sustainable society, one of the pillars of the new Society 3.0, we all have to think hard about the organization of our living and working environments. And we have to question each other on a broad range of topics: our energy supplies, our industries, our logistics, and our place in Europe and on the global stage. What do we want and what should we stop doing?

I'll make the first move by fundamentally scrutinizing a few aspects of our everyday surroundings, and I challenge you to put aside your natural thought process. Will you think with me?

5.1
Politicians and civil servants: ask the 'why' question!

Since the old doesn't work anymore on the road to Society 3.0, many points of view have to be re-evaluated. We need to ask the 'why' question:

Why do we need an even larger port in Rotterdam? In order for us to transit even more goods through the Funnel through The Netherlands to Germany? All this funneling makes for towering infrastructural costs. Think of the modest freight train connection between Rotterdam and Germany, with its €4.7 billion price tag for a 100 mile track, and I'm not even taking the annual exploitation losses into consideration. There is simply very little margin to be made in the transit of goods. Half of our transit goods add (almost) nothing to the Dutch economy. According to the Dutch Central Bureau for Statistics, a product produced in Holland and exported contributes almost six times more to our Gross National Product than an average transit good does. Ask the 'why' question for your country!

Why does Amsterdam Schiphol Airport have to be a so-called Global Main Port? According to their long-standing economic argument, it will benefit the residents of the surrounding cities. For how will it benefit them? Will the sky-high property and land prices benefit them? Will the noise and kerosene pollution? Will the enormous investments by the Ministry of Infrastructure and Environment, as well as the municipalities surrounding this Amsterdam Airport, somewhat maintain commuter mobility around the airport? Amsterdam Airport is no longer an airport, but a mini-state, and, at the same time, a large landowner and speculator in real estate. On the Internet site www.schipholwanbeleid.nl, it says: "Schiphol Amsterdam Airport has such large airport acreage (2,800 ha) and so many runways (not five but already six!), that the two busiest airports in the world (Atlanta 1,500 ha, 4 runways) and Heathrow (1,200 ha, 2 runways) both fit in it. Yet these foreign airports process more than thrice the amount of passengers than Schiphol Amsterdam Airport..."

Thirty percent of Schiphol's profit stems from the development and exploitation of real estate. Schiphol has a double influence: First, through the development company Schiphol Area Development, with 25% of the shares and the right to acquire land through eminent domain 'if necessary' for any possible expansion of flight activities. Second, Schiphol has the monopoly on building within the airport's territory. It has also partakes in lobbying government. Recently, a governmental commission adapted the noise pollution and measurement standards in such a way that the amount of flight movements can increase without any trouble. Noise is not actually measured, it is now 'theoretically calculated'.

Almost 70% of the passengers who arrive at Schiphol Airport will not remain in The Netherlands as their final destination: they are in transit. Most passengers are actually transit goods as well, and their economic contribution is quite limited.

What I especially miss in the megalomaniac decision-making about the size of the Rotterdam Harbor expansion, or the sixth runway at Amsterdam Airport, is a healthy discussion about the query if the growth of the form of transport in question is as large as one thinks.

What is the impact of 3D printing? Will KLM Royal Dutch Airlines' owner, Air France, stick to Amsterdam Airport, or will they chose a French one when it really matters? Or do we leave the ever growing air traffic movements to the oilmoney funded, thus sponsored airports like Dubai and Abu Dabi? For whom are we investing? And, more importantly: do (or should) we actually want this growth in transport? Those are many luxury consumer goods that are being moved. The added value for our society is diminishing, but the burden on the limited financial means and the consumption of land and space is showing a disproportionate increase.

When you replace the Dutch city names with your own local city names I am sure it makes you think twice.

5.2
Overproduction: why too much?

In Europe, we produce more milk than we can consume and manage, and the surplus is too expensive for the rest of the world. Our production costs are too high. The dairy industry also belongs to the zombie economy. Still, over 55% of the annual billions of the European Union's budget is spent on agriculture stimulation and price subsidy, keeping non-EU countries out of the European market.

It is not any different with Dutch pigs. After their horrible stay in those enormous high-rise pig farms, they are transported to Italy. According to the Commodity Board for Cattle and Meat we are talking about 300,000 pigs, and 140,000 metric tons of slaughtered pork, a year. The transport for this costs an arm and a leg (not to mention the environmental pressure). Once this meat arrives in Parma, Italy, it is given the 'Parma ham' seal, and, as a result, this Dutch pork is suddenly worth much more as Italian prosciutto. It is worth more for the Italians, because The Netherlands does not benefit from it at all. We are literally left with shit: the manure surplus. We then use sophisticated high-tech machines to push it into the ground. We call that innovation.

Millions of people world wide take a stand against gen-manupilation of food. Monsanto is their long term target. Also here the power of crowdforcing is showing itself.

Why do we not make a serious attempt to innovate in a sustainable way? Have you heard of the Rondeel egg from Barneveld? The Roundeel concept is a knowledge-operated co-creation of poultry farmers, policymakers at the Ministry of Agriculture, members of the farm feed and egg-processing industry, veterinarians, egg-traders, social organizations, and citizens. All stakeholders – including the chickens – and aspects, such as the environment, energy, and landscape have achieved a beautiful balance in this new concept of intensive poultry farming: a compact self-sustainable eco-system. The Roundeel needs a modest amount of space, and, in addition, is close to our residential area, which reduces the amount of required transport.

Our food chain is getting more transparent. Local suppliers are standing up and getting in direct contact with consumers. This development can be seen in Australia, in the USA, in France and in The Netherlands. The Dutch fruit trader Landwinkel Goense, a collective of 75 farmers, already offers over 125 local products. The public is welcome to pick cherries themselves. On the site www.mijnboerenkaas.nl, you can not only see where your farmhouse cheese originates from, but you can also learn more about the fifteen farmer families who share a passion for their product and trade, showing their real rural authenticity.

Speaking of producing close to home, in New York, a lot of experimentation is taking place with rooftop agriculture. This is being achieved with the aid of a German invention, Rooflite. Rooflite is an easy-to-lay bottom layer, on which anything can be cultivated. This local farming development is, these days, present in bigger cities. And initiatives like The Urban Farmer share their knowledge with Society 3.0 citizens.

5.3
Clean(er) energy

Why are we storing our CO_2 surplus under the ground? The Dutch government has to invest over one billion Euros for a CO_2 storage facility in the Rotterdam Port. Or at least that's what a lobby of nine companies thinks, united under the catchy name of the 'Rotterdam Climate Initiative'. The rest of the three billion Euro project will be paid for by themselves (?), and (obviously) by European Union subsidies.

In my book, this is an old-fashioned, expensive, and ill-considered solution to give the fossil fuel industry a clean tinge. Obviously, it is not old-fashioned in the technological sense because storing some gas in empty natural gas fields is more complex than many people think. Why are we actually still talking about CO_2 storage? Are we not supposed to drastically reduce the CO_2 output? Why are we simply not building sustainable clean power plants instead of power factories that burden us with their waste?

The Netherlands, with natural gas resources, evidently has a strong gas lobby. We are aiming to be the main natural gas distribution center for Europe. A study by the Brattle Group, commissioned by the Ministry of Economic Affairs, Agriculture, and Infrastructure, shows that countries like Austria, Belgium, and Italy have similar plans, and that most of the returns within this plan originate by increasing the national gas production. In short, it's a nice try, but the plan leans on classic, finite, and zombie-economic solutions, which we really have to wave goodbye to.

The new gold rush is called 'fracking'. Chemicals are used to crack rock layers deep in the ground, enabling natural gasses from these rocks to be extracted. It seems to be a big success in the United States, however, there are claims that the optimism concerning this new energy source is grossly exaggerated. In the European countries, however, we lack the vast rural areas like of the US, so this fracking probably will spill our natural supplies of drinking water. Also, due to the fracked energy volume in the US, the global rates for coal have dropped dramatically. CO_2-polluting coal energy plants are now more profitable than most of the Dutch natural gas power plants, so these less polluting plants are hardly used!

Will we never learn? We have to embrace sustainable solutions!

Clearly, we would prefer to burn coal or gas than have a serious look at nuclear energy. Should we skip the discussion on nuclear power? I would love to, but then let's really make an effort to make alternative energy work. It is an absolute disgrace that a company like Shell (with €26 billion in profit in 2012) pulls out of alternative energy projects when the first economic downturn occurs. Why are we still buying gas from these people?

Wind energy is great, especially in the Netherlands. But why build wind turbines near residential areas? Can this not be done instead in the North Sea? Do people not want to 'reside' in residential areas? Who would want a wind turbine in their back yard, dumped there by your own government? I wouldn't, unless it provides me with the energy I need for my neighborhood...

The Rainmaker concept is a system wherein a stand-alone wind turbine is placed in rain lacking regions. This system is especially suited for such environments without proper infrastructure and access to water sources. The Dutch Rainmaker system, literally, makes fresh water from air! The system's wind turbine drives a heat pump, which is directly powered by the wind turbine's blades. With the heat pump, the water vapor in the air is condensed and collected for domestic or irrigation purposes. Depending on local ambient temperatures and humidity conditions, air always contains a certain amount of water. This makes it possible to make water from air almost anywhere in the world.

5.4
Free land in exchange for self-sufficient energy

The American professor Jeremy Rifkin sees only one solution for alternative energy: every house or building has to become its own power plant. This goes a lot further than our contemporary energy-saving new building developments. Simply provide every building with equipment to generate wind, solar, and geothermal energy.

Yes, this can already be done in existing homes. There is a gel that gives windows a higher insulation rating. There is a kind of paint coating that absorbs solar energy. There is a wind turbine made up of nanotubes; they call it Nano-vent skin in Mexico. This 'skin' is fixed to the façade of the house, and turns your home into a wind turbine (this skin can also be applied to the walls of subway tunnels. The wind energy created by passing trains is converted into usable energy). Our own Delft University of Technology has developed a solar foil – the successor of the expensive solar panels – that needs only 35 m2 to provide a home with enough energy for an entire year. And it only requires a €3,000 investment.

Municipalities have to write off their land investments anyway. And, here in Europe, we have ample land. An abundance. The occupants pay only for their house, and on top of that for all these energetic so-lutions out of their own pocket. However, individual citizens no longer have to pay for the land. The land belongs to the community, and we are the community. The price advantage for the land compensates for the additional costs to become an individual energy plant, and this is how, on balance, we can build our houses a lot cheaper. In this way, we can directly save the building and construction industry – and save energy. And seeing that we excel in writing up rules, our civil servants can probably come up with some nice regulations to prevent misuse. Not a bad idea, don't you think?

Any overproduction of that self-generated energy can be stored as hydrogen, and can be transported to our power companies. They can redistribute all this energy, perhaps to the rest of Europe. If we are short of power, we will obviously get our transported energy back first, and free of charge, from our power companies. Rifkin envisions the distribution of all this energy via an Intergrid, a transport network for hydrogen, comparable to the Internet for the distribution of data.

Critics object to such a form of hydrogen distribution, because it will not be simple. Come on! When we supplied every house with gas and electricity in the previous centuries, the circumstances were much worse, and we were successful then, too.

If we do not necessarily have to be self-supporting, then there are always projects like Desertec. In this plan, solar energy is generated in the Sahara desert, and will be subsequently transported to the rest of the world. Greenpeace is evidently on board with this plan: "Concentrated Solar Power plants are the next big thing in renewable energy," said Sven Teske, Renewable Energy Director from Greenpeace International. "After the wind industry took off in the mid 1990s and the solar photovoltaic technology started its boom about five years ago, CSP is now the third multi-billion dollar industry for clean power generation."

The expectations for biomass, in the shape of genetically modified algae, are high. It will take decades before nuclear fusion will be feasible. It is not about making choices. We have to employ every option to put a stop to the depletion of our fossil fuels. And, in view of the rise of the growing demand for energy by nations like China and India, we will have to develop at a fast rate.

5.5
We will no longer work in offices and offices will no longer work

Over the past decades, developing commercial real estate has been a moneymaking machine. Due to the emerging technologies that stimulate virtual coworking, we no longer have to work in designated offices. By now, we have, in The Netherlands as well as the rest of Europe, a surplus of office space, and as our working habits become more flexible and mobile, the demand for office space will only decrease. Where e-commerce is growing faster than ever, a declining demand for retail space will follow.

Still, in the eyes of our administrators, 'thinking big' is nowhere near big enough. Suddenly, every self-respecting city wants a Bio Science Park. Or a Creative Valley. They are swayed by the issues of the day, and their only goal is to hike up their property values. In Europe, we have over 150 Science Parks. In The Netherlands, Bio

Science Parks are offered by the cities of Leiden, Wageningen, Utrecht, Amsterdam (three locations), Rotterdam (three locations), and Delft. The province of Limburg beats them all, with four locations: Parkstad, Venray, Sittard, and Maastricht. Thirteen Bio Parks in The Netherlands? Dream on! To people abroad, The Netherlands is one big city; offering thirteen dens can't be taken seriously.

The focus needs to be shifted toward reuse and renovation. The demand for extra square footage of office space is declining. New developments, therefore, have to make way for replacement and new use.

The municipality of Amsterdam has already struck the right note out of necessity. Due to market developments alone, they have had to cross out a million square meters (10.7 million square feet) of new office space: a loss of €345 million of forecasted revenue. It will now be written off, and, as a result, several municipal initiatives will have to be halted. This is just the beginning of the end for this load of froth, because the European housing corporations are still stuck with plots of land, which are worth billions of Euros. Many cities, organizations, and more money will follow. All of this is in dire need of different legislation. It simply needs to be made possible that old offices can have a different purpose so that they can be reused for other purposes, like living, schools, small-scaled production, or a combination of these. The municipality of Amsterdam even has appointed an 'office-space intermediary' to smooth this transformation of buildings toward new purposes.

5.6
Houses as castles

According to a 2010 study by the Landes Bausparkasse, a house in Germany is, on average, 50% cheaper than one in The Netherlands. On top of that, the building of houses in The Netherlands has been done on a massive scale, creating houses that nobody needs: the wrong types of homes in the wrong places. The surplus of apartments is astounding. However, they are not suitable for elderly people, thus leaving the aging population in the country completely unaddressed. In Dutch cities, there will be a growing demand in the coming years, until 2040, for 700,000 houses. In large parts of our country, the population growth is stagnating, or people are moving away towards the

Interesting, in that respect, is the initiative of Daniele Kihlgren. Striking an unprecedented deal with the local authority, in return for a guarantee of inedificabilita – a blanket ban on new building – he promised to invest serious quantities of money in bringing back to life the ancient village of Santo Stefano di Sessanio in Southern Italy, and after an investment of €4.5 million, Sextantio threw open its doors, and introduced discerning travellers from Italy and elsewhere to a face of the rugged Abruzzo region that they had never seen before, and an entirely new type of hotel: what he calls an 'albergo diffuso', a 'scattered hotel'. No new structures were required; instead, reception, restaurant, and guest-rooms occupied different medieval cottages clustered together on the town's slopes. A second village followed, and the plan is to aquire and operate 9 villages in total.

larger cities, a tendency we see in more European countries. So, no matter how you look at it, the mismatch and shortage is frightening.

Municipalities that are depopulating must devalue their property options. The system of municipal finances is still an enormous bubble. As I suggested earlier, if that land is made directly available to private individuals at no cost, and if such a house were to be its own power station, then that would stimulate home ownership, and people would make a conscious decision to go and live in such a depopulating municipality.

There are millions of empty houses in Spain. Most of them are poorly constructed, but they have served their goal: municipalities and real estate developers have filled their deep pockets. Bankrupt banks, financing the whole scheme, had to be saved with European taxpayers' money. Thank you. So, why don't we give those empty houses to the Spanish population, most of whom cannot pay their mortgages due to the economic crisis? Or give it to the Spanish youth without a future? With youth unemployment at over 50%, at least some people may benefit from this abundance.

The Dutch rental market has been at a standstill for decades. Large groups of people are living in homes that are too cheap, and are blocking the process of moving up the housing ladder, because buying property is unattainable for them. Banks simply no longer cooperate. Only ten percent of the total three million rental properties in The Netherlands are rented on the free market; the rest is locked up in some 'governmental program'. So, lets start a Commons Bank. Or allow credit unions to be formed, just to finance housing again.

New real estate developments need a new approach. Frank Bijdendijk, of the organization Stadsgenoot in the city of Amsterdam, develops housing and office premises according to the Solids concept. It is innovative because the shell of a building is designed, and the inside is not. Liberal regulations ensure that the tenants have flexibility because they are not bound to requirements or a zoning plan. They can do what they want with the premises – turn it into a small company, a home, an office, or a combination of these. You can rent the shell and finish the interior and trimmings yourself. An auctioning system determines the eventual rent price. The canal-side houses and warehouses in Amsterdam inspired Frank. And, because of their flexibility in usage, they are still being used today while the first apartment complexes in the Southeast Amsterdam are being demolished after just thirty years, because they no longer meet the needs of today's occupants. Solids has reduced the risk factor and lack of occupancy with its new vision. Even though (or because) this development is at odds with prevailing legislation and issuing rules, I believe it is a prime example of building innovation.

Surf to Eatmyhouse.nl, an initiative of the East-Watergraafsmeer quarter of Amsterdam. You will find over fifty magnificent examples of innovative construction. There are beautiful and affordable floating houses built according to the cradle-to-cradle principle that generate their own energy. It's brilliant!

On the OECD's list of countries with the most overvalued homes in the world, The Netherlands is in fifth place. According to the OECD, property in The Netherlands is 48% too expensive in relation to family income, and 39% too expensive compared to rental rates. This implies that fiscal mortgage interest relief cannot be sustained. The sooner we end it, the better.

Every country in Europe has its own real estate problems. The key is the artificially created scarcity by the real estate, monetary, governmental, and political elites. We need more flexibility, and to share the communal abundance of land. And I am saying this as a realistic entrepreneur, not as an idealistic socialist from the 1960's...

5.7
City development:
again, use the abundance, not the scarcity

China and Singapore are working on Tianjin eco-city. On their official website it states that:

"The Tianjin Eco-city's vision is to be 'A thriving city which is socially harmonious, environmentally-friendly and resource-efficient – a model for sustainable development'. This vision is underpinned by the concepts of 'Three Harmonies' and 'Three Abilities.'"

"Three Harmonies" refers to:
- People living in harmony with other people, i.e. **social harmony**
- People living in harmony with economic activities, i.e. **economic vibrancy**
- People living in harmony with the environment, i.e. **environmentalsustainability**

"Three Abilities" refers to the Eco-city being:
- **Practicable** the technologies adopted in the Eco-city must be affordable and commercially viable
- **Replicable** the principles and models of the Eco-city could be applied to other cities in China and even in other countries
- **Scalable** the principles and models could be adapted for another project or development of a different scale

The city should be ready in 2020.

The capacity of historic European sites can be an increasing problem. Don't forget that most of Europe infrastructure was built thousands of years ago, and that historic connections are still in place, whether they are covered by a 10 lane highway or not.

Still most European cities approach their development in a traditional way. They may want, for instance, more hotels to stimulate the local economy without wondering if there will be enough for visitors to sustain it in the future. Of course, globally, tourism is on the rise, and in particular, tourists from BRIC countries – mainly China and India – will create an unprecedented surge in the amount of visitors in the short term. And, Europe has a rich past connected with the history of civilization, so we will welcome the majority of these visitors.

Although it seems like a paradox to ask yourself, on one hand, if there is demand for a hotel service, while, on the other hand, the sheer number of tourists will increase. Not only the rise in sharing formulas I introduced earlier in this book, such as Couchsurfing and AirBnb, will solve the need for more beds, but it is the tourist attractions, themselves, that have capacity issues. Because either these 'attractions' were never built to be attractions,or they were never designed for such a mass of tourists.

For a visit to the Notre Dame in Paris, you often have to wait in line. It is normal to wait at least two hours before entering the Eiffel Tower. Do you want to see the Mona Lisa? Sure you can! Just peer over the heads of thousands of other visitors from a distance of 115 feet. Like the Statue of Liberty in New York or a visit to the Alhambra in Granada? They're impossible to visit without booking beforehand. Allowing too many visitors in the Tower of Pisa is downright dangerous. For the average exhibition in The Netherlands, you have to wait in line for hours as well. Do you suddenly feel like playing a round of golf in Spain? You will be confronted with long waiting times on the premium courses. And if you want to drive to the South of France, it is almost normal to wait an hour at each tollbooth or gas station.

The amount of visitors in and around cities is determined by the capacity of the attractions to reach them and the possible presence of obstacles, and not the presence of hotels, airports, and other facilities. It is something our policymakers really need to take into consideration.

People have more choice than ever. The absolute mediocrity of the Spanish Costas is symbolic of the decline of the European vacation-in-the-sun phenomenon. Moreover, tourists from China and India will definitely not visit Europe to lie on the beach, where they are risk of contracting skin cancer. We need to realize that tourists and travelers have limitless choices due to the digital supply of information. Competition has become global. Meta-search engines seek through all the travel websites and give us of the best available prices. The global travel supply is more accessible than ever before. Do you want to go to Europe, to Japan, to Antarctica, or North America? Click here.

There isn't a single solution to the continuously increasing mobility problem. The European public transport system has reached its limit. The railway systems are just as congested as the roads. Car usage has doubled since 1985, train travel has also doubled. The situation will only worsen after 2020. Public transport will no longer function in cities by then, because we will not have enough funds for equipment, and because of the sharp rise in the aging population. There will not be enough bus or train drivers. The old dogmas no longer work here, either.

We really have to pull out all stops to keep our Society 3.0 going. Carpooling, working from home, teleconferencing, Skyping, hub working, coworking, longer opening hours for government services, and healthcare. It's all about using our available time and space a lot smarter.

We need to create legal space for car and bike sharing programs or private car renting programs. We must allow the Google smart cars, vehicles moving around without a driver that can serve as tailormade public transportation. Also, I see an enormous growth of ride/car sharing websites. 'Share the abundance' is the credo here!

and healthcare. It's all about using the available time and space a lot smarter.

Create legal space for car and bike sharing programs or private car renting programs. Allow the Google smart cars, vehicles driving around without a driver that can serve as tailormade public transportation. Also I see actually already an enormous growth of ride-, car sharing websites. 'Share the abundance' is the credo here!

6
WORK 3.0 & MORE

No, this chapter is not about nouveau work. It is about work and income, and how we can all interpret and create it. Work 3.0 is all about the phenomenon of the working human being.

Europe is aging. And that should put some grey hairs on your head. Just look at the data from The Dutch Bureau for Statistics on the country's present and future age distribution and compare that to the age distribution of a nation like India.

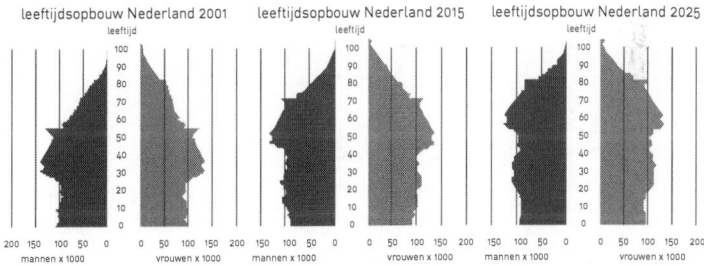

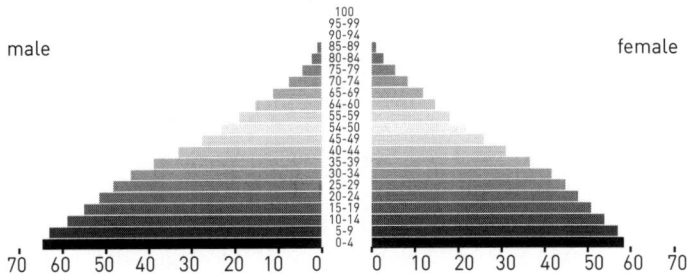

leeftijdsopbouw Nederland 2001   leeftijdsopbouw Nederland 2015   leeftijdsopbouw Nederland 2025

India: 2005   population (in millions)
source: U.S. Census Bureau, International Data Base.

Look at Japan. They have had a huge crisis for a number of decades. Their entire economy relies on exports, and is therefore very one-sided. Keeping a lid on production costs and wages is their only weapon to combat export stagnation. Forty percent of the work force does not have a decent fixed contract; older employees are rarely trained, and they don't train themselves (why would they?). The Japanese costs are shifted unilaterally onto minorities: women and young people. The group with the most initiative in society has the fewest opportunities; productivity continues to decline, and the same goes for Japanese prosperity. In a final attempt to break the status quo in 2013, Prime Minister Shinzo Abe started to pour in money. Lots of it! However, when the clogs are stuck, pouring in more oil doesn't make the wheels turn. So, unless Japan reforms itself and lifts the restrictions and dated legalities, the country will not get out of the zombie state.

This prospect awaits us in Europe as well. In The Netherlands alone, almost 1 million people (out of a labor population of roughly 7 million) will retire in the coming decade. If the market situation does not change, the logistics branch alone will need 55,000 extra people by 2015 (source: Trading Organization for Logistics and Transport).

In the field of education, about 100,000 teachers will retire in ten years' time. And, in the same period, the sharp rise in the aging population in the healthcare industry will create – according to the Dutch Healthcare and Innovation Platform – a gaping chasm between the 480,000 required employees and an influx of just 250,000. If we were to fill all those jobs in healthcare, then 1.7 million people would be working in the field by that time. With today's political insights, we are unable to pay for that. But it's not primarily about the money; because of the aging population, there simply are not enough people. The workforce all over Europe is declining.

The remaining workers want to work less. Collective pensions and healthcare premiums are becoming prohibitive. There are less people paying and more people who will demand these funds over the long-term. This enforced collectivity is bringing us to ruin. The Japanese scenario is lying in wait.

Or are we going to be replaced by robots? Not the human look-alikes, but artificial intelligence around us. Many administrative jobs, middle management, and manufacturing positions will be gone. Even journalism will not be saved from automation.

According to a 2013 study by the University of Oxford, "47 percent of total US employment is in the high risk category, meaning that associated occupations are potentially automatable over some unspecified number of years, perhaps a decade or two."

"The problem with the conventional wisdom is that it underestimates the long-term impact of automation and it expects too much in the way of occupational acrobatics from the average worker," says Martin Ford, a software developer and author of *The Lights in the Tunnel*. Ford argues that this is somewhat analogous to having the agricultural sector mechanized and then expecting that everyone will get a job driving a tractor. "The numbers don't work," he concludes.

Globally, work will be divided in a different way. We see the rise of platforms like Elance, ODesk, and Freelancer.com helping companies to create their own 'circle' of experts around them and serving as the new temporary labor or outsourcing agencies. Corporate value creation will be loosely organized with (global) project teams growing and shrinking quickly, adding and losing different skills. According to Elance's Steffen Hedebrandt, this market for companies like Elance and Odesk will rise between 2013 and the next couple of years from $1 billion to $5 billion, confirming the transformation of 'work' as we know it.

6.1
Solidarity? By choice, not enforced

In the long term, pension funds have to grow to a cover ratio that matches the risks the fund runs. [...] The pension funds have given themselves nine years to achieve this (where a maximum term of fifteen years is permitted). Many funds expect to achieve this with re-calculated investment returns, by keeping indexing on the backburner and asking for a surcharge on their premiums.

– From a publication of the Dutch Central Bank (DNB)
about the Dutch pension funds, July 2009

In plain language, it says, "You are going to pay more and receive less."

The Dutch pension system, supposedly to be one of the best in the world, is slowly but surely going under. In the near future, there simply will not be enough workers to pay the 'pensionados'. Also, according to a 2013 Dutch National Bank study called 'Cost Efficiency of Pension Funds', the system and administration costs remain unclear, but are rising steadily."

So, if 'one of the best systems in the world' is in trouble, what does that mean for the pension funds facing the fast aging populations of the other European countries?

Let's cut all the crap and put a stop to this system.

I keep hearing old directors, politicians, and administrators say that we have to show solidarity. Solidarity? To whom and to what? Enforced solidarity. Keep doing what we've been doing for years with hide-one's-head-in-the-sand-solidarity. How much solidarity are we showing when we are burdening our youth with a dysfunctional pension system? I no longer want to show solidarity towards the mess of the establishment. Why can I not take care of my own retirement as a right-minded citizen ought to? Have we become collectively dumber than all those supervisors and executors with their cushy jobs? Give us the freedom to manage our own pension, and let us decide at which age we want to retire. If I decide to work fewer hours, that is my decision.

People are more than capable of organizing their own lives. Some work like crazy, while others won't. Give them some more say in their self-determination. Some will work independently, and some would like to work as employees. Ensure that employers can customize regulations for each department or sector. At this moment, many regulations are uniform. Let people decide for themselves where they want to park their pension funds. The average citizen is more than capable of making tough decisions, as long as they are aware of the fact they are their own decisions.

6.2
The role of the organization

The balance of power is shifting in organizations. People no longer need these structures to acquire income. They work for and within networks at the same time, and choose the network that earns their 'input'. As an institution, you have to work pretty hard to find people who are willing to add to with your organization.

Dutch recruitment specialist Bas van de Haterd has this to say about it on his blog:

"An organization can position itself in the (job) market as an organization with fans. Being commercial or not-for-profit is then no longer relevant. But, an organization will then have to do something unique, something special. It will have an open structure and strive to optimize value instead of optimizing money. They do not gain revenue from everywhere because they can, and not doing this will lead to a much greater added value. Organizations can then get fans who will help propagate your employer brand, resulting in the fact that people will want to work for you."

Not just potential employees, but actually all stakeholders nowadays chose to create value with organizations, and do so in places they want. This awakening has caused the shift in the balance of power. Who are the new co-creating value network stakeholders, and what do they want?

Let's have a look at the changing stakeholder role of the younger employee, the senior employee, and the non-employee, like your suppliers, clients, and knowmads...

6.3
Generation Y and the senior employee

During a meeting with the Seats2meet.com team, I asked one of our employees, Lukie, "Can you fetch the flip-chart? I want to draw something." Lukie is very smart. This is how she describes herself on her web-profile: "I got my bachelor's in Liberal Arts & Sciences and majored in New Media. During my studies at the University of Utrecht, I researched new media, games and digital culture. I also invented and implemented an open-source cross-media concept."

She is brilliant! Yet, after my request, she looked at me quizzically and a bit uncertainly. I asked her, "Do you know what a flip-chart is?" "No," she replied timidly."

Voilá: the generation Y employees. They are the precursors of the M, S, and Z generations, are in their 20s, and have just entered the job market. They know everything about cross-media, social media, co-creation, crowd sourcing, and user generated content. And they know about augmented reality, embedding, and MMORPGs as well. They have a significant Internet presence. They do not automatically think of money when they talk about value. Transparency and sharing knowledge are second nature to them. But, they do not know what a flip-chart is. The people of Generation Y are looking for a learning and work environment that connects to the way of communicating they have been cultivating privately for years.

On the opposite end, we find the older generation.

Dealing with the sharp rise in the aging population properly is an important issue in manufacturing organizations. Industries that literally need hands to create value will face almost insurmountable demographic problems. We have to cherish these senior employees. BMW has taken the first steps in their plant in Dingolfing. They realized the age of the population is increasing in Bavaria, as well. The average age is rising from 39 years to 47 years. Since 2007, they've been reorganizing their product lines with their employees' concerns in mind. Over 70 small, ergonomic adjustments were made: a wooden floor instead of a concrete one prevents joint issues in the legs; flexible magnifying glasses prevent eye strain, tired eyes, and subsequently, mistakes; a small crane as a lifting tool; relaxation chairs at the workstations; and, strict work diversity to keep production up. A €40,000 investment resulted in a 7% rise in productivity, a reduction of absenteeism by 50%, and a diminishment of errors to 0%.

Or, do you think all these employees will be replaced by robots? Or, will we built fewer cars, due to all collaborative car sharing programs in the interdependent economy? Or, should we just print our cars at home?

6.4
Knowmads: the new employee is a non-employee

Small is the new big, only when the person running the small thinks big. Don't wait. Get small. Think big.

– Seth Godin

In recent years, the business world has been in considerable motion. More and more people no longer experience an employment contract with an organization as secure as they used to, and have decided to start for themselves. The economic recession has accelerated this process. We have labeled this large group of people 'SEPs': Self-Employed Professionals, or Free Agents. John Moravec calls them, in his book, *Knowmad Society* (in which I contributed), simply, 'knowmads'.

"A Knowmad is a nomadic knowledge worker - that is, a creative, imaginative, and innovative person who can work with almost anybody, anytime, and anywhere. Technologies allow for these new paradigm workers to work either at a specific place, virtually, or any blended combination. Knowmads can instantly reconfigure and recontextualize their work environments, and greater mobility is creating new opportunities."

– John Moravec, *Education Futures*

Looking at this development from a generation's point of view, you will see that the so-called Millennials are also knowmadic people. No matter what angle from which you look at this development, these people all share the same behavior.

The Web is a very important tool for them. After all, the Web enables you to connect with like-minded people (i.e., to network), and that is precisely how knowmads gain their knowledge, contacts, and assignments. They drift around virtual networks.

Many of them start their own business and have no staff. It's a movement we are seeing throughout the Western world. At the moment, knowmads comprise about 10% of the working population; I estimate this percentage will rise to 30%, or even 40%, of working people in the next few years. In some Dutch cities, like Amsterdam, already 15% of the labor population is knowmadic. In the US, these percentages are even higher.

The enormous stream of knowmads will be the driving force of the new era of value creation. Let us cherish them, and provide them with technical facilities! Knowmads are not just young people who have taken the leap into entrepreneurship. Their age spread covers a larger spectrum – young and old. Their motivation differs as well. Young people view digital and social networks as a perfect pick-up point, while the older knowmad is searching for renewed certainty, which his old establishment can no longer provide. There are many more motivating factors: a sense of freedom, the importance of independence, practicing a trade or profession, realizing a mission, or professing a passion. The knowmad spends a comparatively long amount of time keeping their network up, which predominantly exists outside the establishment. Social capital is flourishing. Knowmads shape the new ecosystem of and for entrepreneurs. They are globalists.

Knowmads can generally work well together. They have to be good at something; they can't hide behind organizational room dividers. They acknowledge and respect the professionalism of others, and seek out each other's complementary competencies and talents. Together, often in coalitions formed by opportunity, they start companies or enterprises. Thanks to the Internet, small companies can do very large, or even global things. The Internet makes entrepreneurship very accessible. It's striking that the concept of knowmads is not found in current rules and legislation. The establishment does not know what to do with them. Knowmads find it hard to get financing; they are dropped out of government tenders because they do not meet (financial) turnover criteria, or have not been in existence for over three years.

This new value creation force has resulted in a declining interest in 'owning stuff'. Knowmads and new workers share. Access is more important than actual ownership. These people buy fewer goods and services. Why buy a car if you can use Uber or Zipcar?

This generation is far more important than politicians realize. 'Our' knowmads are like elastic bands in the economic community. They fulfill this role now, during the current economic downturn, and will in the future, too. They do not want to rely on part-time unemployment and other benefits; they believe they should simply tighten their belts. They are adverse to enforced solidarity, and would rather handle affairs themselves or with other Knowmads. Sharing is second nature to them.

So, collectivity, or enforced solidarity, in combination with governmental resistance against this innovative development is killing the national economies. Collaboration, or solidarity by choice, makes things work by allowing this generation of people to create value in a new way – yes! Give them space!

At present, there are around one million knowmadic workers in The Netherlands, and their numbers are growing within the rest of the European Union as well. Knowmads form a very flexible labor pool; they are already the flexible 'skin' surrounding the job market, as they continuously (re)train themselves in order to keep up-to-date, make optimal use of new media, and remain active within virtual social networks.

In the US, we see the same movement. According to the latest survey of the US-based MBO partners, "The total independent workforce grew, and so too did the projected future size of this workforce, to be as many as 23-million strong in the next five years. The simultaneous growth in size, satisfaction, commitment, and intent to choose the path, together suggest independence is far from a cyclical economic choice. It instead appears to signal a conscious structural shift and recognition of a new model of work and engagement by innovative Americans."

I have the pleasure of knowing many knowmads, and am always impressed by their knowledge, entrepreneurial spirit, drive, and willingness to collaborate. In short, for me, they are the value creators of today and tomorrow. What a joy it is to work with such a group of out of this world people!

I would like to pass the following message on to knowmads: "Don't let yourself be swallowed up by the establishment. Do not take up any position in a government body. So, not at the social and economic council, unions, or other quangos. Organize yourself informally, via the many networks available, and move outside the patterns of the establishment. You are an independent professional, and you do not need existing structures to create new value. In the very near future, the establishment will desperately need you, so define your own playing field!"

6.5
Co-working

Coworking is a style of work that involves a shared working environment, often an office, and independent activity. Unlike in a typical office environment, those coworking are usually not employed by the same organization. Typically, it is attractive for telecommuting (work at home) professionals, independent contractors, or people who travel frequently and end up working in relative isolation. Coworking is also the social gathering of a group of people who are still working independently, but share values and are interested in the synergy that can happen from working with like-minded, talented people in the same space.

Coworking is vital for organizations without boundaries. Coworking usually takes place in 3rd Spaces, where the reality is augmented by virtual serendipity dashboards, like Seats2meet.com. Coworking is, and was, a typical activity for knowmads creating new value. More and more traditional employees have started coworking, too. Corporations form informal networks with all their stakeholders, including suppliers. When these groups meet and start to co-work, new, economically sustainable value creation will boom.

Research from the Rotterdam School of Management shows that "many people at S2M actively engage in interaction with other coworkers and the pay offs are manifold. Not only does working at S2M increase their social network, it also helps to develop people's business skills, and improve their products and services.

These personal benefits are then followed by concrete business outcomes such as collaborating on a project or targeting prospects together. Even finding a new job or assignment are not uncommon outcomes at the Seats2meet community. Part of these positive outcomes can be explained by the nature of this coworking site. Using this working space asks people to be open to the exchange of social capital, and therefore coworking at Seats2meet.com enables networking. In particular the diversity of people increases the likelihood of serendipitous encounters. These serendipitous encounters positively affect the creation of social ties and in turn increase the likelihood of concrete outcomes such as collaboration and job creation".

6.6
Suppliers and clients become co-workers

Suppliers are in a dilemma: their customers demand more and more from a service or product, but want to pay less for it. Some customers squeeze their suppliers. We notice that traditional, large clients believe that their future success is dependent upon squeezing the last 5% discount out of a deal. Sometimes we go along with this to give meaning to the adage 'we stick together, since we're in this together'. Sometimes, we don't go along with it, and lose these customers.

Well, 'lose'...

We try to set an example in our relationship with our suppliers. I believe their role should drastically change, and that they should play more of a part in our organization. They will be more of a co-creator and partner of the social value network around our services. Within our meeting and congress centers, we no longer invest in matters such as sound equipment and audio/video projectors. Our supplier invests, installs, and services this equipment on-site, including the corresponding virtual information on our website. He no longer needs people who drive around all day delivering and collecting equipment. Thanks to our online reservation system, he is kept abreast of his sales or rentals directly via a Web feed. He can respond immediately to complaints or comments that are created through our review sites and our buzz monitoring. In short, as an organization, we are actually facilitating the connection between our customer and our supplier, without having to be the go-between, as still happens in the old value network. We've moved from value chain to value network. We determine sales prices with our suppliers and share the proceeds. By eliminating a series of costs, the prices can drop, and profits can rise. And, we achieve this without a contract, a service level agreement, or other paper monsters.

Of course, you may still need something like a confirmation letter every now and then. But, in essence, we work together on the basis of trust, and we point out each other's responsibilities. Within our value network, we all have the same stake, after all. It is becoming increasingly more important for us to work with suppliers who understand this new game. This will bring in much more than anybody could by squeezing the last percentage points out of procurement deals, or breaking open, settled contracts.

Smart companies shift a part of their activities to the customer. At our Seats2Meet.com locations, sophisticated Internet solutions enable our customers to manage the entire logistic process around their events. So, we no longer need a separate department for that.

Customers design new constructions at Club Lego, so the Lego design department is history. This open-innovation phenomenon is called co-creating. In part three of this book, the topic will be discussed at length.

7
MONEY 3.0

The banking sector is rotten to the core. Banks do not do what they should be doing: mediating between saver and investors. And they do what should not be doing: selling each other inflated nonsense that benefits no one. This was the situation before the economic downturn and it is still the case today.

− Ewald Engelen, professor of financial geography at the Free
University of Amsterdam, in the Dutch newspapaper
Financieeel Dagblad, December 10, 2010

I think more and more: this is the end of the road, the end of the whole economical system as we know it.

− Joris Luyendijk, a Dutch journalist for
The Guardian, September, 2013

Action leads to reaction. I am talking about our financial crisis. At
Action leads to reaction. I am talking about our financial crisis. At a
national level, in particular, from the political spectrum, there is a call
for more control and oversight over the banking system. The banking
world is reacting as well, although they are singing the tune of 'we
have learned our lesson, now trust us and let us deal with it'. The first
international business banks have − while the crisis is not yet over −
already paid out more bonuses than they have made in profit. So, no
sign of a self-correcting capacity can be found, and control systems
do not work either. But, we can still see the same players shifting
about. That does not instill much confidence. Evidently, change has to
come from outside the system.

Politicians and the establishment are, naturally, calling for more regulations to protect those poor consumers. But does the consumer want to protect himself? Just recently, the most complex financial products, with their high commissions, were selling like hot cakes. Nobody was receptive to the warning signs as we didn't really understand these financial products. As long as the stock markets kept rising, the consumer quickly doubled or tripled his or her returns. Everybody was happy, and everybody wanted more; and yes, we the consumers wanted that, too. We only started to complain when returns and payments fell behind. The term 'usurious policy' was born. It was gradually forgotten that collecting tons of money is coupled to great risk. No regulation can withstand the glitter and glamour in regard to subordinated bonds and other nice financial terms.

The only remedy for a healthy financial market is a critical consumer or a private investor who knows that earning money and taking risk go hand in hand, and who is capable of asking advisors critical questions, whether they work independently, for large banks, or for insurance companies. It goes without saying that providers of financial products have a responsibility to maintain. In other words, their products need to be transparent. The customer has to be able to find out quite easily what the bank is doing with their money. Under these conditions, the consumer can regain control over his or her financial affairs.

Several levels up, we find our nation in a Euro-political system that evidently allows, as we have learned the hard way, countries to be creative with national budgets. How much confidence is there, then, in the Euro? If buyers and financiers of our Western public loans would rather invest their money in the upcoming markets, instead of the no-longer-so-rich-and-influential West, or if they no longer have faith in the Euro market, this will lead to unwanted results. This way of thinking already led to a consumer strike of government bonds for our Euro countries in May, 2010. A Euro meltdown could only be prevented by swift action, taken by European politicians and the European Central Bank with an injection of €750 billion into the system, and central purchases of government bonds, respectively. I am not a financial wizard, so I lost track of how much money, in the meantime, is poured into the Euro system to keep it afloat.

Some people take a gloomy view on our monetary system. The international expert in the design and implementation of currency systems, Professor Bernard Lietaer, predicts the collapse of the dollar in the next five years. Only by borrowing dollars abroad (China) or printing more dollars can the United States still finance its government deficit. You can't do this endlessly. According to formal international standards, the United States is actually already bankrupt. The American economist Lachman predicts the same outcome for the Euro. Euro countries with poor records still may decide to exit the Euro system, simply because they are unable to get their balance sheets in order under the current requirements. Escaping to their previous currency, and devaluing it, could be a way out for them.

These situations always lead to debate. Do we stay in the European Monetary Union, or do we start a new European currency union with the countries in Northern Europe? It's the traditional body of thought: choosing between one and the other.

I suggest making another choice. We let the EMU be and at the same ensure that we will be less dependent on that same Euro. Make the financial system less important. How do we achieve this? By giving new players and new value systems a larger playing field.

7.1
Banking has to become more simple...even boring!

Since the onset of the crisis, we kept saying to ourselves that our banks are 'too big to fail'. Is this to make them appear important, or is it a subconscious cry for help that these institutions are holding us hostage? I believe the banking system should be made up of smaller, (semi) national, ancient, and risk-free operating banks.

When I transfer funds, I expect speed and security. I prefer to keep my savings in an account with a modest interest rate that covers the rate of inflation; in particular, I want my money to be kept safe.

Most of the time, the bank does not even understand you. In my case, the combination of our hospitality, catering, Web, and IT activities unsettles my bank manager. And I can barely explain our innovative Internet and social network activities to bankers who do not even own a laptop.

Banks must make a choice. Do they want high returns, bonuses, and risks? Doing business at their expense? Fine, but do it outside the scope of the existing order and remain self-sufficient. In order to guarantee consumer confidence, high-risk banks should make a financial contribution to a European Guarantee Fund. It's called being responsible. Failing banks should no longer be able to transfer their losses onto the remaining banks or the government because the consumer will then pay for it again. Is it too much to ask for some more stability? 'Steady as she goes?' Small reliable banks? Robust balance ratios? Should this not be a conditio sine qua non in the financial world? To compensate their transaction costs, they can charge a fixed, modest interest rate as a surcharge linked to the Euribor rate (the interest banks charge each other of which I assume will be done honestly in the near future, after the 2013 Libor scandal), but a bank should never be allowed to ask for more returns. Don't you think that banks that make a profit are a paradox?

7.2
Alternative banking services

So, with any luck, we will be left with relatively small banks, bound by rigid rules and legislation, under strict supervision, and run by reliable people who do not have the urge for expansion. So, they are a little bit boring. They may even be partly owned by the government. It is obviously mandatory for the government, the semi-public sector, and other organizations that administer public funds to do business with these banks. Most European countries own, presently, one or more banks, so we can start today.

'Boring' must obviously not lead to a banking bureaucracy: having a grip on procedures with the aim to cover oneself. Opening up a new private checking account – as I have experienced recently, with the state owned ABN bank in The Netherlands – encompasses half a ton of paperwork, and two and a half hours, for three moments of required physical contact. And that's in 2013!

These boring banks do business internationally with other boring banks, so that we can also do business across borders in a safe and boring manner. It's a positive development that ING has recently said goodbye to its insurance division (and if it were up to me, they should divest themselves of their real-estate enterprise as well) in order to just focus on banking. The Dutch state-owned SNS deserves a pat on the back, too, for their new reward policy: any bonuses are capped and are spread out over three years, so they are no longer directly linked to the share price. Yes, it is all very boring, and not very modern.

The customer is tired of invisible mortgage or credit constructions. Thanks to the Basel III Accord requirements, more capital buffers need to be sustained, with the result that less credit can be granted. So, obviously, it is time for something new.

If these boring banks want to do something new, I can think up a few things for them.

How about advising, coaching, and mentoring start-ups and know-mads on financial and economic matters? Existing bank clients can share their experiences with new, potential entrepreneurs and business leaders. Banks could administer the new credit unions, where entrepreneurs lend money to other entrepreneurs. Or, banks could assist the creation of new, informal insurance products, such as the Dutch Broodfondsen.

The bank can act as an incubator and as a facilitator of small enterprise. Instead of playing money shop, they should furnish large bank buildings for flexible workspaces, including Wi-Fi and secretarial support. They should organize training sessions and workshops about personal branding, collaboration, and other handy tips and tricks, for example.

There is plenty of square footage available for such knowmad-flex work lounges in the bank buildings. And if a fee has to be paid, let's say one Euro per hour, then that is a great opportunity to implement an internet-based micropayment system. Maybe the knowmads can make payments through an alternative currency unit. That way, the banks feed innovation, instead of blocking innovative alternate money creation initiatives.

Banks and their monetary affairs may be boring, but they can create a unique customer experience in the facilitation of unexpected meetings between their stakeholders. And just imagine if all banks would organize it together in an open system. Then, they would be on the right track to stimulate the (new) economy. There are so many great things to do at home. Do Dutch, Belgian, Spanish, or French banks really have to be global players? Most European countries are small countries; let us behave as such.

If a business bank is needed for the few multinationals we still have, then they can come from the USA or China. And, on the flipside, multinationals (as well as country governments) should really wonder if it is still socially responsible to work with banks such as JPMorgan Chase (who earned almost $20 billion in 2012 and issued matching bonuses)...

...Or, should we step into the world of micro payments? Paypal and Amazon are already offering e-checkout services, EasyJet is starting up a bank, and a companies such as Google already have Dutch banking licenses! Established banks are being left behind.

The European National Banks will remain supervisors in my view, but let's bring in other managers and administrators, please. Not men and women who think they are above the law, but people who do their work quickly and properly, while keeping an eye on future developments. Just like the police force, which has to become increasingly proficient at fighting Internet crimes, banking supervisors will have to be at the top of their game because danger threatens.

To give you an example, 40% of stock exchange business no longer takes place at the official exchange. This is interesting in light of supervision.

Also, there is an increase in high volume trading, a phenomenon where computer systems trade stock autonomously, using all kinds of mathematical formulas that have been devised by quants, or those who apply mathematical techniques to financial investments. This computer-controlled trading has an edge of a couple of tenths of seconds(!) over the rest of the market, and that market reacts to it within tenths of seconds. This generates high volumes at an incredibly high pace. All of this means that the next global financial crisis can literally take place, completely 'underwater' within an hour.

7.3
Peer-to-peer lending

Society 3.0 is a paradigm that characterizes itself by moving around the establishment, and whose citizens organize things as much as possible themselves. You will find people in social networks prepared to lend and borrow money to and from like-minded people. This is called peer-to-peer lending.

In the distant past, we used to do this as well; in fact, this is how the Rabobank in The Netherlands, the Raiffeissen Bank in Germany, or the Credit Agriculture in France came into being cooperative banks.

Now, we have a website for that, and you can look further than your street or your family – you post how much money you want to lend, what you need it for, the interest rate you want to pay, and in how many installments you intend to pay off the loan. People who want to lend you the money can sign up for just a small part of the desired amount. Even here, the level of interest is linked to the amount of risk. Some sites even give you a credit rating, so moneylenders can decide how much of a risk they want to run. The amounts that are loaned and borrowed range from €1,000 to €25,000. Like-minded people understand each other's needs, businesses, and risks. Experienced IT professionals can, for example, help starting IT workers in their start-up businesses.

The peer-to-peer initiatives have exotic names like Zopa, Prosper, and Fosik. There is Smava in Poland, and Paidai in China. At the American company Prosper, almost $600 million have already been distributed, and over 1,850,000 people are participating in this peer-to-peer lending enterprise.

Start-up companies or producers can turn to Kickstarter.com, a website that mediates venture capital on a small scale for projects that have a clear start and end. The amounts can run up to, and even over, a million dollars. During the re-editing process of this book, I learned that Ubuntu, an open source software platform, is running the biggest crowd funding action so far on the site Indiegogo: their goal is to raise over 30 million dollars.

The importance of these platforms is not only the availability of money, but also the presence of (prospective) clients. If nobody wants to give money for your idea, perhaps you should rethink it?

In Belgium, over 100 organizations, from unions to NGOs, are working together with over 40,000 civilians to found the NewB, a new, co-operative, peer-to-peer bank. This initiative started in March, 2013, and is presently in the process of becoming a real bank – however, a bank whose values, according to their manifest, are 'simplicity, modesty, transparency, and only investing in local, sustainable initiatives'.

In The Netherlands, various groups are working to establish credit unions, however, the establishment is resistant, and our legal system doesn't make this an easy journey.

The Swedish bank JAK operates without using interest rates. Members save up money, and then borrow from the big pot. So, they are an old-fashioned, reliable cooperative savings bank, provided they operate without calculating interest.

"The JAK Members Bank is for a just and fair economy. By this, we mean a sustainable economy that takes all environmental costs and gains into account and aims to increase long-term prosperity for everyone. Through its savings and loan program and its efforts to spread information about the ill effects of interest on money, JAK is working actively to promote an economy that does not exploit people or nature."

Individual participants, and also community projects, can borrow money, but it all starts with saving. The savings serve as a foundation for a loan that can be increased by a certain factor. This is connected to the available liquid assets. During the loan term, money is paid off and saved, so at the end of the term, the saved amount is equal to the loan. Saving points are used as a monetary unit. Only a fraction is paid for system costs, plus a 6% deposit as a standing security. Nowadays, there is no need to save money first at JAK. The bank has become a 'real' bank, according to Swedish legislation. As a result, the deposited savings are covered by state guarantees. The amount of repayment is much better than with traditional banks. And, because no interest is charged, the capacity for installments from participants is very high. That is why the average term of a home loan ranges from nine to eleven years, which is, in old monetary terms, 'pretty quick'.

7.4
Alternative currency systems

In 1934, two Swiss businessmen, Werner Zimmermann and Paul Enz, founded Wirtschaftsring Genossenschaft. This was an alternative banking system meant to circumvent the credit shortage of 1929. It was mainly aimed at small to medium enterprises. Now it is called the WIR Bank. The WIR-system has about 60,000 participants, which amounts to 20% of all Swiss small and medium enterprises. About 1.6 billion Swiss Francs are turned over, and spread over millions of small transactions. In 2008, the total balance was SFR 3.4 billion. How does WIR work? An entrepreneur is accepted into the system after a simple screening, based on reputation and solvability. He sells his products or services, partly for money, and partly for a WIR check from the purchaser. This check balance is booked into a central register after 1% is deducted for administrative fees. The entrepreneur can use this balance to purchase products or services from other WIR participants.

Notice that this is principally about small amounts, up to a few thousand Francs per transaction. In this manner, a lot of value goes around for relatively little money. Many products and services can even be purchased with just WIR checks. The 1% administration fees are invoiced periodically, and can only be paid for with real money. If you want to purchase something and you do not have sufficient WIR credits, you can borrow credits, as long as certain securities are put in place. Like, for example, a mortgage that can be paid off in ten years. A modest interest rate is calculated over the amount borrowed in WIR-credits: about 1%. Approximately SFR 2 billion in mortgages have been issued. All in all, WIR has strong points like low risks, low costs, quick transactions, and a lot of turnover within the own circle. The system has expanded into a self-basting, commercial-social network that organizes fairs, workshops, training, and network gatherings. The checks have been partly replaced by an internet-based payment- and transaction system. Your Swiss satellite navigation system can direct you to a restaurant, hotel, or retailer that accepts WIR-credits.

The Calgary Dollar from the Arusha Center in Calgary, Canada is described as:

"The grassroots currency system that brings together local talents and resources to strengthen our local economy and build community. A community's true wealth lies in the skills, talents, and capabilities of its members. We believe that every person has something of value to offer to his or her neighbors. By encouraging local production and consumption, we are committed to creating a healthy economy that is rooted in a healthy society and a healthy ecosystem."

The Canadian Government itself in the meantime, started a currency initiative called the MintChip.

In the United States, ITEX is the marketplace for bartering, or transactions without money. The annual turnover is over $100 million, and over 25,000 companies are members. Similar, private local exchange and trade systems (LETS for short) have been in existence since 1983. You will find them all over Europe, including in The Netherlands. In Amsterdam, there is Noppes. The membership fee is €20 annually, plus 3 Noppes per month. Flarden can be found in the city of Vlaardingen. One Flard is equivalent to half a Euro; the minimum hourly rate is 15 Flarden, and the subscription fees are 12 Euros a year. There are no transaction costs. The local social services grant welfare recipients a turnover of 250 Flarden a month, before his benefit is cut. Now that's a great initiative! Most of these types of systems – about a hundred are active in The Netherlands – have a bit of a woolly image. The systems work in an old-fashioned manner, with books of coupons or paper checks. But they work.

The Dutch Social Trade Organization is mainly active in South America, and has an open source software package at its disposal. It is called Cyclos, and others can use it free of charge. This kind of trade by barter could grow to a large extent, and then the 'L' of local could be exchanged for the 'C' of community. From LETS to Community Exchange Systems, or CES. New Internet software makes trading by barter possible on a global scale.

Japan has the successful homecare system Fureai Kippu. If a Japanese person cannot care for his or her mother regularly, someone can do it for him. The other way around, he can return the favor for somebody else. In the USA, you have time banks, where people can perform a service in exchange for time dollars, units of time. It is proven that these systems improve the social cohesion in an area or in local communities. The social digital solidarity of people could make a 'local' neighborhood into a very large neighborhood. After all, the Internet has no boundaries.

The new kid on the block is called Bitcoin, a crypto currency, wherein the creation and transfer of Bitcoins is based on an open-source cryptographic protocol that is independent of any central authority. More and more companies from all over the world are accepting this currency, which is completely based on trust. There is no central bank watching, or any other central, regulatory organization. However, there is a central Bitcoin website.

Bitcoins can be 'mined'. You need a mini-supercomputer and the software. I am always interested in innovations from a couple of smart guys, and I invested in four computers for €5,000, and 'mined', using computational-intensive software, a number of Bitcoins. However, mining becomes more difficult, as there are more miners every day, and a dwindling supply of Bitcoins to mine... Enthusiasts, like me, believe that Bitcoin's peer-to-peer architecture and low barriers to entry will allow the creation of a new generation of innovative financial services, in much the same way that the Internet's open architecture led to innovative, new online services.

The bitcoin protocol makes money programmable, making numerous innovations possible, from fraud-proof voting systems, to branded currencies or digital rights management systems. So it not only virtual money!

The successor of the Bitcoin could be Ripple ⦁⦁ or the Nxtcoin ⦿.

The government, itself, does not necessarily need to mine Bitcoins or to go to a bank; they can become a new financial player by creating money themselves. After the World War II, the Dutch government created promissory notes in the form of 'mint notes'. So, why not do it again? Why do only banks have the right of money creation? In 2009, the State of California did something similar. Under the leadership of governor Arnold Schwarzenegger, the state issued IOUs due to lack of funds, and in doing so, they bypassed the banks.

7.5
A Seats2meet.com currency unit?

Together with the Dutch organization Tradecoin, we are investigating the possibility of an alternative monetary system for our own social-business network, Seats2meet.com. Then, the S2M knowmads could do business with each other without having to use money. Many services and products are already exchanged among 'seatsers'. Social capital subsequently gets its feet on the ground without having to translate into old money. In this manner, social networks can develop into sustainable ecosystems. And in the near future, we will accept Bitcoins or Amazon coins as well.

When you combine peer-to-peer lending with community exchange systems, a whole new economic structure comes into being: in the area of development cooperation, international business, or by helping each other out locally. Social capital that is generated within social networks suddenly obtains tangible value. Banks (in particular, the reliable, boring ones) should be able to facilitate this process effortlessly. They should consider helping society create new, sustainable value systems.

The Netherlands as a model country? Why not?

The role of The Netherlands as a financial global player – if it ever was significant – has been played out. However, our industrial designers, like Daan Roosegaarde, belong to the best in the world, like our creative industry. Our DJ's, such as Armin van Buuren, and our Dance festivals are renowned. Viktor & Rolf are leading fashion designers and guys like Boris Veldhuijzen van Zanten and Patrick de Laive have turned the *The Next Web* into a global leading techblog & event platform. We Dutch have been fighting the sea for centuries. Not strange when you realise that almost 50% of our land is below sea level. Our technical knowledge on building dikes, bridges and weirs is huge. Our dredging industry is leading in the world. So, why not use that creative knowledge when it comes to the pioneering work in the new parallel banking processes? We could facilitate the alternative payment systems as the trendsetters of the Interdependent Economy. I think this will suit us; we have what it takes: the infrastructure, the knowledge, the living examples, our tradition of working and acting with many different cultures, our entrepreneurial spirit, and a country capable of finding consensus – a balance. In this case, not the traditional balance between the Anglo-Saxon or Rhineland system, but the balance between social and monetary capital in the Interdependent Economy of Society 3.0.

8
DEMOCRACY 3.0

As restrictions and prohibitions are multiplied, the people grow poorer and poorer. When they are subjected to overmuch government, the land is thrown into confusion.

– Lao Tzu, Chinese philosopher, 6th century BC

Our political and administrative elite are at loss. Every day, on national levels as well as on international levels. Old systems no longer work. Our governments are divided along class lines, and that is an understatement. Ministries are closed bastions, even to fellow ministries. Municipalities do not work well together; they would rather compete. The police are not the fire department. Dozens of supervisory and investigative authorities get in each other's way. And, the administrative intermediate layer of quangos makes these issues more complex.

Social, economical and financial problems are so complex today that many ministries, and therefore, many officials or other external consultants, are no longer capable of finding solutions. The quest for solutions turns into a bureaucratic process, and the big picture disappears from sight. Loads of committees produce mountains of reports, and they just get pushed through. Something goes wrong: more rules. Governments are desperately trying to get the dynamics of our time, all the innovations, and all the new ways of value creation back into the old 'boxes' to bring them under control. A certain amount of modesty by the establishment would be appropriate. But no, many of our administrators are just arrogant.

In the report *Guide to Owning Transparency for Federal Agencies*, one of the solutions to have a better government is called an open government:

"An open, transparent, and participatory government is a government of the people, for the people, and by the people. These are the democratic principles upon which our country is built. Internet-based tools and technologies have made it easier to realize these values. Two-way, interactive Web 2.0 tools and technologies make information sharing, citizen participation, and public and private sector collaboration easier than ever before. Transparency of government practices and information, both within government agencies and between the government and its stakeholders, is the heart of open government.

[...]

Transparency is as much about open-mindedness and information sharing as it is about increased communication and information access. Citizen engagement, public-private sector partnerships, and inter-agency initiatives are all predicated upon transparency.

Transparency fosters the engagement of government employees and citizens alike, so they feel a part of the conversation, process, and decisions; and, thereby, a part of their government. This heightened sense of ownership, accountability, and trust makes government more responsive and enables agencies to more efficiently and effectively accomplish their missions: from government operations to government products."

During my lectures, I often hear that higher-ranked officials believe that citizens are unable to take a position on issues, and have little to no knowledge of subject matters; it is necessary that the government takes the lead.

Well, if someone thinks he is a hammer, everyone around him is obviously a nail. It's a pity that so many officials believe they have the solution, or are even the saviors. As it happens, a lot of knowledge is hidden among citizens. It is just a matter of mobilizing it. If you succeed in doing that, you will have better solutions and more public support for said solutions.

8.1
Ask the turkey...

By now, we all know that we have to make drastic cutbacks to the tune of billions of Euros. The political parties involved come up with all kinds of measures in their election campaigns, and after the elections, we have to reach 'consensus', and the political principles are just given away. F**k the voter. Most of the cutbacks have one thing in common: we will pay more for a lesser product (government). If this is not sufficient, then a few ministries, provinces, or police departments are consolidated. In the meantime, the alleged efficiency benefits are booked as yields and political gains.

Unfortunately, as a simple citizen, I miss real solutions. Let's start by making big cuts in the foundations of our democratic society, like our costly institutions. Shall we just shut down our regent quangos – remember those 3,000 Dutch institutions that burn up over €150 billion annually? That would be a nice opportunity for creative destruction. And what about our participation in Europe, our spot in the modern world? I had expected much more from all those brilliant minds.

According to a professor in the science of public administration, Roel in 't Veld, we need a participating democracy, "a society where citizens are creators of institutions, next to politicians and professionals. This will lead to a say of the parties concerned in the nature and content of collective provisions. The government will limit itself to a coordinating quality assurance." In 't Veld believes in massive argumentation and communication in meticulously constructed Internet dialogues.

Guus Berkhout, a professor at University of Delft, takes it even further in his essay *How Do We Make Democracy More Effective?* He is in favor of establishing a series of small ministries as back offices, to be formed into ad hoc project ministries. These project ministries, consisting of trade officials complemented with external experts, occupy themselves with national themes and operate horizontally outside the current paradigm of compartmentalization. National themes are environmental planning and public infrastructure, defense and national security, housing and care, education and work, industry and innovation, agriculture and foreign aid, and immigration and integration. Before and during elections, citizens influence the political agenda of these project ministries directly.

The line of reasoning among the aforementioned visionaries is clear to me. We convert the self-created shortage of people, means, and time into abundance: Society 3.0. Our government actually has no choice but to directly appeal to its citizens to take responsibility. In this manner, we achieve a higher level of quality, and, at the same time, create public support. This is how the government and politics can achieve a permanent connection with society. The government does not actually have to step down if a policy proposal does not pass through parliament due to lack of support – find more support, or come up with a new proposal. Of course, this transcends party politics. It would eliminate a lot of political tension and involve the electorate directly in issues that really matter.

8.2
Relationship between government & public: open data, closed Internet

Here's quote from the report *Nouveau Work at the State*, which was written by a group of Dutch officials:

"If you want officials to perform cross-border work, it is a bit strange that they have to do so in one building. With 'Nouveau Work' there is more demand for meeting places than workspaces. So the government should open the doors of government buildings to the public."

Our Seats2meet.com program enables civil servants to find a workspace in their vicinity on their cellular phone, and book a seat at the same time. We also provide insight into the knowledge that is present at the moment with other officials who are working there as well.

The municipality of Molenwaard no longer has an official brick building 'town hall'. The activities are physically spread over existing buildings in the municipality, like schools. On the Web, there is one official gateway for its civilians. Other Dutch municipalities are not so brave yet; they keep on spending money in the 'old-fashioned' way and build little palaces...

Ultimately, it would be great if we, as citizens, could make use of the existing governmental workspaces as well. Share the abundance! That is when the much needed co-creation will develop and after all: we paid for it by paying taxes.

All in all, citizen participation can be organized easily. *The Nouveau Work at State* report continues:

"The government can take a step back in their role as organizer and administrator. They must, however, facilitate the advancement of our society. A Government 3.0 creates a system of regulated basic provisions that are at the service of the whole community: education, healthcare, and infrastructure. We will find system banks, energy supply, and road and railway connections under the infrastructure category. And don't forget about our data connections in order to offer super-fast Internet access. These provisions are all ours, so why would you privatize them?"

"In a democracy which is permanently adapting itself to technological and social developments, government has to manage the unmanageable. This only can be done if the policy makers leave a decent space for civilians. They have to know when they are needed, otherwise they have to stay away."
– From the 2013 report of the Dutch Scientific Council for Governmental Policy, *Trust in Civilians.*

So, the picture becomes clear. Let's see how the government distributes information. And, how they get information...

It is estimated that the Dutch National Government, and our quangos, have over 4,000 websites in cyberspace. The government is trying to bundle the sites that are directly run by ministries. That seems like a good idea, but it will cost a lot and will solve nothing. The total volume of information is simply too great. This is also the case for cities like Utrecht, Amsterdam, or Rotterdam; they publish too many information pages, too. Working with a central content management system will not solve the control issues. The Dutch population still has to look for a needle in a haystack. The system has to become smarter. The person requesting information has to be presented with the data out of that haystack that fits his need, situation and place.

We see the same, or even worse, development in other European countries.

Widgets are mini-websites that can be built into other websites. They can contribute to solving this problem. But, is not wise for the ministries to build these solutions themselves, especially if this is done from the perspective that 'we know what the people want to know'. In this way, the information remains controlled by the supplier. The solution is to let information trickle down, in fragments, to the right place, at the right time, and in the right form. The government would be wise to seek collaborations with private parties to achieve this. All the government has to do is make all of its data available: open data! The market will organize this data according to supply and demand. Just imagine what kind of great packages of information and services could be produced. Additionally, this will cost the government little to nothing.

So, what happens to all that information about us, gathered by (governmental) organizations? More insight should be provided into that. We need new privacy guidelines for this in Europe. In the UK, there are a relatively large number of cases of data being found 'on the street'. That is because companies have a legal duty to report if something happens to their data. These mistakes happen in other countries as well, of course, but we are simply not aware of them. It's not just about the Internet. The new Dutch National Debt Information System is not at its strongest in meticulously organizing personal data. According to the Dutch Data Protection Authority, people will be stigmatized by this system. In other words, if you do not pay your wrongfully-received phone bill, you will be pilloried. So, our traditional administrators are, yet again, not setting the right example.

Face recognition is a new step in technological development. It has been used during Super Bowl XLIII in Tampa, USA. Faces of all the attendants were digitally captured and run through the FBI criminal database. With special software, a match can be found automatically. Which is more important: safety or privacy? And since this kind of software is used by Facebook as well, you can be sure many governmental institutions around the world are using this software too. So, beware! Big Brother is watching you!

8.3
More privacy issues

"I'm worried about safeguarding privacy in The Netherlands," says Samir Elloui, Chairman of the Dutch Pirate Party on the VPRO blog. "We have implemented a dangerous infrastructure in recent years. Developments are ongoing. In a couple of years, people can be followed from the moment they wake up, on the street via CCTV, and in the subway with the Public Transportation Pass. Or, just by following their cellphone. People are hardly aware of this, as are politicians. It is not just about protecting people who download, but also about protecting, for example, whistle-blowers. We have confidentiality of our mail in The Netherlands. Why is this not the case on the Internet? It is no coincidence that many people who are involved with pirate parties work in the information technology sector. I have a background in information security."

Since the publication of 250,000 confidential documents from the U.S. government on the website Wikileaks, a discussion has at least been started on how far our tolerance with regard to transparency reaches. In the meantime, all documents are being translated, by bloggers, and through official channels, into Arabic and Chinese. It is strange that the U.S. government is trying to prosecute the people behind Wikileaks, while the free press was seen as the guard of (American) democracy during the Watergate affair. The U.S. government allowed the vice-president of Afghanistan to travel scot-free to the Middle East with $50 million in his suitcase, according to Wikileaks.

We, the public, give the majority of our data away on the fly. But, a larger and larger portion of the collected data is not shared freely. In the US, the National Security Agency is building a new data collection center. It will contain over 10,000 server racks with a storage capacity of 12 exabytes. I will not even explain to you how massive that is, but it needs a power supply the equivalent of that used to power 75,000 U.S. households per year. The NSA is even checking, under the so-called Patriot Act, all the Internet traffic around the world, with the assistance of Microsoft, Yahoo, Google, Facebook, Paltalk, YouTube, Skype, AOL, Apple, and most of the other 'democratic' governments of this world.

The NSA is capable of collecting 5 billion records a day on the whereabouts of cellphones around the world. Prism, the name of these global spy-programs, and Edward Snowden, the whistle blower, have made the history books. And, after further revelations by Snowden and press investigations, it is almost like James Bond during the Cold War: everybody in the Western World seems to spy on everybody.

Other countries are no exception. China supposedly has over 2,000,000 Web-watching 'monitors', with special software from Western companies (some from those named above), which are scanning Web traffic for words such as 'Taiwan' or 'Tibet', and pornography is not tolerated. Furthermore, the monitors are used "strictly to gather and analyze public opinions on microblog sites and compile reports for decision-makers". So, be careful about what you say about the government.

Porn filters were (as of summer 2013) an issue in the UK, but Dutch conservatives would like to install them. Rumor has it that our Dutch (or US?) intelligence community is already illegally tapping all Internet traffic going through the Amsterdam Internet Exchange. Anyhow, since the NSA already tapped the exchange in Brazil (2013), one of the largest in the world, why wouldn't they do it in Amsterdam?

I often hear people say, "I have nothing to hide, so why should this Big Brother stuff bother me?" We underestimate the impact of the data revolution. The risk that the wrong algorithms are used on the wrong questions, will increase strongly the coming years. Our fear should not be Big Brother but The Trial by Kafka: that we are being accused of something without knowing why and on the basis of which information.

– From the Dutch *Trendspeech*.

The number of telephone taps per capita of the population in The Netherlands is the highest in the world, and our government has a higher-than-usual interest in drones. Trust your civilians?

I appreciate that countries are trying to protect their citizens. But, where does protection stop and anti-democratic controlling begin?

The biggest advantages of the Internet – its openness, its global connectivity, and the free flow of information – are at stake. The response of the Brazilian government to the NSA breach of privacy is to force cloud-based companies like Google to set up server farms within Brazilian borders, and to investigate the idea that e-mail shouldn't be provided by the national telephone companies. The Web could loose its transparent strength if countries are going to 'border' it. Iran is working on an 'Islamic Internet'; in China, the Web is not open and strongly controlled. Even in The Netherlands, where, in 2002 a law giving our intelligence community more power to access Web traffic was adjusted by parliament due to 'privacy issues', our civil servants presented stubbornly in 2013 the evaluation of this law, pleading for more freedom for the Dutch intelligence community.

The next step for regimes could be to 'prepare' mobile phones before they are sold...and, you and I thought Big Brother was long gone...

In China, Google was initially willing to cooperate with a certain level of censorship in search results from Chinese computers. Google worked implicitly with the Chinese government. At a later stage, Google went back on the agreement, because the Chinese government allegedly 'broke into' Google as a way of thanks:

"In mid-December (2009), we detected a highly sophisticated and targeted attack on our corporate infrastructure originating from China that resulted in the theft of intellectual property from Google. However, it soon became clear that what at first appeared to be solely a security incident--albeit a significant one--was something quite different. First, this attack was not just on Google. As part of our investigation we have discovered that at least twenty other large companies from a wide range of businesses--including the Internet, finance, technology, media and chemical sectors--have been similarly targeted. We are currently in the process of notifying those companies, and we are also working with the relevant US authorities. Second, we have evidence to suggest that a primary goal of the attackers was accessing the Gmail accounts of Chinese human rights activists."

- David Drummond, SVP, Google

There are several active Internet spy networks. Ghostnet is one of them. The Information Warfare Monitor (apparently we need one those!) wrote about Ghostnet in March 2009:

"GhostNet represents a network of compromised computers (>1000) resident in high value political, economic, and media locations spread across countries worldwide. Our investigation reveals that GhostNet is capable of taking full control of infected computers, including searching and downloading specific files and covertly operating attached devices including microphones and web cameras. The most obvious explanation, and certainly the one in which the circumstantial evidence would be, that this set of high profile targets has been exploited by the Chinese State.... and many of the high value targets are clearly linked to Chinese foreign and defense policy."

Finally there is the Deep Web, the underground world every society appears to have. The best known website here is Silk Road, where users could browse goods anonymously and securely without potential traffic monitoring. It was a marketplace for drugs, rent-a-killer, and more criminal stuff. Payments in this world? The virtual currency Bitcoin was widely used for that purpose.

Some organizations are still not thinking long-term. The Amsterdam Internet Exchange decided to open up a U.S.-based location. In spite of all the promises, it makes us vulnerable to all kind of U.S. laws, giving institutions like the NSA an open window to European data. Short-term shareholders' monetary value trumps the interest of other stakeholders. Where have we seen that before?

8.4
Facebook, the Internet as drugs, and who has the (copy)rights?

The government is not the only ones to hassles our privacy.

The social network site Facebook – the largest in the world, with over 1.2 billion(!) users – amended its privacy policies completely unilaterally in 2010, and kept on doing so afterwards. That illustrated how information that could only be found privately was suddenly made public. It led to fierce reactions. The authoritative publication Wired threw the following into Facebook founder and CEO Mark Zuckerberg's lap:

"I think Facebook, itself, is a major agent of social change and by acting otherwise Zuckerberg is being arrogant and condescending. 350 million people signed up for Facebook under the belief their information could be shared just between trusted friends. Now, the company says that's old news, that people are changing. I don't believe it. The change of the contract with users based on feigned concern for users' desires is offensive and makes any further moves by Facebook suspect."

Another flip side of the Internet is its risk of addiction. We are talking about 'sociodicts': people who are addicted to networks, to Internet porn, or online games. Former addict and Seatster Kees Romkes shares his experiences:

"You have the feeling you are alive because you interact with others, not because you 'are' yourself. The urge to be connected all the time is frightening. I come from an online game world where addiction is the order of the day where people are actively busy to continuously improve themselves, to earn more money, to be the best, and to amass status. World of Warcraft is a fantastic, but frightening, game where rewards based on time are paramount. With these rewards, you can show your friends that you are the best. You can show that you are spending all your time on gaming, where the effort (sixteen hours or more a day) is given a 'heroic status'... 'That guy is awesome'... Until I found a different challenge in my job and life, I had spent over 6,000 hours gaming online..."

Copyright or right to copy?

We need a new copyright structure, and quickly, please. The Dutch copyright law goes back to 1912. According to the Foundation of Copyright and New Media, 40% of the Dutch population runs the risk of infringing upon the current copyright laws daily.

The most recent report from The Dutch House of Representatives on copyright laws advocates, 'upholding the law and subsequently prosecuting offenders'. Barely three pages later, you will find 'thanks to technological and social developments, the boundaries of upholding the copyright laws are coming into view' Which is it to be, dear lawmaker?

What about your LinkedIn profile? It is built up as an employee in a company, probably during working hours. Is this profile, with all its linked business relations, yours, Linkedin's or your employers?

Internationally, it gets more complex. Think about the fast-growing trend of video conferencing. On the American site Meetings.com, lawyer Stephanie Cason says:
"With virtual conferences, ownership of material may be unclear. A presenter might submit an outline or record a speech, which the conference organizers then include in a larger publication, adding to or changing the presenter's material. Can the organizers reproduce this on their website? Can the presenter? The answers are often unclear."

A digital tsunami is coming our way that will merge and intertwine our intelligence and information. Unconsciously, we are all becoming a part of the 'Global Brain'. It is not a question of whether we want this. How we want it is something we might be able to influence. As an individual, and as an organization, we have a choice to make. Do we dig our heels in, and hope the wave will roll over us and leave us unscathed? Or, will we learn to skillfully surf this tidal wave, and, in the process, make maximum use of its boundless energy?

8.5
Taxes 3.0

Governments need income, and raise taxes in order to receive it. On the one hand, that is understandable, because certain issues need to be dealt with collectively; on the other hand, paying taxes is a fine for productivity. meaning that taxation is also one of the most market-disruptive elements in economic society.

In most European countries 40% to 60% of the Gross National Income is absorbed by the national governments. Let's not forget that we 'redistribute' in The Netherlands, alone, about €150 billion a year, through over 100 regulations, with the help of 3000 quangos. Do you have any idea how much that costs? Our systems have become too expensive. Controllers must be controlled. An army of legal advisers are needed to explain even the simplest of fiscal laws and rulings.

Even a simple tax like the Value Added (Sales) Tax has been made complicated. Some Dutch examples:

Books are taxed 6%, but E-books 21%. Rabbit feed is 6% but hamster feed 21%. Schoolbooks with 32 pages or more 6%, but with less than 32 pages 21%...

The tax system can and must be simplified. In a well-intended plan (from October 2009) from the Dutch State Secretary of Finance, you can read that, for 'simplification of reimbursement and provisions for employees, the employee will have to split his lunch bill from a business lunch under the new regulation, into tax-exempt intermediary costs and actual costs for said employee' Thanks to that business lunch, this employee does not have to eat his homemade lunch, and that can't just happen in Calvinist Holland! But, is this a simplification?

In European countries, where even simple tax collection is below standard, you will see corruption rising. That is also an unwanted situation.

I am a big supporter of the so-called 'flat tax'. The British economist and Nobel Prize winner Sir James Mirrlees argues, in his calculations, that a flat tax is more of a blessing than a dilemma. As it happens, it is a uniform tax rate for all work earnings. Everyone has the same tax rate. The additional advantage is that the European Tax Administration will function properly again. As citizens – but companies are good at this, as well – we will no longer need armies of tax specialists to find the loopholes in the system. Paying taxes will just become your contribution to the costs of our society, and there is nothing wrong with that. Especially if those costs of society are reduced sustainably, in which Society 3.0 gives every reason.

Levying taxes can be simplified too. In the past, it may have been useful to levy advance tax payments (or income tax) through employers. At this juncture, it may be smarter if every citizen paid a monthly advance to tax authorities, and then settled up periodically. And, let go of the end of year deadlines – this will eliminate a lot of bottlenecks at the Tax Administration Offices. We do it all the time with our energy bills: we pay a monthly, fixed amount, pass on the meter readings, settle up, and, if necessary, adjust that monthly amount.

Let's accept the fact that most employees have to work until they are at least 70 years old (if there is still work, but I will address that later). Life expectancy has risen enormously over the past years. We need to allow people to privately build up a nest egg for lifetime schooling, possible unemployment benefits, and pensions themselves.

That's what those very safe, boring savings banks are meant for. Banks will provide the people with excellent budgeting tools, and will arrange their affairs with ease, and those who are unable to achieve this can ask for help from their unions, banks, or a clever cousin. And, don't forget the many knowmads who are willing to step in, at very reasonable rates. Many such consulting groups are already active in the Seats2meet.com network. Together, we can make this work, smart, simply, and sustainably.

9
EDUCATION 3.0

Schools should not use new technologies to teach the same old crap. 3.0 schools will need to rebuild themselves not on software, not on hardware, but on mindware that builds our imagination, creativity, and capacities to innovate.

– John Moravec, Education Futures

I detect a change in the kind of discussions in our meeting rooms. Whereas, in the past, there was an emphasis on one-sided transfer of knowledge, I notice a shift toward mobilizing the existing knowledge in the group. So, there is a shift from a trainer, flip-chart, audio/video projector, and twelve person horseshoe arrangement to a dialogue with interaction, a moderator, chairs in a circle, slouching on the couch, and writing ideas on the wall. There seems to be more learning and interactive knowledge exchanging, which I find to be a great development because learning is obviously not limited anymore to the formative years at school.

In the educational world, terms like 'flipping the classroom' enter the scene. But also, education has to face things like MOOCs, iPad schools, collaborative learning, and more.

In The Netherlands, schools are closed because they are teaching in an 'immeasurable' way.

Our lead Web developer at Seats2meet.com did not finish school; and, in our network, having a graduation somehow seems less and less important. Many students are also some kind of entrepreneur.

On *The Daily Riff*, blog flipping is explained:

"'Flip' is a verb. We are actively transferring the responsibility and ownership of learning from the teacher to the students in a Flipped Classroom. When students have control over how they learn content, the pace of their learning, and how their learning is assessed, the learning belongs to them. Teachers become guides to understanding rather than dispensers of facts, and students become active learners rather than receptacles of information.

Secondly, we are flipping the instructional process and using technology to 'time-shift' direct instruction where appropriate. Direct instruction (or lecture) is still a valuable tool for teachers in some cases. Rather than relying on lecture, we simply utilize the process where appropriate to help reach a learning goal."

The dynamics of Society 3.0 have obviously entered the educational landscape.

9.1
Life time learning?!

The old, educational process is like a traditional, industrial process. Start at four years old, go through the educational pipeline, and after graduating college or university, you are ready to start working. You learned the same stuff as your student colleagues, and can compare scores due to the standardization of our examinations.

I guess there will be many more locations in which to learn in the near future, in addition to greater variation in available content. The experience would be more tailor-made, if you like. So instead of going to school for 6 years, you can pick up learning opportunities, when and where you need it, about 1,000 times per year, for a period of 30 years...

If we want to be usable as interdisciplinary junctions in the value network, remain employable in the process of value creation, and keep our new organizations up to par in these dynamic times, then we will have to assume an attitude of learning for life. By 'being usable', I mean as a human being who is aware of the qualities and responsibilities that reach far beyond technical skills. Learning is becoming more accessible. Information and knowledge can often, and easily, be found on the Web. Knowledge is shared with people from all over the world, and, as a result, new insights and new knowledge come into being. This is what we need to prepare our children for.

So, the question is: should we still send our children to schools, and, if so, what do we want them to develop?

I am looking into a direction in which our educational institutes have to deliver autodidactic people, who can produce knowledge by sharing existing parts with others, and then remix it with new ideas; who find change and development necessary and quite common; people who present themselves and behave like meaningful beings; and, people who can mobilize their knowledge, experience, and information for themselves, and in relation to others.

"At schools, we are educating people for professions that will not be around in five years time while we have to educate people for occupations that will only come into being in five years time."
          – Martijn Aslander, Dutch thought leader

161

In order to join that global game of value creation in the future, our educational system will have to be fundamentally changed. Pumping improvement money into a dead system, like many governments presently are doing, in order to get a competitive advantage, is disastrous. We no longer need a closed institute, but an open space, dazzling, creative, and social; virtual and physical, with places for meetings and activities in the community, village, or city where the school is located. Also, the locations wherein we create value are learning locations, as well.

The rise of alternate learning venues, such as coworking centers, tech labs, and corporate in-house innovation departments, open to internal peers of an organization, is excavating the exclusive right of a physical school (building) to be the center of education and learning. Boundless and blurring are Society 3.0 themes, obviously also in education.

The city as a university?

"Major social and commercial hubs now offer learning opportunities alongside existing products or services to satisfy demand: libraries, high streets, theatres, galleries, public transport interchanges, and cafes all form part of an informal network of knowledge exchange and dissemination. The boundaries between work, education and leisure have blurred and the city has started to respond to this opportunity. New city educational networks have become a valuable piece of social and financial infrastructure, giving purpose and employment to those seeking to learn or teach for enjoyment or enrichment..."

– Source: *Treehugger blog.*

As more organizations are working like networks, with dynamic groups of people, one of the key elements of these organizations is a need to store their knowledge somewhere, and present it to newcomers the moment they need it. Otherwise, there will be no progress, since everybody would be busy reinventing the wheel.

Could that be a true learning organization?

And, in case if you wonder what the new roles or tasks (or jobs) may be, you will find exotic titles, such as gamifier, data pilot, environmental scanner, content curator, knowledge guardian, cloud service broker, relevance analyst, barrier fighter, team builder, network recruitment specialist, and trust agent. Some of these roles are already being played within our organization, Seats2meet.com.

There are role requirements, such as, "we are looking for an expert in cutting-edge technology, like EC2, Hadoop, Solr, JBoss, and Hibernate," or, "an expert on NLP and machine learning techniques, such as data mining and Bayesian classifiers." I have no clue what these acronyms mean.

But, when I read that, 'the team is looking for a reasonable, mature coach, helping us to keep our entrepreneurial focus without spoiling the fun', I still may have a role to play. How about you?

9.2
How do we learn?

In an interview with the blog *Leading & Learning*, Salvina Muscat, an official at the Maltese Ministry of Education, had this to say: "In this busy, fast-changing world, educating children for the future is the real challenge. Children need self-confidence, to be adaptable, to utilize their natural creativity, to understand their strengths and weaknesses, to be increasingly self-aware emotionally and intellectually, and to be capable of building relationships quickly, effectively, and often virtually. Entrepreneurship will be a vital tool for their success and for our economy's future stability..."

And yes, it is impossible to imagine life without learning for life. If people want to remain employable, they will have to go on refresher courses or retrain during their working life. Finishing school is not the end of your learning process; it should be the beginning. The Web ultimately accommodates this development.

I can learn a foreign language via the site Livemocha.com, free of charge, by connecting with native speakers from other countries who love to teach me their language, including languages such as Mandarin Chinese. I can get over 2,000 (predominantly math) tutorials via the Khan Academy. These are short, instructional videos that explain mathematical and physics principles. Or, I can go to Videolectures.nl, where I

> Colleges and universities are indecisive, slow-moving, and vulnerable to losing their best teachers to the Internet.
> – Google Executive Chairman Eric Schmidt,
> and Anne-Marie Slaughter, professor at Princeton University,
> *Bloomberg Businessweek*, 2013.

can choose from about 4,000 guest lectures by professors from all over the world. On YouTube, there are over 200,000 instructional how-to-videos that can teach you how to skate, make Excel spreadsheets, or cook complex meals.

Our own Seats2meet.com network offers free Internet workshops, and with the Dutch recruiter Rise, we organize free LinkedIn application training for job seekers. In short, even costs will not stand in the way of us as life-long learners!

Take MOOCs (massive open online courses) where hundreds of thousands people from all over the world are frequenting top-notch universities, both online and in real time.

Universities are moving in 'big'. On http://www.mooc-list.com, you will find over 600 MOOCs. Started in 2012, Coursera, an initiative of some of the US's top universities, is now offering close to 500 'free' courses from 85 institutions. Over 4 million students have already participated.

The educational principles that make MOOCs different from 'going to school' are:

Aggregation. The whole point of a connectivist MOOC is to provide a starting point for a massive amount of content to be produced in different places online, and later aggregated as a newsletter or a Web page, accessible to participants on a regular basis. This is in contrast to traditional courses, where the content is prepared ahead of time.

The second principle is remixing, that is, associating materials created within the course with each other, and with materials elsewhere.

Re-purposing of aggregated and remixed materials to suit the goals of each participant.

Feeding forward, sharing of re-purposed ideas and content with other participants and the rest of the world.

We will also see new locations emerge besides the traditional school.

Offices of the Organization 3.0, like Google and coworking spaces like S2M, will facilitate and stimulate this life-long learning by offering an environment where serendipitous meeting of other people creates an unexpected learning experience. At S2M, we use real-time dashboards to show what personal knowledge is available and up for grabs.

The question remains of what we are still going to learn. With the use of Google Goggles, I can literally get my mobile phone to read a text, whereupon Google will find corresponding information. And via Word Lens, my phone will read text and translate it to another language in an instant. Google Translate and Bing are improving all the time, so the question exists if our children should even learn foreign languages.

9.3
A passionate vision

During one of the round-table sessions I organized in preparation for this book around the theme of education, I met Bert van der Neut, a genuine educational innovator. I believe he has an excellent view on the future of education. I quote from his story:

"The key question of this book *Society 3.0*, is if old solution strategies and old systems can also help us in the future. With regard to education, it leads to the essential question what children and youths of today need to be successful in the future. The counter-question is if we can say anything sensible at all about this, when the jobs these young people will take, the systems they will work with and the organizational forms they will operate in, might not even exist yet... After all, nothing is certain and the predictability of developments is only decreasing. In a world where there will be almost no fixed structures, there is no reason to adapt yourself to them. The next decades will expressly be about 'what mark you want to make in the world' and how you want to do that. Economically, but perhaps also socially, more and more it will be about your added value. It will be about the speed at which you can adapt to changing circumstances, while maintaining your strengths. It will be about self-management, discipline, social qualities, the insight that you can learn anywhere, and the knowledge that you will have to keep learning. [...] As a consequence of the expected shortage of teachers, there needs to be a pointed difference between the positions of coach or course plan guide on the one hand and teacher on the other. The studiehuis (Dutch secondary school form in which students are expected to learn independently, work in groups, and perform independent research) and other important educational innovations were partly bogged down because the right people were not found to do the job. On the whole, the passion of teachers does not lie in the area of coaching and guidance. If we assume it is necessary to expressly emphasize personal development, an important role is granted to coaches and trainers in education. There will be a new master-mate relationship where – thanks to technology – a continuous physical presence is not necessary. In our nation, we can draw from a large reservoir of trainers and coaches, and nothing is stopping us from bringing them into action in regular education. Preferably this should be done on a part-time basis and with the expectation that they will earn part of their income outside the educational system. This is how a natural bridge is built between worlds inside and outside of our schools."

It is a beautiful vision. Bert pointedly explains the understanding that change affects the larger whole; it affects all people involved, the physical learning environment, the educational tools, and the new leaders who have to carry the load. Education should be the link between our youth and our society, both locally and – thanks to the new social media – internationally. It's evident that new skills are needed for this. Society is becoming more complex. What Bert is actually saying is that, at this juncture, when we have to learn fast and where the old and the new clash, our students need to gain the confidence to make the right connections in this area of tension. This means that the student needs to occupy center stage.

In 1968, the Sudbury Valley School was founded in the United States. It is a school where children enjoy complete freedom. There are no school timetables, no tests, no report cards, no classes, and no diplomas. By now, we can find schools all around the world that work this way. At a Sudbury school, they assume that all people are naturally curious, and that learning is easier if people take initiative and are left free to creatively develop their own talents. This freedom is essential for personal responsibility. The school is governed together by members of staff and children. They find it important to work together and devise creative solutions together for concrete situations. The children chose what, how, with whom, and when they want to learn, from their own interests. Everyone follows their own personal development path. De Koers (www.dekoers.org) in Beverwijk is such a school. Students from ages four to eighteen are welcome there. Recently, the Sudbury school

De Kampagne was opened in Amersfoort... and forced to close down by a Dutch judge, because the school did not fit into the Dutch schooling system. And, as long as the law didn't allow these new schooling approaches, he had, 'no other choice than to close the school down.' Or so the judge said.

So, we see people are trying to renew the system because of their displeasure with the current one: not from within, but by trying to bypass it, and I think that is a great development.

A new computer school in Paris has been overwhelmed by some 60,000 applicants. The school, called 42, was founded by a telecom magnate who says the French education system is failing young people. His aim is to reduce France's shortage in computer programmers while giving those who've fallen by the wayside a new chance. In the hallways of 42, suitcases and sleeping bags are piled, and people are stretched out on mattresses in some of the corners. There are showers and dozens of colorful bath towels. Living here for the next month are some of the 4,000 potential students who already made the first cut by passing cognitive skill tests online. Now, they have to clear another hurdle: they're thrown together and challenged with computer problems for 15 hours per day. Only 800 students will earn a place, says 42's director, Nicolas Sadirac. Youth unemployment in France is at a 14-year high. At the same time, French companies cannot find enough IT specialists, and thousands of young computer enthusiasts cannot get training. That prompted 42's founder Xavier Niel to invest $90 million of his own money in the school.

I realize that a chapter like Education 3.0 could be much longer than this one. I believe that every analysis of the current educational system is an addition that limits space. Our learning environment has to be so completely overhauled, that nowhere is, in fact, the best starting point. Who will take the ball and run with it?

I know John Moravec of Education Futures does good things, as well as Claire Boonstra of Operation Education, but there are already many, many others!

10
HEALTH 3.0

The healthcare system affects us all. The number of senior citizens is increasing, we are living longer lives, and we are expecting more from our medical scientists. The healthcare sector is quite large – from health insurers to the pharmaceutical industry, and from out-patient care institutions to hospitals. The sector is heavily criticized. Every discussion turns into a financial one. We are dealing with a strange system of payments, wherein everybody – from consumer to insurer, from specialist to the Ministry – has lost their way.

The problems in healthcare are well known. Healthcare, as we now know and have come to expect, is becoming prohibitive. In the mean-time, demand will only increase. We will have to contribute more. But, we have to do that for our pension as well, and perhaps for other ser-vices, too. A hospital or other healthcare institution will never become a company, and doctors will never become managers. Managers will never become doctors. They don't have to. That is probably where the crux of the problem is, but because of the independence of patients and the diligent drive of the government for control and issuing of rules, fed by nontransparent structures and rewards, healthcare or-ganizations are forced to act like companies. The Baumol Effect, the phenomenon where a rise of salaries in jobs that have experienced no increase of labor productivity is a response to rising salaries in other jobs which did experience such labor productivity growth, may play a role here too.

Every country in Europe has its own system. For some reason, in The Netherlands, we pay an annual fixed amount to get basic care.

However, this money is given to health insurance organizations which have only one goal: to make as much money for their shareholders as possible. Endless struggles between healthcare providers and these companies are a result, and, for the first time in history, in 2013, Dutch hospitals went bankrupt.

When health organizations should behave as a (efficient and effective) company, they do not. The bickering about the electronic patient file all over Europe is yet another example of old and imperious thinking. It is made too complex, and is therefore going rapidly down a road to failure. Just give patients a chip in their medical ID card or keyring, containing their basic medical data, and have that card updated during every visit to a physician. Combine that with files patients can keep up to date themselves on Google Health (free of charge), and we have made a huge first step, at little cost.

We can stimulate a healthier lifestyle by applying gamification, however strange that may sound. The website healthmonth.com is literally child's play, encouraging children to become more aware about their own lifestyle. They set monthly goals, and are rewarded for reaching them. The website GoodGuide.com rates over 60,000 products. The impact of these products on our health is rated scientifically on our environment and our living conditions.

Patients are becoming more independent, and they are getting organized. They are forming communities, too. One example is the association Per Saldo, 'an association for people who need care and support and who want to arrange that themselves, without governmental involvement'. It already has over 24,000 members, and is provided with a professional support system. The site Patientslikeme.com is also noteworthy: tens of thousands of patients exchange information on this website about doctors, treatments, hospitals, and more.

Thanks to the Internet, we have all become specialists, and we can find the answer to many of our medical questions. I can, for example, find out how my medication works on surveyorhealth.com, including advice on whether it can be combined with other medications. Knowledge is no longer limited to a select medical community. If only for this reason, our healthcare is getting more expensive, because medical practitioners feel they are forced to work more defensively. Because of the many websites with reviews of physicians and medical institutes, the required transparency of successes and failures, and the increased personal responsibility in the future, risks are increasingly being avoided. Why don't you run an extra test, or ask for a complete lab report and a second scan, to be on the safe side? It is no wonder that the American healthcare system is so expensive. Doctors are being sued there at the slightest provocation, and the premiums of their liability insurance range from $20,000 to $50,000 per physician per year! Are we headed that way as well?

Yet, doctors can use all this available global information, too. You can find over 2,500 case studies, including videos, scans, and other shared information on medting.com. Or you can turn to eyetube.net to find out more about eye-related diseases.

10.1
Hospitals or prevention?

Ultimately, it is much better if we ensure that fewer people get sick, and more people grow old healthy. 'Prevention is better than the cure', is that not the saying? In ancient China, doctors were paid as long as their patients were not sick. We have become alienated from our roots; we are fixated on the treatment, and hardly on the causes. Our food chain can be organized to be a lot healthier, with smaller production units, local or regional production, no hormones or other stimulants, and no 'saccharification' of products. We need a cleaner living environment, re-using instead of dumping in the ocean. That is how we can stay healthy.

I got to know Lucien van Engelen through Twitter. His username is @lucienengelen. Lucien is the Zorg 2.0 ambassador/innovation change agent at the Radboud University Nijmegen Medical Center. Of course, he is a great advocate of new media, and he started an in-house Seats2meet.com co-work location called the REshape center, open for everybody involved in healthcare to come in, work, and meet other people.

Lucien sees huge changes starting to take place, especially in the area of transparency and communication. He relates:
"Six months after I started at Radboud, I was confronted with frag-mented information in emergency care. After some research and ad-vice, I took the initiative to form a community for professionals around this issue, where a scientific library can be found as well as current developments: AcuteZorg.nl (Emergency Care). During the prepara-tion and implementation of this platform I discovered how strong the role of the Internet is and the relative absence of it in healthcare. In particular, I saw possibilities for social media and communities in a sector which I believe will move more from a point of functionality in-stead of functionaries. Position this in a world that, in itself, is chang-ing, a world where Generation Y will surpass the Baby Boomers in population size. It is a world where over 80% of people will first surf to Doctor Google before going to their own physician. If you consider that an average consult takes ten minutes and that people do not re-member over 50% of what was said, then you will understand that there needs to be different ways for a doctor to communicate with a patient. And that way has been found because 60% of patients share

their experiences in one way or another on the Internet. The Internet is being used increasingly more to determine which hospital or which doctor to visit. This is widely accepted in the US: based on ranking and rating sites, a physician may be chosen. If this is done on the basis of objective, verifiable and transparent criteria, there is no problem. It becomes an issue if there is talk of blunt criticism without retort. I think and hope that this will become a self-regulating process, based on social control."

Marcel van Marrewijk has done a lot of research into patient experiences as manager and owner of the agency Research to Improve. I asked him to share his vision with us. Marcel emphasized the particular role of healthcare as an institute, and the unusual role of the patient:

"Healthcare organizations are special companies. They distinguish themselves in one essential aspect compared to regular industrial organizations: the patient – the person who requires care – is, as it happen,s a very unusual customer. The patient has a very strong dependent relationship with the healthcare professional(s): he can be seriously ill, be in chronic pain, or experience existential fears which will result in feelings of vulnerability and insecurity. Dealing with these issues as a healthcare professional is a completely different kettle of fish than providing a service to a customer. This is what makes healthcare institutions, like hospitals and nursing homes, so different to other organizations."

And:

"The emotional and psychological dependence that many patients have in relation to their healthcare professionals, make great demands on the quality on the mutual relationship. That requires specific competencies from the professionals; and, in particular, the willingness to treat patients with sympathy and courtesy – and to show mercy and compassion when the situation (and the patient) asks for it. In healthcare, unlike with service organizations, the patient – often a vulnerable and insecure person – has a strong need for empathy. The healthcare professional must have the capacity to open oneself up without prejudice unconditionally, and to connect on an emotional level. Only then can compassion and mercy come into being. And it is these qualities that are crucial to win the loyalty of the patient. Even if healthcare professionals are mostly recruited on the basis of availability and expertise, in reality, many individuals, in particular in nursing, poses these essential values, motives, and competencies to realize the personal rapport with the patient time after time again. It is usually not the healthcare employee; the healthcare system is the restricting factor most often – leading to great frustration and eventually cynicism and dropouts. Recent experiences with Presentatie (presentation), developed by professor Andries Baart, connect to the personal directed approach. Baart says: 'Healthcare is not fixing. Healthcare is caring for somebody.' His Presentatie theory is all about getting very close to somebody, opening your self up to that person, and, in that relationship, trying to figure out what their needs are. You enter into a relationship with that person, and you are there for her or him, unconditionally. Good healthcare should be the basic principle, not the residue – the unintentional effect – of a self-referring system that is optimized by efficiency and market forces."

I care for all this! Don't you?

11
A REVOLUTION ON THE MOVE: MOBILITY, REAL TIME, AND 3.0

In a nutshell, I have explained so far in this book that Web 2.0 – the social Internet – enables the transition to the interdependent economy and Society 3.0.

Social networks, infinite access to knowledge, and unlimited forms of collaboration can bring an end to economic thinking in terms of scarcity. From this point of view, you can regard the Internet as the basis of our future welfare. But what is the future of the Internet itself? We are now entering the world of Web 3.0, and Web 4.0 is already on the horizon. So, before having a closer look at the Organization 3.0, let's first look at which direction the context of organizations is moving. In other words, let's look at the future of the Web and its related technologies.

Web 1.0 was all about supplying information.

Web 2.0 is based on the interaction between people based on the supplied information, which results in new information, new connections, and thus, new value.

Web 3.0 is about the Internet getting more contextually intelligent: information is interpreted and handled semantically. The new Internet systems comprehend the meaning of data, and are able to distinguish the coherence between different chunks of information.

You may wonder if we still have time to look for information. The American Web 3.0 guru Nova Spivack introduced the philosophy of

'Nowism' and the real-time Web. He explains on his blog: "We will spend less time searching. 'Nowism' pushes us to find better alternatives to search, or to eliminate search entirely, because people don't have time to search anymore. We need tools that do the searching for us and that help with decision support so we don't have to spend so much of our scarce time doing that."

Google's Knowledge Graph is a nice example of how information will be presented to us. Google navigates the Web by crawling through all 60 trillion Internet pages and puts them in an index. Their smart algorithms know what we are looking for. According to Google, 'for a typical query, there are thousands, if not millions, of webpages with helpful information. Algorithms are the computer processes and formulas that take your questions and turn them into answers'. On Google Knowledge Graph, instead of giving a flat result as an answer to our search question, the given answer is more like a story, where our requested information is linked to what Google thinks is relevant for us to know.

The Web 3.0 is also called 'The Internet of Things'. Millions of devices are connected to the Web, thus making devices and machines capable of retrieving information to enhance their intrinsic value. Tracking that information allows us to manage 'stuff' remotely, or will stuff manage us? Running late for a meeting? No sweat, your online calendar communicated that already to the other participants. A chip on the tail of a pregnant cow will tell the farmer when to cow is about to give birth. Smart 'Bag2Go' suitcases travel parallel with you, but, besides tracking the suitcase on your smartphone (still a phone?), you will see your suitcase again only at your final destination. Smart sex toys for women allow them to sync up the toy with audiobooks on their smart phones for solo play, and the toy will switch up its vibration depending on how juicy the book is getting. Or, drink a beer from a Heineken Interactive Beer Bottle.

And, are we mobile? Yes we are!

Computers and their software have become more service-oriented. Many services are available at no cost, and content is freely available. All our virtual networks are inter-connected. We share knowledge and information all the time with each other. Information is available to us wherever we are, 24/7. It is available to us via our cell phones, glasses or contact lenses, gadgets like rings and jewelry, and even woven into our clothes. With this, data has become completely mobile.

"By 2015, five billion people will be connected via a mobile device. That is a 100-fold increase in networked traffic. The Mobile Society is completely different to the industrial society. It requires a new logic and a new way of thinking of how to create business, civil governance, health care, and education. The mobile society is seen as both an opportunity and a threat because it signifies a reordering of business models, new flows of communication, and the appearance of new gatekeepers in the information distribution wars."
– Allen Moore's *The Glittering Allure of the Mobile Society*

Print, recordings, cinema, radio, television, and the Internet are the six mass media we have known until now. Mobile technology is seen as the seventh mass medium. According to Moore, being mobile has six unique benefits that you do not find in other media:

1. The first personal mass media.
2. The first always-carried media.
3. The first always-on media.
4. The first media with a built-in payment mechanism.
5. The first media always present at the point of creative impulse.
6. The first media whose audience can be accurately identified.

11.1
More about Mobility, 3rd Spaces, and Big Data

In China, Japan, and South Korea, mobile is already much larger than accessing the Internet via the computer. In Japan, €6 billion of products are bought and sold through mobile devices annually. In Africa, where there is a demand for infrastructure for computers, the development of the mobile market is much faster than the advance of the Internet.

There is simply more revenue to be made with mobile technologies than compared to many Internet service platforms: satellite navigation systems, music shops, and many other applications are just the beginning of the many possible payable services. This is achieved because there is a direct link between the consumer and the service provider which makes it easy to charge for the services.

The website www.navitime.com does not just show pedestrians the fastest walking routes, but it also presents indoor locations in case it starts raining, and what kind of CO_2 output you produce, depending on the choice of your route or method of transportation. Delays in traffic or transportation are shown in real-time, including suggestions about disembarking or transferring to a more favorable connection. These kinds of applications have millions of paying customers in Japan.

Augmented reality demonstrates that mobile is almost a bigger revolution than the Internet itself. You point the camera of your smart phone at something (a building for example). This building is identified (with the help of GPS-tracking, directories, or the shape of the building itself), then information is collected that could be relevant at the time you are looking at the building. If it is a cinema, it will give you the opening times and the list of movies that are playing. If it is a house, it will present you with the latest property value. If it is a railway station... you get the picture. The information is also linked to you, the mobile user. If the building is a restaurant, your mobile device will tell you if friends of yours are having a meal there... and how they rate the food!

In augmented reality, the virtual world and the physical world come together where digital information enriches your real and physical experience. The American management thinker Joseph Pine identifies nine of these combined virtual and physical worlds: from augmented reality to warped reality, from mirrored reality to alternate reality, and much more. In his latest book *Infinite Possibility*, Joe calls locations '3rd Spaces', places where virtuality and reality are blurred.

Our Seats2meet.com coworking locations are 3rd Spaces. On top of every physical S2M location, we augment the transformative experience of our visitors by showing a real-time dashboard of digital information, showing not only who is present, but also what knowledge there is to be shared, what the general sentiment is among visitors, and various contact possibilities. We call this our Serendipity Machine. Accredited residents of S2M have more options: they even can look ahead in time for this information!

Around 2010, the term 'Big Data' entered the scene. The sharing of information with our networks, supplemented by data from machines and devices around us, created an amount of data never seen before. In addition to the enormous amount of data, the quantity of sources and the speed of data traffic are elements that transform data into Big Data. Organizations have to collect, analyze, and understand data in order to use it in a meaningful way. Thus, realizing a better stakeholder experience in order to create stakeholder transformations as the ultimate value creation of that organization is its right to existence.

A group of people are gathering Big Data around themselves and share it afterwards. This movement is called 'quantified self'. It is an international collaboration between users and makers of self-tracking tools, and its goal is to help people get meaning out of their personal data.

Organizing personal Big Data opens the road to developments such as persuasion profiling, wherein 'you present customized content to your website visitors, depending on which persuasive strategies have historically proven to work best on that particular visitor', according to the Science Rockstars company, so the behavioral data of consumers on different sites are combined.

New software and hardware that are bigger, faster, and smarter will help organizations, using data better than others, and give a competitive advantage. If you, as a consumer, are happy with this remains to be seen, as other people may know you better than you know yourself.

11.2
Via the stratosphere to Singularity & Web 4.0.

We are connected to everything, everywhere. Of course, many countries have an infrastructure, but what about when traveling or living in remote areas? In the desert, use BRCK, a smart, rugged device, that can connect to the internet in any way possible, hopping from one network to another or creating a hotspot for multiple devices, all while plugged in or running on battery power. Or, even more remote? Hook up to the Google balloons...up in the stratosphere (20 kilometers up), and a series of connected balloons become your hotspots. This is called Project Loon, and, according to Google, 'Project Loon is a network of balloons traveling on the edge of space, designed to connect people in rural and remote areas, help fill coverage gaps, and bring people back online after disasters'.

Besides connections, we need more speed. Moore's Law is a rule of thumb in the history of computer hardware whereby the number of transistors that can be placed inexpensively on an integrated circuit doubles approximately every two years. It's just that the end of this advancement is coming into view, even according to Moore, because of physical limitations that are placed on technologies. At a certain stage, a transistor can't be 'smaller than small'. This constraint is enhanced by Wirth's Law: software is getting slower more rapidly than hardware is getting faster. This development could slow down the rise to the new mobile order.

On the road to Web 4.0, we will increasingly monitor data flows, and be continuously connected to the Web and with each other. A set of intelligent tools and agents will filter and customize our information to our needs continuously. This requires different computer systems.

In his Law of Accelerating Returns, Kurzweil sees technology in a broader context. He believes that many other issues are more important than the computer chip or software development. His start-ing point is an extraordinary combination of technology, economy, biology, physics, and sociology, which causes an exponential accel-eration of innovation.

Kurzweil named this the 'Technological Singularity'. There will be a time when ingenious combinations of technologies will slow the aging process in people, so that the sharp rises in healthcare costs will be completely solved. One day, there we will have technology that can read someone's emotions from a distance. If we can follow the principles of the Singularity, we can shift into top gear, and human and artificial intelligence will amalgamate into the so-called Global Brain. Some have predicted this will happen in 2040. So, Web 4.0 may be this Global Brain.

The scientist Peter Russell mentioned the Global Brain in 1983. He explored the idea that the Earth is an integrated, self-regulating liv-ing organism, and asks what function humanity might serve for this planetary being. It suggests that we stand on the threshold of a major leap in evolution as significant as the emergence of life itself.
Vernor Vinge calls this global brain the Digital Gaia. But Vinge warns us too: "in the 20th century, there was the specter of nuclear warfare. In the 21st, nuclear terror is very real, but there is also distributed terror and the consequent government drive to use embedded net-works for ubiquitous law enforcement". And Vinge had no knowledge, in 2000 when he wrote this article, of the NSA actions of our time.

The Dutch academic Gerard Jagers op Akkerhuis advocates an 'Op-erator theory', He argues that this Singularity is to be the next logical step in human evolution. On the website www.hypercycle.nl, you can explore where and when artificial intelligence will overtake human intelligence.

We can only hope that the benefits and necessities of all these de-velopments will be measured in relation to the wellbeing of the whole of humanity.

11.3
The road to Society 3.0: is the ultimate goal in sight?
Dear reader, you would almost forget that there are still many

quangos and governmental organizations that have huge, overhead budgets. And they are putting up a fight for their own survival. However, the revolution is imminent, as their monetary reserves are diminishing at a high speed. So, be prepared for the tidal wave that is crashing in on us. We have the Internet, social networks, value networks, mobile technologies, 3D printing, and we global citizens who want to create new value, globally as well as locally.

These global citizens ask themselves the following questions: 'How are we, as global people, going to reap the biggest effect on society as a whole?' And 'how can we contribute, as effectively as possible, to the path of Society 3.0?'

I am convinced that the biggest impact can be gained through our memberships to organizations: memberships of new network organizations, and of old conventional organizations. We spend much of our time in them. Organizations, especially large ones, are more boundless than governments, for example. Organizations generally have good communication facilities. Imagine if we, as global people, transformed our organizations into Organizations 3.0 that acted and flourished in reciprocity and interdependence. What would be the effects on society? I suggest we tackle our organizations from the inside out, and help them develop into Organizations 3.0. If not, or if the resistance is too fierce, don't accept that, and move around them quickly to be the cause of their disruption. Ignore them, and by doing so, make them disappear!

And let's create more space for independent startups. The political establishment has to act. In the BRIC countries, according to a study by the international accountancy firm RSM, the birth rate for startups is 7 times higher than in Europe. However, the report says:
"France registers the highest growth of new company formation in the group. This result is surprising given the widely held view of France as an over regulated economy with a rigid labor market... However, in 2009, the government launched a program for small businesses called 'Auto Entrepreneur' that prompted a surge in startups. The scheme simplifies and reduces the tax liabilities of small businesses, enabling Auto Entrepreneurs to avoid many of the heavy social charges levied on employers in France. While critics argue that the Auto Entrepreneur program has merely created a tax haven for

the self-employed, the scheme is widely credited for stimulating new business growth and invigorating French entrepreneurs."

This way, we will create some very strong change agents for the interdependent economy, as is our task (and what a beautiful task it is) for Society 3.0's global people.

I see already many initiatives in various fields of operation. Individuals are really making a difference and inspiring others. We also see a struggle as the establishment fights innovation, and tries to get the situation under control. Sometimes these fights are nasty: court procedures, lawyers, police, and even more governmental regulations. Let's not forget that the Industrial Revolution lasted, in some countries, over 100 years. Times are faster. Our revolution started somewhere in the early 1990s, but we may have to keep working on this transformation for at least another decade or two.

Let's focus, in the next chapter, more on these new kinds of organizations – their business models, their leadership, and their dynamics...

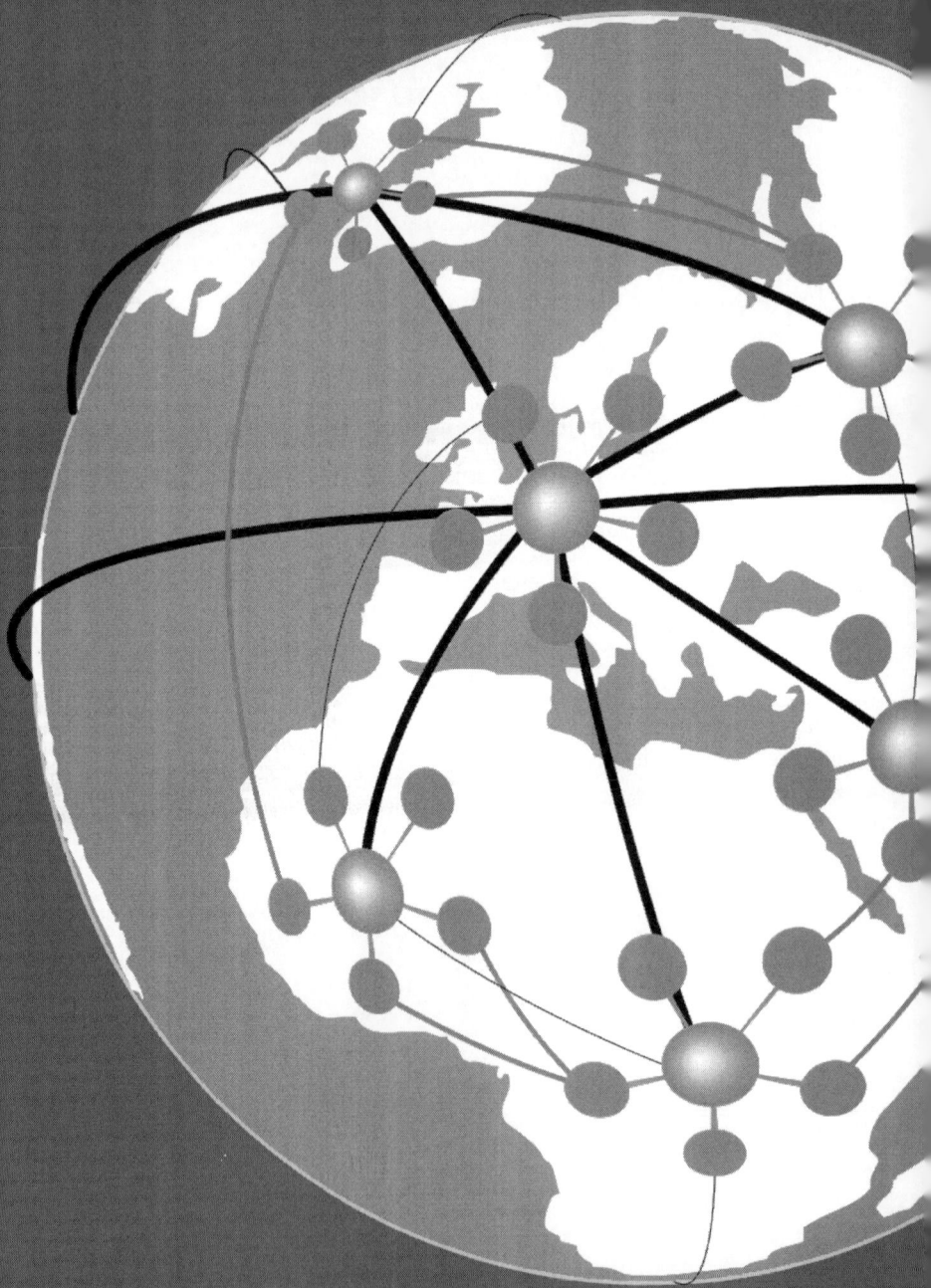

Turquoise is
the color of
systemic openness
and collective
connectivity.
Typical qualities of
3.0 organizing.

Hidden road and path

Seasons to explore,
fields to find

Vision is a gift

12
ORGANIZATION 3.0

Change is a big part of the reality in business. Willingness to change is strength, even if it means plunging part of the organization into total confusion for a while.

– Jack Welsh

The word 'organization' stems from the Greek word οργανον (organon), which literally translates into 'tool'. An organization is the main instrument that brings people and resources together to add value, within a certain timeframe, to (part of) a product or service, where parts may or may not have been outsourced. From this point of view, the organization cannot be a goal in itself. In addition to this, a real craftsman is one who constructs his own tools...

Value creation is the reason of existence for organizations. Management thinker Peter Drucker called this 'The Theory of the Business'. Value creation is centered on:
- Performing activities that increase the value of goods or services to clients.
- Actions that increase the worth of goods, services, or even a business.

Traditional methods no longer work. Many organizations have lost their touch with relevance, as Drucker states, 'they no longer fit reality', Hence, they are no longer capable of creating value, and thus lose their right to existence.

In 1994, Peter Drucker wrote an article with the title *The Theory of the Business*:

"An organization is built around assumptions. Assumptions that shape any organization's behavior, dictate its decisions about what to do and what not to do and define what organization consider meaningful results. These assumptions are about markets. They are about identifying customers and competitors, their values and behavior. They are about technology and its dynamics, about the company's strength and weaknesses. These assumptions are what a company gets paid for."

We see organizations that have changed the traditional value creation into what is called 'shared value creation'. The concept of shared value can be defined as policies and operating practices that enhance the competitiveness of a company, while simultaneously advancing the economic and social conditions in the communities in which it operates. Shared value creation focuses on identifying and expanding the connections between social and economic progress. The concept rests on the premise that both economic and social progress must be addressed using value-based principles. Value is defined as benefits relative to costs, not just benefits alone. Value creation is an idea that has long been recognized in business, where profit is revenues earned from customers, minus the costs incurred. However, businesses have rarely approached social issues from value-oriented perspectives, but have treated them as peripheral matters. This has obscured the connections between economic and social concerns.

"Value co-creation is not efficient when using a traditional value creation process. It requires a complete reconsideration of how a company operates and cannot be approached within the context of a traditional value creation system."
                                                        – Tanev, Knudsen, and Gerstlberger (2009)

Don Tapscott, author of the book *Wikinomics*, sees opportunities in using the Web, and all its possibilities, to create 'shared value creation'.

He argues:

"Corporations are going through profound changes that are affecting their strategies and business models. The Internet is dropping transaction costs, triggering deep and unprecedented changes in the deep structures and architecture of the firm. 'People' who provide capability for firms can now be outside corporate boundaries. Companies participate in complex networks and can innovate through Ideagoras -- open markets for uniquely qualified minds. They can turn customers into producers or 'prosumers.' They can tap into vast peer production communities outside their boundaries like Linux. For corporations, there has never been a time of such turmoil."

The Dutch professor André de Waal, after investigating 1,500 companies in 50 countries, argues that successful organizations, or 'High Performance Organizations', as he calls them, have a number of characteristics in common, and in which they have better performance than others. These are the five key factors:
- Quality of management
- Openness & action orientation
- Long-term orientation
- Continuous improvement and renewal
- Quality of employees

All the above may be already obsolete. Where virtuality blurs with reality we see the rise of so called Crowd Companies (Owyang, 2013). The crowd can get anything they want from each other and may go around your organization. So in order to survive as an organization, you have to connect with the crowd. Engage with the crowd. Work, design, produce and sell with the crowd and again, they may do that by themselves. Hence the name 'Crowd Company'.

So, in order to become a successful organization in Society 3.0, we have to change our organizational thinking, in terms of value creation, our raison d'être, the justification of our existence as an organization, and we have to do that within different organizational structures. We must do so with a different philosophy than we have used traditionally. It is time to reinvent ourselves.

Let's have a closer look at value creation.

12.1
Human Transformation as economic value

According to Pine & Gillmore in their book *The Experience Economy* (1998), when making an economic offering to your clients, there has been, from a historical perspective, an economic progression of value.

Progression of economic value consists of:
- Commodities
- Goods
- Services
- Experiences
- Transformations

Each level is totally different from the others, and each is enveloped by the next.

Now, using coffee as an example, imagine a coffee bean. A coffee bean is a commodity. For the large part, commodities are extracted. Prices are set by the market.

Goods are tangible items that are created from commodities, and are a main component of the industrial economy. They command a higher price because they can be used immediately. Now, imagine roasted coffee beans. Goods are made.

Services are what you do with goods, like obtaining a cup of coffee at McDonald's. Services are delivered or provided, and thus create the Service Economy.

Experiences are a mindset, staged and authentic to the business. Experiences are a 'distinct economic offering' that are as different from services as services are from goods. When buying coffee at Starbucks, you not only buy the coffee, but a dynamic 'hot spot' environment in which to spend some time and use the free Wi-Fi. You are buying the Starbucks experience, but at a higher price than the coffee at McDonalds.

Customization allows you to move up the ladder of economic value. However, concepts can be copied, or the operations may lose connec-

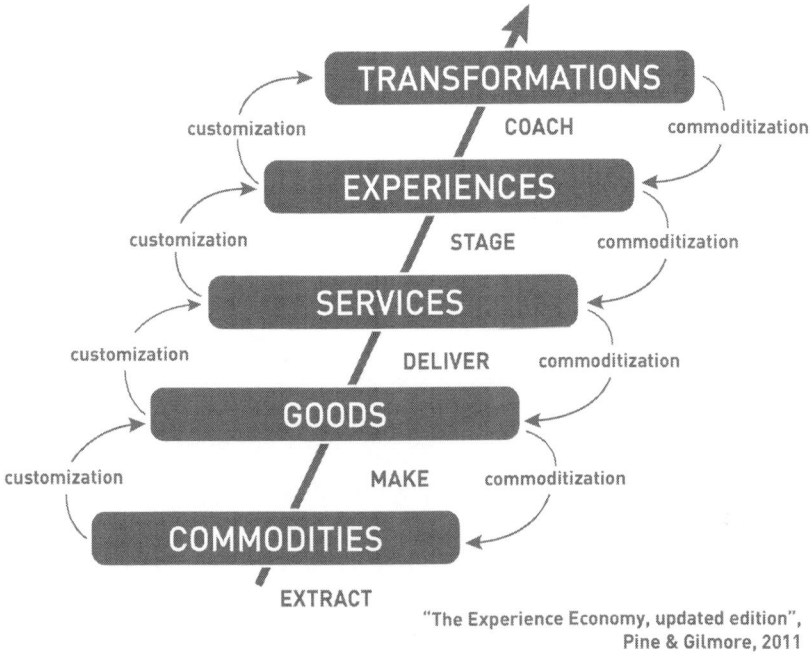

"The Experience Economy, updated edition",
Pine & Gilmore, 2011

tion with the concept. Or, the element of surprise becomes smaller: 'been there, done that'. Then, your offering is commoditized, and you move down the ladder.

After the economic offering of experience, we approach the next steps, according to Pine & Gillmore, which are referred to as 'transformations'. Transformations are becoming the ultimate economic offering for any corporation, value network, or independent contractor.

By customizing an experience to create a learning experience, making it just right for an individual – providing exactly what he/she needs right now– you cannot help changing or transforming that individual. You coach your client to change. Transformations, a changed person, are a result of what the company does. In other words, the customer is the product, and hence, transformations are the last and final economic offering.

So, in brief, 'a transformation is a tailor-made experience with an educational element and a changed individual as a result'.

Working from this point of view, we learned at Seats2meet.com that the 'educational element' for our stakeholders is the 'unexpected relevance', or serendipity, of an experience. Since we are in the people-meeting-people industry, we realized that, by offering a stage for stakeholders to act upon, and by facilitating the process of 'unexpected, relevant, serendipitous, meetings' between stakeholders while visiting our S2M locations, we achieved co-created transformations as manifestations of our added value, and thus, our right to existence.

How we facilitate the process of serendipitous meetings will be discussed in a later chapter.

Your challenge is to figure out how to co-create unexpected, relevant experiences together with your stakeholders in order to ensure your right to existence in the interdependent economy of Society 3.0.

12.2
Value chain, or rather profit chain?

Value chain: it seems like such a nice concept. Yet, it is 'old school'. In this so-called value chain, people, means, and time are pressed through and between organizations with just one single purpose: that there will eventually be someone who is willing to pay for the service or product for a higher price than your cost price. The manufacturers higher up in the value chain, and the suppliers who are lower down in the same chain, all perform the same trick. As long as the buyers in the value chain are not yet the consumers, a producer will try to produce something which he believes the last customer wants.

Via 'terms and conditions', the manufacturer pushes the entrepreneurial risks as far as possible down the chain towards the consumer. And, as a consumer at the end of the chain, we actually have no choice other than to purchase what rolls out. Don't believe you have freedom of choice. The fact that there are seventeen different types of jam available – most of them made by the same machine – only ensures that you will consume more jam on your bread. Through all kinds of market research, we can determine the needs of buyers, so that we think we know what the end user really wants. Then, we mix it into something mediocre and offer this in all kinds of 'self-competitive' versions.

This is not the same as real freedom of choice. What it is doing is keeping the product-driven profit chain going. It is the same with our governments. Politicians think they know what the people want. The platform (from any political color) is an average message of what is good for the citizen. After the electoral mix (or coalition formation) with other colors, policies are shoved into society through a policy chain from which many, many officials drain their income and whose ultimate added value can be strongly challenged. Value chain? Profit chain? Who wins? Who loses?

But we do have a problem. Time, people, and means are in short supply, particularly due to the archaic structure of our nations and organizations. The aforementioned Coase Ceiling constantly limits us. The corresponding thinking, in terms of value chains, does not offer a solution for the current economic crisis or for the future of our countries, our organizations, or ourselves.

In fact, the limitations of the Coase Ceiling are only getting stronger; we are swiftly and surely losing our traditional means. Once it's gone, it's gone forever. Fossil fuel reserves are depleting. Our money is gone – the traditional banking system is holding us hostage. Working people, a shrinking group due to the rise in the aging population, will still work with you, but no longer for you in traditional terms of employment.

In short, the value chain is, all in all, no more than a typical pyramid scheme, where the next one in the chain generously compensates the previous link, but remains in debt themselves. In most countries, pyramid schemes are a criminal offence...

12.3
The rise of value networks

In a disconnected world, the costs of [being] evil are minimal. In a hyper-connected world, the costs of [being] evil explode.

– Umair Haque's Law, *HBR blog.*

In Society 3.0, people share their knowledge on their own accord; the actual intellectual property of information is of marginal importance. The opportunity for sharing knowledge makes people autonomous to engage collectively in a new way of value creation.

Connected through social networks, people constitute an almost inexhaustible potential, not the least thanks to the abundance of free software and all kinds of useful apps. Thanks to the Internet, we are not only connected to each other 24/7, but also with each other's information and collective knowledge. And this is how knowledge ceases to be scarce. There is an abundance of knowledge, information, work, and more on the horizon.

That is how 'access to' becomes more important than 'ownership of'.

Access to what?
- Information about your stakeholders, supplied by those same stakeholders.
- The collective thinking and creative power of these stakeholders.
- The workforce capacity of your stakeholders.
- Knowledge and all kinds of smart knowledge-enhancing software on the Internet.
- Funds of your stakeholders.

In the past, when we talked about the properties of knowledge and information, it was in regard to organizations and individuals who built an organization around their knowledge. And when we talked about access, then it was mostly in regard to the individual who had to make the effort to gain access. In a value chain, it is relatively easy to screen out knowledge and information. It is very different in a value network. Suddenly, this is no longer the exclusive domain of organizations (in the traditional style). Now this network consists of all kinds of individuals, and their personal knowledge and information. Private property, therefore, slowly (de)generates to collective property.

Access is becoming increasingly implicit: as soon as people in organizations connect with people outside said organizations or with people in other organizations, it soon becomes point to point, and everyone has access to everything. And, that is when it starts to be fun. Then, you can no longer sneakily abuse the gullibility of isolated individuals because they will quickly warn each other. Together, we know everything.

That is what Umair Haque means, I believe. Then, I read an article by Yochai Benkler. In 2006, this Harvard professor of entrepreneurial legal studies wrote in his book, *The Wealth of Networks*, that:

"A new economic value creation becomes a logical consequence of the availability of an increasingly larger amount of information and knowledge, among an increasingly stronger connection between groups of people, by the increasing technological developments in and around the Internet."

When I read this and tried to fathom it, I suddenly understood that value creation is in a transitional phase: a transition from thinking in terms of value chains to coworking in value networks.

12.4
The dynamic balance of the value network

It is not a matter of a fixed alliance between the network members in a value network. The network is not always visible as a group. Usually, a value network has a few core members – including a possible client – complemented with the occasional co-creators, and some more people who incidentally provide a requested contribution (resonance). The core members often do not even know the peripheral members, while the source of the knowledge is not always visible. It is more of a cloud or a social value network – I prefer to call it a Social Economic Entity – it almost exhibits Al Qaeda-like structures and movements. Beckstrom and Brafman have named this, in their book *The Starfish and the Spider*, the Starfish Model.

In their book *The Starfish and the Spider*, Beckstrom and Brafman introduce organizations without an evident leader and with apparent little structure. The difference between starfish organizations and spider organizations is staggering. A starfish has no discernable head and will survive if it loses a leg; a fully-fledged starfish can grow out of that lost leg. If a spider loses a leg, it does not move along that well; if the spider loses its head it will die. In which organization would you rather be?

Teamwork is a nice concept, but working in a value network goes further than the time-honored team notion. It starts with another perspective on objectives. In the traditional team organization, the objectives are usually clearly defined, as is the road that leads to it, like the division of tasks and the responsibility. A value network is predominantly characterized by shared starting points and a path of creation, in a context of collective responsibility, to be discovered collectively

In the cooperation with or within organizations, the community leader facilitates the process as much as possible, but you can't call it 'managing'. There is an open structure: an appeal can be made for new knowledge and contacts across the entire world outside of the organization. The same can be said for recording and making available the acquired collective knowledge of the value network. The old team thinking is more inclined to keep this to themselves, but value creation, of course, benefits a lot more from open connections.

Therefore, it is not always clear to the customer who has the ultimate responsibility, while it is not always evident for the participants how any revenue is divided up.

We actually need (do we really?) a new legal form for these kinds of provisional networks, or constellations. We need provisional formations, pop-up organizations, crowd companies or pop-up value creation groups that somehow legally organized as a Social Economic Entity (SEEs). Within these SEEs, insightful agreements can be made for all stakeholders, including the customer to be. These SEEs can be quickly registered and deregistered in the Registry of Companies (or perhaps even this thinking is outdated). Specialized organizations will start up to facilitate these processes for a modest fee and the organization of the end customer can fulfill a leading or facilitating role, itself.

Whereas regular organizational teams or departments have the tendency to mark their territories and compartmentalize, value networks have the capability to connect among themselves. Individual members of value networks can organize themselves from one spot or another. The data portability between networks is (because of this) increasing on a daily basis. This is how boundaries continue to dissolve: value networks are exceedingly dynamic, and flow into each other. That is why they are hard to comprehend for outsiders. It is not always a clearly identifiable team or project group that is at work. The work is also no longer done between four walls under one roof, with the name of the organization on the façade of the building. The places where new value is created are hard to distinguish... However, they can, after all, be found in 'The Mesh'.

12.5
The Mesh. How to create your own...

A Mesh describes a type of network that allows any node to link in any direction with any other nodes in the system. Every part is connected to every other part, and they move in tandem. ... Mesh businesses are knotted to each other, and to the world, in myriad ways.

– Lisa Gansky in The Mesh.

Meshworks focuses on 'meshing' or integrating, aligning, and synergizing people and resources on specific challenges, goals, objectives or outcomes, using a transcendent purpose.

– Dr. Don Beck, Center for Human Emergence.

Stakeholders in the Organization 3.0 want to be increasingly involved with the realization of its services or products. This contributes to that special user experience. Every experience, from incidental co-creation to a full collaboration, enhances the feeling that it is all about you, and, as an additional advantage, delivers a much more superior product or service. So much better, in fact, that the eventual sticker price, whether that be monetary or social capital, has become secondary as a selection criteria for doing business, procurement, and collaboration. In order to give the stakeholders that feeling of authenticity, and in order to co-create with them, the organization has to connect with them and start a dialogue.

In that way, the organization can create its own mesh of value networks. Most of these networks are like mini-circular economic systems in themselves. Acting from abundance, social capital, reciprocity, and trust complements the traditional monetary systems. The value creation locations are 3rd Spaces; virtual and reality are one.

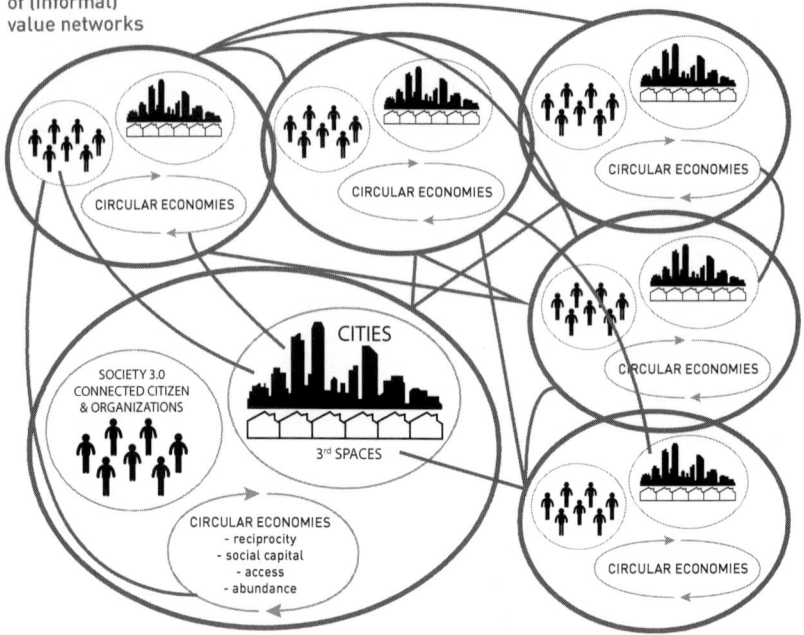

THE MESH
a chaordic system
of (informal)
value networks

Stakeholders of organizations are interconnected, so they will form the connection between an organization and the outside world. In that way, the organization may be active in many formal and informal networks in the value creation process.

To gain access to a whole network of stakeholders, the modern decisive organization can do itself a favor by developing a solid social media strategy. The starting point is that all communication moments (so-called touch points) are engagement opportunities between all stakeholders, inside and outside the organization 3.0. This requires dynamic and flexible internal processes, and a large extent of operational freedom for the people involved. But when you are succesfull in doing this, your organization becomes resilient and always ready to anticipate on the dynamics of our times. Some innovative companies let stakeholders interact between themselves, even without any 'employee' involvement in the official form of a Web care team or a help and sales desk, like at the UK-based Telco Giffgaff. The Seats2meet. com helpdesk is the largest in Europe. Thousands of stakeholders assist each other on the Web, 24/7. Still, it is not OUR helpdesk.

So, if you want to claim your position in the clusters of new value networks, called The Mesh, as an organization en route to tomorrow, you will have to work with minimal standardization, and with a new, informal corporate culture, based on trust and with open communication. Only then can you seriously make an appeal to autonomy and entrepreneurship in order to excel internally, as well as externally, around a dynamic organization. It is not a matter of 'being social on the side'. It requires a completely new vision of organization. A vision to rethink the order of things. A vision that answers the question of how to challenge someone within the new value networks to feel, think, and operate with his entire capacity for the value of co-creation; and, how to supply stakeholders with relevant information at the right time, so that they can operate independently, and thus perform. A vision of a style of leadership to keep all of this on the right track is further required.

"An ant colony forms a very powerful organization. Thousands of ants work hard and effectively in good cooperation. Together, they manage to cope with all kinds of threats, whereas a single ant would stand no chance. Yet, they do not use a top-down command structure. It is interesting to notice that, on average, half of the ant colony population is without work. They are ready to go into action, should any shortages in ant power occur. This combination of anticipating ants and a large reservoir of inactive ants causes the colony to serve as a mechanism with a hugely adaptive capacity.The organization3.0 resembles an ecosystem which largely maintains itself and provides opportunities of value creation for its members, just like an ant colony is an independent ecosystem serving its own ant population."
– Evert Jan van Hasselt and Pauline Romanesco,
Ecosystems for Business

The value creation of Society 3.0 is born out of the mobility of people, knowledge, and energy. People, operating from within their social networks, with the same objective. They share goals. Knowledge is also being shared, with the generation of new knowledge, and thus, new value, as a result. In Society 3.0, we collaborate in a different way. We do that within open and flat organizations: social network, resilient organizations that are in harmony with their Mesh eco-system, and are therefore sustainable.

12.6
More on value networks, new workers, and the organization, SEE

On their way to renewal, many organizations have experimented or even adopted the 'New Way of Working'. It can be seen as the first step in the process of new value creation and towards opening up an organization to seek connection with the outside world in order to start co-creating.

The 'new workers' form self-managing, multi-discipline teams within their value networks, which operate smartly and open-mindedly. Every individual new worker represents one or more organizations, and is open to support and realize fundamental changes in these organizations. New work is about people who organize 'chaordicly'; people who behave as wandering knowledge workers: Internet-connected nomads, or knowmads. These coworking people are independent professionals, suppliers, customers, and employees – in short, all stakeholders of a process or a problem. Even the 'old new' employees work in a decent time- and place-independent manner. And, when they make agreements, they do not talk about the number of billable hours, but about performance.

New work that is predominantly developing in the new social value networks is also called 'meshworking', a term coined from the neurological field that explains how our brain is able to combine hierarchical and self-organizing network structures. It is clear that I view new work as the most powerful motive to reinvent organizations. The great thing is that it starts with the individual, any individual, and preeminently, with readers of this book, of course! New organizations do not arise because they are reinventing themselves. New organizations are formed because new workers create it. These organizations, as value networks may be very informal. These informal pop-up organizations are SEEs.

There is no particular fixed connection between network members in a SEE value network as the network is not always visible as a group. Generally, a SEE value network has a few core members – including a potential client – complemented with occasional collaborators and some other people who contribute incidentally and/or if required (resonance). The core workers often do not know the peripheral participants, while the source of knowledge is not always visible, either. It is more of a cloud. Teamwork is a great concept, but working in a value network goes beyond the old team philosophy. It starts with a different understanding of objectives. In traditional team-based organizations, the targeted goals are usually clearly defined, as is the road that reaches them, such as with the allocation of tasks and responsibility. A value network is mainly characterized by shared points of view, and a path of creation that is mutually discovered in a context of collective responsibility. In collaboration with or within organizations, the community leader facilitates the process as much as possible, but you cannot call this 'managing'. There is an open structure for new knowledge and contacts one can use to make an appeal to the entire outside world. The same goes for capturing and making the acquired knowledge of the value network available. The old 'team thinking' is disposed of to keep this within their walls, but value creation is, of course, best served by open connections.

For 'customers', it is therefore not always clear who bears the final responsibility, while it is not always clear to the network members how the revenues should be shared, or how copyright issues are dealt with. Within these entities, arrangements can provide insight for all stakeholders, including the final co-creating client. Whereas regular organizational teams or departments tend to mark their territories and build ivory towers, value networks have the ability to connect with each other. Individual members of value networks can organize themselves from one spot. In part, this increases the data portability between networks on a daily basis. This is how boundaries continue to dissolve: SEE value networks are extraordinarily dynamic and flow into each other. That is why it is so difficult for outsiders to understand: it is not always an obviously recognizable team or project group that is on the job. The work is also no longer done within four walls, under a single roof, with the name of the organization on the façade of the building. Seats2meet.com locations offer an excellent 3rd Space experience for SEEs.

12.7
How to become an open organization.

Opening up takes a lot of guts for organizations. Boundaries are crossed, and unknown territory is entered. Scary. Management has to let go of control. Even more frightening!

Management author Kevin Kelly gives us in his book *New Rules For The New Economy*, four tips for traditional organizations seeking to 'open up' more, and thus create value and enhance their survivability:
1. Make customers as smart as you are.
2. Connect customers to customers.
3. All things being equal, choose technology that connects.
4. Imagine your customers as employees.

Maintaining sound connections between an organization and its stakeholders is unfortunately not something that goes without saying. These moments of contact – or moments of truth – are becoming even more rare when we realize that stakeholders no longer need the organization to connect with each other.

There is an opportunity here for organizations! Moments of contact between stakeholders offer opportunities to offer and gather information, and are therefore of vital importance to the organization. A kind of question-and-answer game has to originate. After all, as an organization, you have to (or want to) know increasingly more about a stakeholder. At least, if you want to customize your communication, repeatedly supply your customer/stakeholder with the right information at the right time, or create the next branding moment.

Smart organizations establish and facilitate that network – The network wherein event driven communication (EDC) is the key word. With EDC, every event is the starting point for an activity in the communication stream between organizations and their stakeholders. EDC is always active, right through the organization. EDC facilitates the continuous connection between the four main elements of Organization 3.0 (culture, leadership, transactional business concept, and social business concept), which will be explained at length further on this third part of this book.

Within that communication network around an organization, it's all about optimizing the experience a stakeholder should have with each random moment of contact with the organization and/or its other stakeholders. That puts great demands on the product, and, in particular, on the service around it – whether it is about informing, reserving, buying, selling, after-sales, or customer complaints. As a consequence of this, I believe an organization should deal with the issue of which services or production processes can be outsourced in a different manner. This is a pity for all call centers, but telephonic contact with customers need to be done by your own staff, because, as entrepreneurial employees – not limited by a script – they are preeminently capable of making autonomous decisions. It's a shame for Internet hotel room booking portals as well, but communicating with a potential hotel guest and registering their information should be done by the hotel, itself (with the added advantage that you will own the information of your customers). It is not smart, as an airline, to outsource the check-in process to another specialized company. Just do it yourself.

And when saying 'do it yourself', I should add 'or ask your community of dedicated fans to help you'. These nearby stakeholders who lvoe your brand will be more than willing to assist in a very professional and authentic way. We at Seats2meet.com have the largest help desk in Europe. It consists of over 40,000 fans, available 24/7. So, just ask your question about our organization on Twitter, and see what happens...

12.8
The real-time organization

The best teams might be temporary, but their company's success is enduring.

– David Burkus, HBR blog network, 2013

In the 1970s, Gerard van Endenburg put the ideas of a sociocratic organization into practice. According to the Wikipedia article on the topic: "Sociocracy is a form of management that presumes equality of individuals and is based on consent. This equality is not expressed with the 'one man, one vote' law of democracy but rather by a group of individuals reasoning together until a decision is reached that is satisfactory to each one of them. The structure uses a hierarchy of circles corresponding to units or departments of an organization, but it is a circular hierarchy—the links between each circle combine to form feedback loops up and down the organization. Because representatives overlap the circle with a linked circle and each circle makes policy decisions by consent this forms a strong and integrated structure of communications and control. Feedback moves up and down the organization and can't be ignored."

Zappos is the largest online shoe store in the world with an annual turnover of over $1 billion. CEO Tony Hsieh announced in 2013 it would change itself into a holocratic organization , also a sociocratic approach. Instead of a top-down hierarchy, there's a flatter 'holarchy' that distributes power more evenly. The company will be made up of over 400 different circles and employees can have any number of roles within those circles. John Bunch, who is leading the transition to Holacracy at Zappos said, "one of the core principles is people taking personal accountability for their work. Everybody is expected to lead and be an entrepreneur in their own roles, and Holacracy empowers them to do so." In its highest-functioning form, he says, the system is "politics-free, quickly evolving to define and operate the purpose of the organization, responding to market and real-world conditions in real time. It's creating a structure in which people have flexibility to pursue what they're passionate about."

This holocratic or sociocratic organizational structure, its interdependency, and transparency makes sense in Society 3.0 organizational thinking.

These sociocratic circles could (should!) also include 'outsiders'. Because of this permanent interaction between all stakeholders within the increasingly hazy boundaries of organizations, a creative culture originates that makes the organization cyclically innovative. Innovation is finally no longer a goal, but an imbedded strategic weapon that can push the distinguishing abilities of the organization to great heights. This applies to all forms of innovation: product, process, and business innovation. All scientific studies show unequivocally that innovative companies perform fundamentally better than their competition, even in bad economic times.

Resilient organizations that understand the art of Event Driven Communication grow into so-called real-time companies, especially if they can change the more traditional EDC into easy accessible subject-centered communication streams. These organizations become a network with permanently connected stakeholders, where informal and formal relationships flourish. They optimally use the Internet and other technologies to create value. They are continually facilitating the co working process. They are convinced of the fact that thinking in terms of here, now, personal, relevant, and reliable can maximize interconnectivity. Organizations that can achieve this will be happy with a successful right to exist in an innovative and creative manner, together with and in the interest of, all stakeholders, a significant product or service of real value is created.

This is what I like to call Organization 3.0: a sustainable eco system wherein people can be proud of the stakeholder value that is created, and where the people of the organization are stakeholders, themselves. This Organization 3.0 has a slightly different design than is customary, and, in building it, a large role is reserved for global citizens. If you want to read the following pages as management literature, you are obviously free to do so. But, it is actually food for thought for global people.

12.9
The fundamentals of the Organization 3.0: N=1, R=G...

In his book, *The New Age of Innovation*, C.K. Prahalad, with his co-author M.S. Krishan, redefines the organization as 'The New House of Innovation'. Prahalad poses that the traditional organization, as the epicenter of value creation, is a thing of the past. Rather, value is created by having access to knowledge and information, and not by having ownership or control. Value is something that is overwhelmingly created outside the comfort zone, or paradigm, of the traditional organization. Social networks shift the power of organizations to their stakeholders, in particular, their consumers. If the organization wants to capitalize on this, they will have to emerge as a communication interchange, with the main goal of facilitating and optimizing cooperation between all stakeholders.

According to Prahalad, every customer wants a customized and co-created experience in every moment of contact with the organization, its service, and the product. Only then can we talk of distinctive capacity. This requires an unprecedented decisiveness and flexibility in the company processes. This is one of the three qualities of his New House of Innovation.

The second organization quality is N=1: the customer is unique. Human, material and immaterial sources for organizing are available everywhere.

Their key to success is collaboration between all stakeholders. The high measure of Internet connectivity enables even the smallest organizations and free agents a role on the world stage. Or, as Chris Anderson puts it in his book *The Long Tail*: 'The webification of the supply chain in many industries, from electronics to apparel, now means that even the smallest companies can order globally'. With that, he subscribes to the third organization quality Prahalad postulates: R=G, resources are global.

THE NEW HOUSE OF INNOVATION

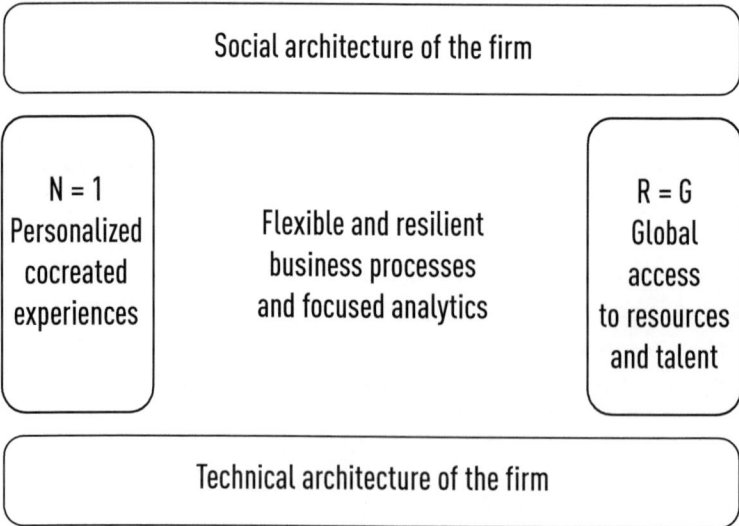

Social architecture of the firm

$N = 1$
Personalized cocreated experiences

Flexible and resilient business processes and focused analytics

$R = G$
Global access to resources and talent

Technical architecture of the firm

With this model for The New House of Innovation, Prahalad and Krishan designate an organizational architecture that, as far as I'm concerned, deserves the designation of 3.0. It is based on a social structure and a technical architecture, and excels in the qualities of flexible company processes, 'N=1' and 'R=G'. Their insights confirm that organizations, small and large, have to focus on the individual instead of the masses.

For me, this means a connection with Anderson's Long Tail theory. So, let's have a look at that.

12.10
The Long Tail & the Long Snout
The Pareto principle, also known as the 80-20 rule, does not work anymore. This principle states that 20% of the customers bring in 80% of the revenue. Or that 20% of the suppliers supply 80% of the materials. That way, you can do a high volume with a few processes, and that is quite efficient for traditional organizations. In this picture of the Long Tail, you can see clearly that a traditional organization, in this case, one of our former meeting centers in Utrecht, The Netherlands, focused on the 'head' of the tail (greyish area). The nitty gritty stuff to the right had to be ignored. It was too expensive to work with.

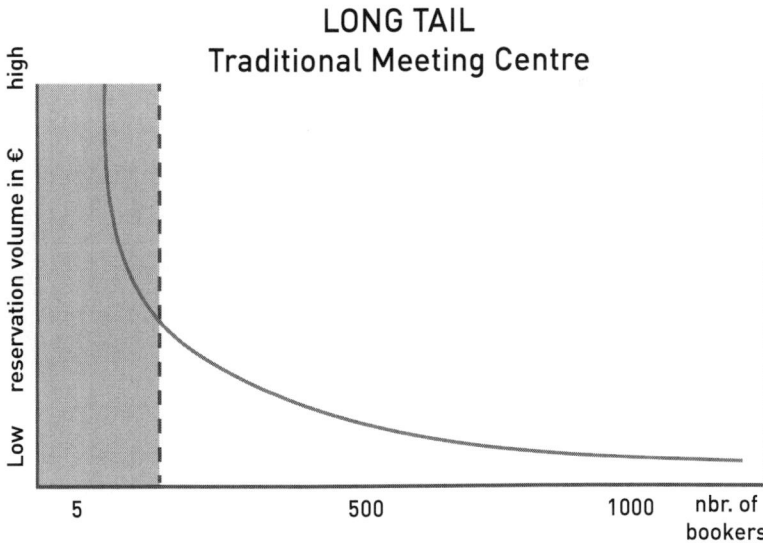

However in the rising Interdependent Economy of Society 3.0, we see thousands of small and individual buyers hanging in the Tail. In our case at Seats2meet.com, these are knowmadic workers, looking for one dedicated desk for a week, one meeting room per month, and perhaps two desks at a coworking center.

It's a 1-to-1 situation, if you want the business. C. K. Prahalad called that, as we saw in the previous chapter, N=1.

Why is it that Chris Anderson is so adamant in his book, *The Long Tail*, that his Long Tail theory will replace the Pareto principle, and thus fulfill the aforementioned Law of Prahalad? His answer is:
"(retail) space for the Long Tail is made possible by the unlimited 'shelf space' on the Internet, the first distribution system in history that is suited for both the niche- and mass market. Shelf space is only unlimited if the space does not cost anything. Because 'marginal costs' of digital distribution – the extra costs for shipping an extra copy in addition to the 'fixed costs' of the required hardware – are almost negligible, we can make unlimited use of it."

Anderson likes to use Apple's online music store, iTunes, as an example. This store is not limited by old economic restrictions, such shelf space, opening times, production of leaflets, distribution, and sales staff. Therefore, iTunes is able to present an extremely wide assortment of products, which can be bought 24/7. Even if a track is downloaded just once a year, iTunes earns a healthy profit margin on it. In fact, someone who wants to buy his favorite music is prepared to pay a higher price for it, and so improve the profit margin. Meanwhile, the annual turnover has risen to billions of dollars. And this sales volume was realized without costs for storage, stores, salesclerks and everything else that is needed to run a brick-and-mortar retail chain. That is one incredibly profitable store!

Our Seats2meet.com coworking and meeting space locations are active in the Long Tail. We handle hundreds of thousands of individual desk, office, and meeting seats (all individually priced) per year through our Web reservation systems. We offer our Knowmads 'free' coworking, including desk space, Wi-Fi, coffee, tea, and, at some locations, even a free lunch. These knowmads pay by means of social capital. They are willing to create value with others by sharing their knowledge.

LONG TAIL
Seats2meet.com

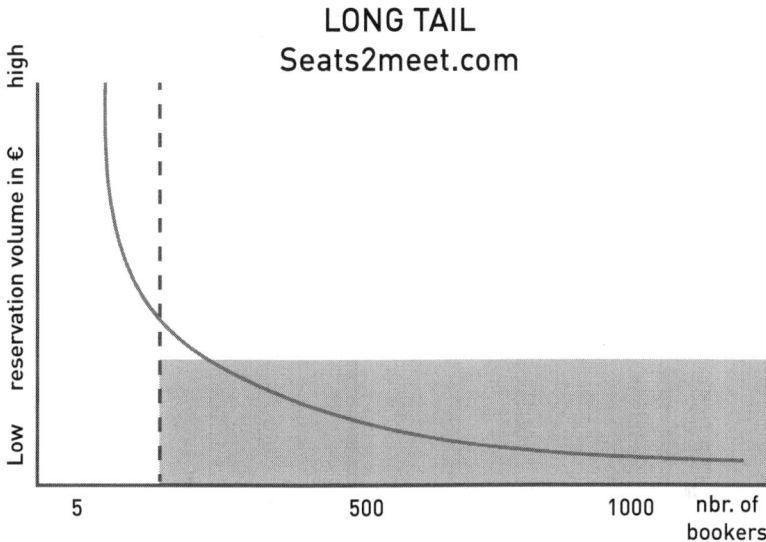

Also, when you realize that these stakeholders and buyers in the Seats2meet.com Long Tail are connected with other individuals, and that all these prosumers and knowmads have their social networks at their disposal, you start to appreciate their real value for our organization. Their and our networks are connected to other social networks, and become a part of The Seats2meet.com Mesh, the domain of value creation within the Interdependent Economy. These knowmads form the only(!) link to new markets, and are therefore of the utmost importance to the Organization 3.0's right to exist.

With our new, 'disruptive' meeting concept, Seats2meet.com, we have focused on the Long Tail of the Dutch market for meeting spaces since this Long Tail does not only hold Euro value in seats sold, but every booker represents a tremendous value (social capital): they appreciate our products and services tremendously, and help us to position Seats2meet.com in The Mesh. They create an enormous flow of buzz on the Web (we used to call that PR in the old days); they feed us with tips, reviews, knowledge, and their time (that used to be called marketing), and actively promote us to other knowmads and to corporate and governmental organizations (that used to be called sales). Whenever they have 'real' business, they book their training and meeting rooms at Seats2meet.com locations without asking for a discount.

So, at Seats2meet.com, we no longer have a PR, sales, or marketing and reservation department. How do you think that works out for our operational costs? Moreover, the still-growing army of 'fans' who do our commercial activities is staggering.

When we changed the axis 'reservation volume' and renamed it 'total value', to our surprise, all of a sudden, a reversed Long Tail showed itself, which, from that point on, we called the Long Snout.

LONG SNOUT
Seats2meet.com

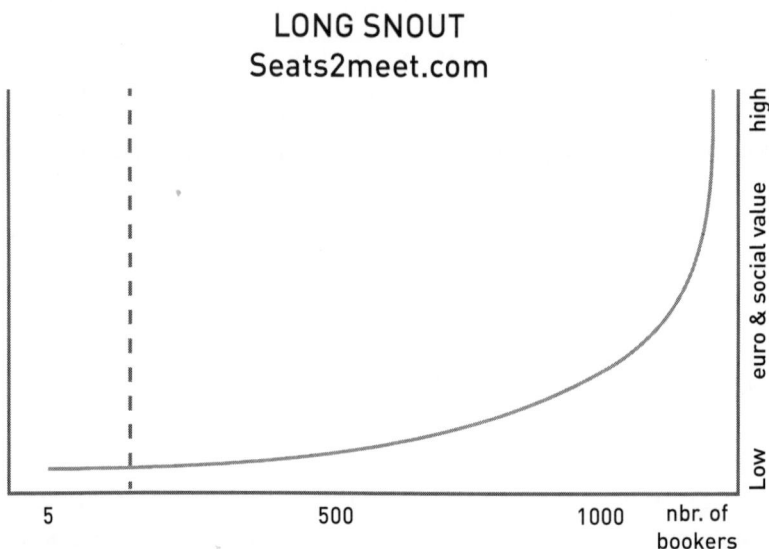

12.11
Nothing beats FREE

'There is no such thing as a free lunch'. These words date back to the 19th century, when bartenders in the United States were serving free lunch to attract a crowd. The cost was incorporated in the sale price of the liquors, so 'free' was not really free, or was it?

The word free may mean without cost, but it definitely does not mean without value. There is a clear sense of value, but you need to think of it in terms of intangible benefits such as social capital. You receive something, and you give something else in return. If you offer a free download of your book, sales of the physical book will rise. This much has been proven in recent years. By giving a lot in one place, you can earn in another place. Sometimes, this is in the shape of money. It is tricky that the relationship between giving something and receiving something in return is not always a direct or equal one. This is called asynchronous reciprocity. Do as you would be done by; you just do not know exactly how and when.

You read in the previous chapter that we offer free coworking at out Seats2meet.com locations, and of the tremendous reciprocity we experienced as a result. The German scholar Sebastian Olma has studied the concept of Seats2meet.com. In his book, *The Serendipity Machine*, he describes our asynchronous reciprocity as follows:

"What Seats2meet.com experiences is the manifestation of an archaic principle, albeit in very modern form: the potlatch. A potlatch is a ceremonial feast that has been found to be an integral part of many archaic economies. The word comes from a native North American dialect term meaning 'to give away' or a 'gift'. Anthropologists have long been fascinated with the potlatch, because it is the cornerstone of an economic system in which acts of exchange do not take place in a space abstracted from personal relations. In our modern economies, a transaction is sealed by paying a price, thus alienating the previous owner from the good or service. Paying the price, one might say, cuts off the previous owner's bond with the object of exchange and also prevents the emergence of any social bond between the two parties. The potlatch, in contradistinction, is a form of exchange designed to establish a social bond between the parties engaging in the exchange. The gift is never alienated from the giver. Rather, he or she enters into a relationship of asynchronous reciprocity with the receiver of the gift. The exchange establishes a strong social bond between the parties involved in the gift exchange, obligating the receiver to repay his or her gift debt. However, the reciprocity is asynchronous, meaning that when and how repayment takes place is left to the will and capabilities of the receiver."

On the Internet, you will find quite a number of free applications, products, and services. Or at least, they seem to be free of charge. In his book, *Free*, Chris Anderson explains that this is the case, because certain Internet-related costs (bandwidth, data storage, and software) are approaching a zero point, and, as a consequence, more and more can be offered for nothing.

One of the companies that are very good at giving is Google. Google's Eric Schmidt calls it the Google Max Strategy: "Take whatever it is you are doing and do it at the max in terms of distribution. The other way of saying this is that since marginal cost of distribution is free, you might as well drop things everywhere."

Using an Internet music service, like Spotify, you can listen to music free of charge, but in between the songs you will hear or see advertisements. If you want to use all the goodies offered by the platform, a monthly fee will be imposed. Although the traditional music industry has fought these services for years, they are slowly starting to see the impact and potential success of the new business models. In 2013, in The Netherlands, for the first time in twelve years, the music publishers saw an increase in turnover caused by their share in these Internet music platforms, and I hope, for them, it is not too little and not too late. Some artists are complaining again that their share is too little, as the establishment greedily grabs a too-large share, and their added value is almost nothing, so the battle between traditionalists and Society 3.0 citizens is not yet over.

12.12
Reciprocity needs a network.

Giving only makes sense if you have a good network to give to. Only then will giving be a part of the social capital system, and someday you will receive something in return. So, giving something for free is something different than giving away something free of charge. Organizations who do not have access to a surrounding social structure cannot give. They can only literally give something away, because there is no possibility for the receiver to do something (indirectly) in return.

The free of charge phenomenon has many industries in its grip. As a traditional organization, you can't fight against free. But, eventually someone is paying for something somewhere. It's true that Google offers many applications for nothing, but it receives a lot of data and information about you and me in return. That data is worth a lot of money to others. For example, Google gets paid well for its professional trend analyses. By giving, Google also generates a lot of visitors to its websites, so it can earn with its ads. Not everything can be paid for with alternative or non-tangible currencies. A book can be downloaded for nothing, but you do need to purchase a computer and Internet access to do so.

And, as mentioned before, by giving free seats at our Seats2meet. com coworking locations, we get back online buzz, help desk assistance, market information, and sales assistance, saving us lots of real money and earning lots of real money in return by our loyal bookers.

The freemium model is quite popular: the first step, or basic version, of a freemium product is free. Then, a price is charged. An example is a psychological test (pay $ 4.95 to view the full results). Or a simple piece of software that is free of charge, but the 'pro' version has more, or better, or faster features, and costs little bit of money.

Our S2M event software is free, as long as the event itself is free. The moment an admission fee is imposed, the organizer starts paying a small fee for the software.

Or, you can design your own woolen hat, gloves, and scarf for free on www.granniesinc.co.uk/, and then it is knitted for a fee by a granny in the community.

12.13
What do the guru's say?

In his book, *Theory of Business*, Peter Drucker (1994) explains that – in our fast-changing world – traditional ways of organizing (arranging) lead to a corporate structure that can no longer move along with external dynamics. The preservation of the structure has become an objective in itself, and has drifted far from the means that it should be. The traditional organizational structure mainly determines internal boundaries: job profiles, duties, responsibilities and competencies, the division of work, processes, procedures, and instructions. The human being is of secondary importance to this. The structure also determines the relationship between the organization and its environment: how we deal with customers, how external communication is managed, what kind of information can be published, and what cannot. The familiar organizational structures employ the basic principle that 'to measure is to know', and have an immense measure of control. The organization restrains itself with this type of structure and experiences the limits of the Coase Ceiling as a traditional organization which creates its own limitations in terms of available people, means, and time.

Joseph Pine and James Gillmore, the authors of *The Experience Economy* (1999), are looking more at clients' perceptions of experiences when dealing with organizations and/or their products and services. This is the raison d-être for a company or organization. They base this view on their hierarchical model, which starts with the cultivation and selling of agricultural products, the fabrication of products using fossil fuels, setting up a provision of services around these products, and subsequently creating a special user experience.

Pine & Gilmore, in the 2011 update of their book, take this experience to the next step, to transforming the client as the ultimate experience. The transformed client becomes the actual service or product.

Ron Ashkenas recommends in his 1995 book, *The Boundaryless Organization*, that you literally break the traditional chains in order to enter the dynamics of the unbounded organization. Meeting each other within value networks simply happens in complete openness. You get to work together, whether you are an employee, a knowmad, a supplier, or a customer. This requires a completely different set of demands on the setup of the organization. It has to be predominantly 'open'. What does this mean? Data are freely available, ranging from the source code of software to Web services and APIs (software hooks that can be connected to external websites, which makes data more freely and widespread available for third parties). Intranet no longer exists as limited Internet usage. Transparency, information, and sharing knowledge, both internally and externally, are relevant keywords. Knowledge is no longer the symbol of the power of possessive managers; knowledge is there to share and to be shared. This is boundless organizing.

Dee Hock made sweeping changes to his credit card company, Visa. In his book, *Birth of the Chaordic Age* (2000), he describes how the structures within traditional companies particularly spur the people within that organization to apply their thoughts, feelings, and actions for the benefit of themselves and the enterprise. Words like 'together' and 'stakeholders' do not exist within that vocabulary. The preservation of the established structures and processes has become the goal, instead of the means. The person in the company invariably complies with the main structure, and is inclined to renounce themselves and their abilities. Hock has named his new way of organizing the 'chaordic organization'. 'Chaordic' is an amalgamation of chaos and order. According to Hock, a chaordic organization is 'self-organizing, self-governing, adaptive, nonlinear, and complex, which harmoniously combines the characteristics of both chaos and order'.

In the book, *Blue Ocean Strategy* (2005), Chan Kim and Renee Mauborgne talk about a Red Ocean situation in the market. It's a bloody mess, wherein the parties involved try to maintain their market share by endlessly lowering their prices, even if it is partly at the expense of the organization. This situation can be characterized by hostile takeovers, price wars, reorganizations, outsourcing, redundancies, and a complete lack of stakeholder loyalty. The unwillingness to innovate (in other words, not supplying the ultimate customized product or service, and not advancing to the next phase of economic value creation as an organization) will irrevocably lead to commoditization, a situation in which all products and services look alike, and where the consumer is left with a single criteria for purchase: price. This is the zombie economy market.

Yochai Benkler wrote in his book, *The Wealth of Networks* (2007): "I see the emergence of social production and peer production as an alternative to both state-based and market-based closed, proprietary systems."

As a Harvard blogger, Umair Haque talks about awesomeness:
"Insanely great stuff. Awesomeness puts creativity front and center. Awesome stuff evokes an emotive reaction because it's fundamentally new, unexpected, and 1,000x better. [...] Social strategies are about reinventing tomorrow. Their goal is nothing less than changing the DNA of an organization, ecosystem, or industry. Want to get radical? Stop applying 20th century principles ('product,' 'buzz,' 'loyalty') to 21st century media. The fundamental change of scale and pace that social tools introduce into human affairs – their great tectonic shift – is the promise of more meaningful work, stuff, and organization."

In his book, *The New Capitalist Manifesto* (2011), Umair Haque names the critical success factors of his so-called 'meaning organization'. The meaning organization only provides products or services if they are truly meaningful – not just as value for the short-term profits for shareholders, but also actually contributing something to society. The organization puts the wellbeing of the stakeholders at the forefront.

217

This is how economic effort can enrich society. These companies ask the following question: What binds our stakeholders to our organization? It is not just about free trade, but also about fair trade; not only about doing business, but about doing it ethically as well; not solely about innovation but about integrity, too. It is no longer enough to like what we do within a company or organization, but to do what we like within those organizations. The new organization is bursting with ambition. It has the desire to turn the organization into a platform that will really enrich the world and humanity, both locally and internationally.

12.14
What do your stakeholders say?

The 'crude' delivery of a service or product is no longer good enough. Stakeholders want much, much more: they want a complete and meaningful experience, which will transform them.

Stakeholders want an increasingly richer user experience or brand perception during all moments of contact with their supplier. They have to feel that the product, the service, the employees, and the production processes are authentic, and are made just for them. This is tricky, because, all things considered, not a single product or service is authentic. After all, these products and services are made to be sold. So, it is important that consumers and stakeholders experience a sense of authenticity. Involvement, transparency, honesty, responsibility, openness, and sustainability in all sections make an organization very authentic.

Stakeholders want to be increasingly involved with the realization of services and products. This contributes to a special user experience. Every experience of co-creation strengthens the feeling that you are a part of it, and co-creation has the added advantage of yielding a vastly improved product or service. It improves so much that the ultimate selling price, whether it be actual money or social capital, will become subordinate as a standard of choice for doing business, purchasing, or collaborating.

In order to give the stakeholders a sense of authenticity, and in order to co-create with them, the organization will have to connect with them and start a dialogue. In short, an organization has to form its own Mesh, create engagement by starting a dialogue, be transparent, and start a co-creation value process.

To gain access to an entire network of stakeholders, the Organization 3.0 has to plan and execute a social media strategy. The basic principle is that all moments of communication, or touch points, take place immediately and directly between the stakeholder and the person directly responsible for that service or product. This requires resilient, dynamic and flexible internal processes, a high degree of freedom of movement, and decision-making power for the people involved.

The network of inter-human contacts creates a permanent solidarity between the organization, its people, and its other stakeholders. This social exchange of information and knowledge leads into co-creation, and ultimately results in 'doing business' with each other in these value networks. On one hand, 'new organizing' comprises a social relationship with the stakeholders; on the other hand, it comprises a business relationship. These relationships are not necessarily the same.

If you really want to claim your position in the clusters of new value networks as an organization on the road to tomorrow, in the global Mesh, then you will have to operate with minimal standardization and an informal company culture based on trust and with open communication. Only then can you make a serious appeal to autonomy and entrepreneurship in order to excel both internally and externally within such a dynamic environment.

12.15
My vision of the Organization 3.0

So, new organizing is not a matter of replacing the old model with a new one. The reform mainly occurs from a vision on organizing. All in all, there was not that much vision for organization in the past: there was a structure for organizing, which was predominantly aimed at preservation. The vision of new organization is directed at breathing along with, moving along with, and experiencing. This does not fit in any model; it is a new structure. Every new structure will have the tendency for self-preservation. What I'm trying to say is that the new style organization, at its core, is led, managed, and guided by vision. Vision

– to keep looking at developments and continuously adapt to them, including birth and death – will be the new management paradigm.

Serendipity, the phenomenon of finding something unexpected and usable while looking for something completely different, enters the scene. Serendipity stimulates the transformation, and is the ultimate product/service of the Organization 3.0, and of your stakeholder. Make sure to be part of this serendipity generation process, because remember, your stakeholder will start to ignore you as he/she doesn't need your organization to get what he/she wants...

Stakeholders want to deal with meaningful organizations that are in balance with their environments. 'Social enterprise' is a term we see popping up. A social enterprise is an organization that applies commercial strategies to maximize profit and enable the organization to improve in human and environmental well-being, rather than maximizing profits for external shareholders only. Social enterprises form a new economic sector within the Interdependent Economy: the 4th Sector (beside the traditional sectors of Government, Commercial, and Non-profit). 4th Sector organizations may be self-organized, non-formal swarms of people, or more structured, value-creating social network around an Organization 3.0.

We see that many successful, new 3.0 companies, like Facebook, Twitter or LinkedIn in the end turn to the traditional stock market in order to get the resources needed for further growth. That is funny: a new initiative turns to old solutions, making these exciting companies

> The Spanish MONDRAGON Corporation is the embodiment of the co-operative movement that began in 1956, the year that witnessed the creation of the first industrial cooperative in Mondragón in the province of Gipuzkoa. Its business philosophy is contained in its corporate values:
>
> Cooperation, participation, social responsibility, and innovation.
>
> The corporation's mission combines the core goals of a business organization competing in international markets with the use of democratic methods in its business organization, the creation of jobs, the human and professional development of its workers, and a pledge to develop with its social environment.

turn into traditional, short-term thinking, shareholder/profit driven organizations, putting the community, which initially created the success, in second priority. So the real Society 3.0 organization may be the one with a cooperative conversion commitment.

Suddenly, boundless, experience, chaordic, and awesome have become qualities of the same phenomena – which, for recognition's sake, I'll continue to call 'organization' – namely, a meaningful organization whose behavior adapts to circumstances, and whose leadership and vision have nearly become synonymous. Such a purely vision-driven organization – where, as it happens, semantics define the quality of (stakeholder) communication, and not the syntax – I would like to label as Organization 3.0.

> In Brazil, the Semco group of companies also adopted a 4th Sector approach. From their website:
> "A company based on innovation, Semco Partner does not follow the standards of other companies with a predefined hierarchy and excessive formality. At Semco Partner, people work with substantial freedom, without formalities and with a lot of respect. Everybody is treated equally, from high-ranking executives to the lowest ranked employees. This means the work of each person is given its true importance and everybody is much happier at work."

Within the vision-driven Organization 3.0, all the stakeholders are, in one way or the other, involved with and have a vested interest in the enterprise. This can be in the role of an employee, supplier, guest, customer, family member, or member of a social network in the broadest sense. The concept of the vision-driven organization has the mission statement as a benchmark for these stakeholders, and as a realization of the collective vision of all stakeholders on issues around the organization. We are not talking about that bit of obligatory text that is made up by a select group and then dished up. We are talking about a shared mission. With that, the mission automatically has a dynamic character, and every stakeholder can – or they should be able to – explain, in their own words, what their vision is on issues that touch the organization on their own personal level. The right mission statement also contains a vision on that entrepreneurship in itself, or what you are able to do with it while you work.

12.16
The Organization 3.0 model

The Organization 3.0, comprised of the formal organizations as well as the informal pop-up organizations or Social Economic Entities, organizes its activities around four crucial starting points that I have named as follows: leadership, culture, transactional business concepting, and social business concepting.

- The culture of the organization is based on trust. Key words are openness, self-responsibility, and self-management.
- Leadership is, and will remain, extremely important to the org-

anization. The new leaders are no longer 'the boss', but they interpret, give direction, and form a source of inspiration for the stakeholders.
- The transactional concept bears upon the business model of the organization: what we do, for whom, and how we ensure the co-creation of a sustainable company, product, and/or service.
- The social concept points to the organization of stakeholder communication and interaction to achieve a permanent stakeholder engagement.

Event-driven communication streams will be the binding activities between these four main ingredients, internally as well as externally. As far as it is possible to talk of a structure within the vision-driven organization, it is mainly a communication structure that is meant to facilitate the conversations around the aforementioned starting points with and between all internal and external stakeholders. Tasks have been replaced by roles; these are not clear-cut, but rather a tool to facilitate the internal communication, feedback loops, and the work itself. Someone can hold several roles, even in more than one organization. The management strategy is aimed at drawing on the inspiring force of talents. That is how there is no longer a substantial distinction between talents of internal or external stakeholders.

At first sight, the migration to an Organization 3.0 is quite a challenge. It is indeed. This migration is really more than the shift from one organizational structure to the next in an attempt to hold the grip on the surrounding dynamics. It is a shift from the old paradigm to a cyberdigm approach, a much more open and fluid attempt to create a position in the chaordic world of the Organization 3.0. It is no longer sufficient to do an appeal on the economical productivity of human talents. Society 3.0 can only flourish if it is founded on the chaordic mesh of organizations collaborating with their interconnected stakeholders, daring to use the complete human capability of feeling, thinking, and self-steering.

So, lets have a more in-depth look at leadership, culture, transactional business concept, and social business concept in the next chapters.

High sea, a huge storm
Leadership is a talent
Security for all

13
LEADERSHIP 3.0 IS MASTERY

A leader leads by example, not by enforcing it...
–Chinese General Sun Tzu, *Art of War* (600 BC.)

The master is at the back; that is why he leads. He is independent of everything; that is why he is one with everything. Because he has detached himself, he is completely fulfilled.
– Lao Tzu, *Tao Te Ching* (600 BC)

Leadership is all about vision and strategy. Strategy is about realizing that vision. Vision is always about the developments around and within the organization and its leader. The vision is a collection of points of view. The leader makes sure the stakeholders know what's going on within and outside the organization. He or she knows what the developments are in the home market and beyond. The leader has insight into society. The leader sees the future, sets a good example, builds bridges, and connects. The leader is visible, gives clarity in conveying their vision, is honest and dependable, and acts from their own place of authenticity. Everybody in his or her vicinity knows what the leader stands for. In light of the aforementioned profile, an organization can accommodate many leaders. Leaders can no longer be identified by the fact that they are in charge (or that are trying to be in charge). That is very 20th century. True leaders receive leadership.

Cees Hoogendijk, a Dutch organizational developer and contributor to the Vertical Dialogue movement, begins with a question in his book, *Strength without Power*:
"What do managers do? And, whom do they manage? And, how do

they manage? Everyone has his or her own assignments and someone is in charge. Or, is it somehow different? In reality, managing has degenerated to taking charge. Do managers just seek control? Do they claim power? But where do the parties involved stand, the employees? This leads us to the Vertical Dialogue. Just imagine that such a manager, when plans have to be made or problems need to be solved, would switch off his 'power' and stand on equal footing with his staff. Imagine that he would weigh their professional knowledge and experience to reach a collective strategy. Would this result in acceptance and support? Would it be possible that this manager would now actually be in charge? I believe that a manager can only truly lead if he has earned the ability to be in charge. What do you think?"

In his book, *The Chaordic Organization*, Dee Hock says that leaders need to be focused chiefly on their own personal development. Leadership requires the ability to ask questions more so than the ability to answer them. It is all about ignoring your own ego and actually engaging in a dialogue with stakeholders.

Capelli and Singh (The India Way) see leaders in emerging nations, like India, acting as stimulators for the organizational strategy, guards of the organizational culture, and example setters for employees. Guarding the shareholder's interest only comes in fourth!

People who can inspire other people to move away from their comfort zone are true leaders. Instead of reacting and fixing problems after the fact, these leaders enable others to self-manage on the road to fundamental changes in thinking about society and the organization of it. Claus Otto Scharmer says in his book, *Addressing the Blind Spot of Our Time*, that the road to this fundamental change is the biggest challenge for leaders in the 21st century:
"On all four levels – personal, group, institutional, and global – shifting from reactive responses and quick fixes on a symptoms level (Fields 1 and 2) to generative responses that address the systemic root issues (Fields 3 and 4) is the single most important leadership challenge of our time."

These root-level issues refer to an improved balance in entrepreneurship and leadership. We call this socially-responsible managing; as well as to the monetary interest, attention is also given to social and ecological interests. Thus, Organization 3.0 is realized as a social enterprise operating in the 4th Sector.

13.1
Leaders & vision: inseparable

A leader is a visionary, somebody that has an eye for his or her environment, and is continuously monitoring the changing circumstances. He or she sees the future and analyses the impact of the changing playing field on his/her organization. A leader is a trend strategist.

The vision of an organization is the collective sum of the individual visions of the stakeholders. These include visions of events, developments, and other things in its surroundings, with consequences for the organization. They need a vision of how to create shared value. Leaders should realize that a vision is dynamic, so visionary leadership is about trendwatching, creating a situational stakeholder awareness of the future environment, and enabling the organization to adapt itself to the dynamics of modern society.

The mission statement is the embodiment of that vision and can (and should) be used as a point of reference for all stakeholders in their daily (business) life.

The stronger an individual stakeholder's (shared) vision, the better this person operates independently, with a capability for self-steering. Processes gain speed and the whole organization rocks!

Leaders are aware of the position the organization in the living and working environment of its stakeholders. This 'eye for the own environment' encompasses many points of interest: technology, society, economy, politics, and government. Leaders of organizations keep a close watch on the moral ideology of the organization, on their own level, and, with it, its sustainability. In this case, I define sustainability as the sum of financial returns, social renewal, and an ecological awareness. This goes much further than simply 'being green'. It is great to transcend the whole, but an organization eventually finds its bed in the local community. 'Think global, act local'.

Vision is something that relates the present in to a certain goal in the future. Leadership is also about winning (or conquering). There is nothing wrong with that. Leading an organization means identifying future obstacles and leveling them, thus making sure that the or-

ganization does not lose momentum. Many strategic insights may be acquired from the Art of War. This chapter began with a quote from the Chinese general Sun Tzu, but we can also learn from warlords like Genghis Khan and Karl von Clausewitz, the Prussian general who is recognized as the founder of modern warfare. They all identify the same factors of success to turn leaders into victors:
- Be aware of what is going on around you (situational awareness)
- Have expertise, but also have metacognition (how do I impart intelligence?)
- Communicate (knowing something before the opposition on all levels, enabling a faster decision-making process)
- Delegate (people within the coordinating vision who have the relevant information and knowledge follow their own strategy)

Governing is akin to looking forward. Leadership is about anticipating. Arriving too late, and, consequently, only reacting is deadly. This requires vision as well.

13.2
Leaders enable, connect, and engage

We have consciously chosen for minimal structure in the companies that belong to Seats2meet.com: we attach a lot of value to the informal feedback loop. The basis of this is our vision that we trust that people are able to self-organize and self-manage, and consequently, can stimulate each other to perform value-driven work. This puts great demands on our employees, and it is a great challenge that requires constant attention. It is actually a lot more exciting than boarding up an enterprise with measures, which is really no more than a supposed form of control on the realization of the strategic targets.

The old-fashioned 'drawing up' of job competencies, responsibilities, or competency management no longer works. To illustrate my thoughts on new leadership, I would like to introduce Transforium, a preferred method of working to monitor and support the development of people and contact with stakeholders in the vision-driven organization.

The Transforium virtually follows the development of the individual, without wanting to define or dictate that person's development.

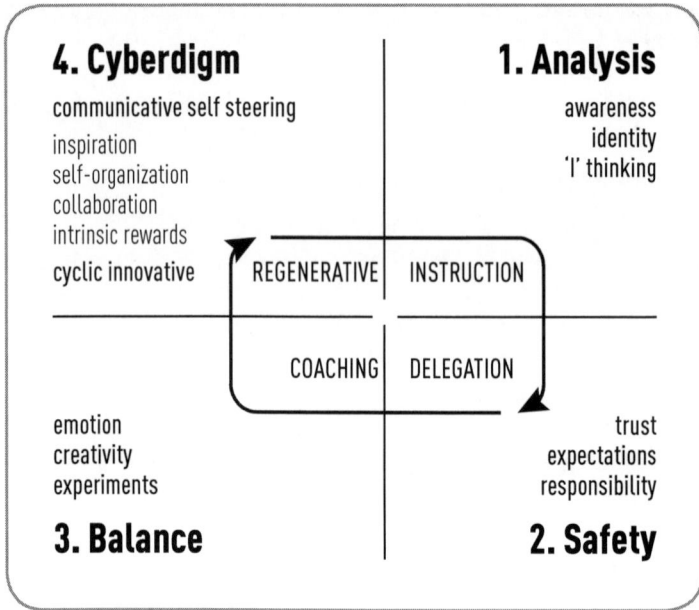

4. Cyberdigm			1. Analysis
communicative self steering			awareness
inspiration			identity
self-organization			'I' thinking
collaboration			
intrinsic rewards			
cyclic innovative	REGENERATIVE	INSTRUCTION	
	COACHING	DELEGATION	
emotion			trust
creativity			expectations
experiments			responsibility
3. Balance			2. Safety

The model is not necessarily a leadership rule; it is a guideline for managers and employees. It is a guideline to calibrate and re-calibrate the realization of the mission statement of the organization on the level of the individual, group, team, and organization.

The Transforium was created by us as a management tool to understand the dynamics of the behavior and development of people, as individuals, as part of a team, and within our organization or social network. It is not Neuro-Lingüistic Programming or any other official human theory, but a model developed within our daily reality, and we found it works very well with people/stakeholders who are not trained in this field. For management, it helps with recognizing the deeper causes of operational and/or relational problems, how to deal with them, and which management style is the most suitable in a particular situation.

It is an hierarchical model: if you skip level 1 and/or 2, you will never reach 3!
So be patient, and when working with this model, make sure not to move too fast...

The model is explained in depth on the website of this book. You will find it here.

Within the organization, in the broadest sense of the word, leaders need to recognize, acknowledge, and know the talents of the stakeholders. Based on this, they have to create the conditions that will ensure everyone can make far better use of their talents, and they have to challenge people in and around the organization to utilize and develop their knowledge, strengths, and capabilities to solve problems. Leaders incite others to learn, and learning processes usually take place in interactions between people. These people need to be connected to each other. This may be the most important role of the leader. It is not just people who are connected. When connecting people, you will connect their knowledge as well.

Many books can be written about the connecting possibilities of the leader. Naturally, my goal is to serve up these words as succinctly as possible. As it happens, Organization 3.0 is preferably a product of you. A vision can be found on the website www.verbindendleiding-geven.nl (connected leadership) which is dear to my heart: "People and organizations are happy, work well, and perform sustainably with leaders who connect people, values, processes, and systems with each other." As far as I'm concerned, this is a great prelude to the next success factor of Organization 3.0: culture.

A genetic string
Human participation
Time is relative

14
CULTURE OF THE ORGANIZATION 3.0

An organization has to be involving, it has to be fun, and it has to exercise your creative instincts.

– Richard Branson

I believe an organizational culture is something very personal. I am not sure it can be captured in a model, or if it should be. And I do not think I'm the right person to offer an alternative for all models available in the area of organizational culture. Regulations in this area do not give any solace. I do not want to prove anything here. In whatever form I may find the culture of Organization 3.0 important, I want to limit myself to the experiences of the people around me. Please take stock of my filtered fragments and determine how you would like to define (your) organizational Culture 3.0.

Organization 3.0 has a different culture than we are used to within traditional organizations. It is a culture of openness, of an almost radical transparency, and one where links outside the company are almost continuously sought. It is a culture of trust, of taking responsibility, and learning for life. There is permanent social innovation. There is social innovation in the form of creating added value by cleverly utilizing the talents of people: We are talking about wanting something and being open to change. This is how a culture is created in which people can think freely and creatively. It is a culture where people name their passions and goals, even if these passions and goals lie outside the organization, which is the case with most of the value networks, as people are only temporary and not exclusively attached to the organization. As an organization, you can make good use of people's talents. And these people can make good use of the organization to develop and grow their talents, because interdependence obviously takes place within Organization 3.0, as well.

"We simply do things differently within our Seats2meet.com companies. We have an eye for talent, we have the conviction to create corresponding positions, and we no longer need to pigeonhole people in our organization. We have entrepreneurial employees, who know what our customers want and who develops new services and products in co-creation with our customers and other stakeholders. Our organization anticipates and is cyclically innovative. We do not have rigid control systems, but we trust right-mindedness, entrepreneurship, and the ability to do business by the stakeholders themselves. Stakeholders have access to all available information, except when the privacy of our people is at stake. Employees have access to all financial figures and statistics and other 'exciting' data. It's striking that in an environment where everyone can access and know everything, the need for information suddenly receives focus. It seems that the creed 'knowing everything does not make you happy' has come true. People are aware of the kind of information they require to operate optimally. We have a low-hierarchical and open organizational culture. Our parent company is named CDEF Holding, an abbreviation for Cada Dia Es una Fiesta (everyday is a party), to stipulate that is should be fun to create sustainable value with your network every day!"

– Mariëlle Sijgers, my business associate
and co-owner of Seats2meet.com

14.1
Organization 3.0 has a learning culture

What is it that you like doing? If you don't like it, get out of it, because you'll be lousy at it. You don't have to stay with a job for the rest of your life, because if you don't like it you'll never be successful in it.

– Lee Iacocca.

There is no organization without knowledge creation, but this is mainly aimed at personal development of all stakeholders within Organization 3.0. It is aimed at increasing self-knowledge, and thinking and operating autonomously in order to establish a place in an enterprise with dissolving boundaries: the value network of the Interdependent Economy. It is more about process knowledge than content knowledge. This is the challenge for every organization that wants to flourish in the new cyberdigm. Investing in expert skills is no longer enough. The distinctive value for the enterprise and for the individual changes with the infinite availability and accessibility of information and knowledge via the Internet. In other words, our competitors have access to the same information. The distinguishing value capabilities of the enterprise will only emerge when the individual stakeholder becomes mobile, stays in touch with coworkers and other stakeholders, and is mostly able to create a transforming experience for the customer by him- or herself. So, the key question is, what is your degree of stakeholder employability?

Employability is defined by the theory that knowledge is dispersed among individuals, and isn't necessarily restricted to a select group within the organization. The place of knowledge and experience with regard to a particular problem is the same place where ideas and solutions are formed for said problem. Today, individual participants in an enterprise are used to making choices from an increasing supply of services and products outside of their work. They are organizing their lives to suit their interests and ideals, and they bring this behavior along with them when they enter an organization. The vision-driven enterprise makes emphatic use of these self-managing capacities. The structure of traditional organizations does not really invite participants to fully utilize the entire spectrum of thinking, feeling, and performing, so if you want to stay on top of the game, here is another reason to change and adapt.

The 70-20-10 theory teaches us that we pick up 70% of the knowledge we need 'on the job', 20% is learned from our peers, and only 10% is picked up through 'formal learning'. We distinguish explicit knowledge, which can be counted, documented, and easily distributed, from tacit knowledge, which is difficult to define and share, like informal relationships or 'why we do what we do'. This organizational knowledge cannot be easily documented, and is locked in the minds of your stakeholders.

The idea is to facilitate stakeholder learning by through three components: resources, time and channels. If stakeholders have access to the right content from accessible resources, at the right moment, on the right device, they are capable of managing their own learning needs during the value creation process. Within the vision-driven Organization 3.0, people are invited to get in touch with their entire spectrum of feelings, thoughts, and actions. The effect of which is that people will dare to give themselves something to hold onto (again), and can then switch companies, networks, and /or positions a lot more easily.

The question is to what extent this manner of transfer of knowledge needs to be completely facilitated and financed by the traditional employer. I believe that, in this area, one can expect more from individuals' responsibility. The big advantage of working with knowmads is that their personal development is their own responsibility, and if they want to be 'employable', they need to make sure that they learn everyday, formally and informally.

Internal stakeholders in our enterprise are therefore encouraged to be active in external social networks. External stakeholders are tempted by using gamification techniques to do the same. Sharing stories and knowledge – storytelling – both on- and offline ensures that new knowledge is generated, which is beneficial for the organization, as well as to someone's personal life.

This corporate-knowledge storytelling, and the curation of this corporate content storage, ensures that the organizational knowledge becomes part of the organization's DNA, and further ensures that the players, who enter and leave the corporate Mesh all the time, don't have to re-invent the wheel...

Different forms of knowledge exchange contribute to the continuing process of social innovation. Within our Seats2meet.com organization, we have good experiences with the following forms:

- Frequently creating physical network meet-ups for all stakeholders, where knowledge and experiences are exchanged. What's characteristic about these occasional sessions is that the content is valued as much as the physical setting.
- Permanent coaching of the cultural bearer-ambassadors of our network. The mission and vision of the organization are put to the test with regard to personal values and norms, and are under the supervision of a coach.
- Facilitating entrepreneurship, particularly made possible by creating trust within and outside of the organization. Only leadership that advocates open communication can help people deal with far-reaching empowerment.
- Creating intervisionary moments to enrich and put the dynamically subjected vision to the test in order to remain cyclically innovative. These moments are around a certain topic and characterized by creativity, high involvement, and open communication by the invited participants from in- and outside the organization.
- Cross-pollination: connecting with organizations that appear to be outside the sector, offering a stage to the energy of young entrepreneurship. This leads to unexpected, but innovative co-creations, which create value for our various stakeholders, and also for ourselves.

According to me, there is no need for much organization in Organization 3.0, except when it comes to the facilitation of learning and development.

14.2
The disruptive bypass: the organization bypasses itself!
You never change things by fighting the existing reality. To change something, build a new model that makes the existing model obsolete.
– Buckminster Fuller

In the culture of the Organization 3.0, there is no fear of change, even when the change is disrupting the market in general or when it disrupts the organization, itself.

Designing or planning is one step; implementation is two, three, four or more steps...

In the traditional economic model, we dealt with the limiting factors of means, people, and time, but we implemented both good and bad products and services. In the Interdependent Economy, the limitations have been replaced by opportunities – in particular, with transparency. At this juncture, I believe that you simply should not market a product if it does not reach the top. The new proposition needs to disrupt, in an economic sense, the current market. This (market) disruption has almost become a goal in itself when launching new products and/or services. You create your own Blue Ocean market, and make the competition irrelevant. However, mind the chasm.

Geoffrey Moore's classical book, *Crossing the Chasm*, deals with the gap between a product's early adopters and the rest of a market. Written in 1991 and revised in 1999, he concluded that there was a 'chasm' between the early market and everyone else. The essence is that the first users, the early adopters, are different than the rest of the market. These innovators (almost by nature) are comfortable with changing their behavior, and are eager to do so to get a jump on the competition. In contrast, early mainstream purchasers "want evolution, not revolution. They want technology to enhance, not overthrow, the established ways of doing business." Later mainstream purchasers do not want to change at all; they do it because they have to. So, crossing the chasm, the gap in motivation of users (which results in a standstill), is a challenge. When you want change, look at it as a product with which you have to surprise your market, which includes your colleagues, your boss, or share- and stakeholders.

At the start of WWII, the German Army advanced at an unstoppable pace. They used the Blitzkrieg model. Their mechanized advance guard was never tempted to delay and fight resistance. They maneuvered around the larger centers of resistance and then cut off their supply and communication lines. This tactic was enormously disruptive, and it was often too late before the enemy knew what was going on.

Implementing an innovative, disruptive concept is not easy. A lot of resistance needs to be overcome. The existing organization needs to be brought on board. You have take into account the competition and stakeholders who have freedom of choice. It takes a lot of energy and time to beat the competition and to stay on the right side of the stakeholders. The result is usually not strong, and the victory is always temporary. There is an alternative. As it happens, you can bypass the establishment by using your innovation or new business model. Just like the German Army did.

I call this movement the disruptive bypass.

When implementing a new product or service, every organization can choose between the hard way and the smart way. I believe the disruptive bypass belongs in the latter category. Red Ocean – the hard way – is defined as changing an organization, or cornering a small stake in an existing crowded market, and so spending a lot of energy with little result to show for it. Blue Ocean – the smart way – is defined as launching a new product or service around the existing market with a 'wow!' effect, and is a lot more effective. Moreover, a concept like this can appeal to people within the organization, the aforementioned new leaders, enticing them to join the new model. It is easier to create support this way, and those new leaders can 'take' others with them from within the organization. The existing group will then shrink by itself, both physically and influentially, enabling the innovation to have full play, and, almost organically, a new organization will announce itself.

A tip for global citizens you can apply this strategy easily if you hold a lower (management) position in a company or organization: Move around existing structures and just implement something new. This can be the launch of a knowledge group or an intranet site/service, or organizing trend sessions. Speakers and experts for these sessions can be found on the Web at little or no cost. Do not forget to invite your stakeholders! Or tell stories on the corporate message boards, comment on external blogs, start a wiki library with videos, text, and photographs about a topic, give Twitter training courses to your colleagues, organize field trips to other stakeholders, etc.... In short, do something – something unexpected and disruptive!

14.3
A social enterprise named Appreciative Inquiry

My friend and Society 3.0 ambassador Cees Hoogendijk, who, in 2007, initiated the social enterprise called AI100, wrote this chapter.

– Ronald van den Hoff.

Since the global citizens are the building blocks of Society 3.0, we should pay attention to their (preferred) behavior. They are independent, self aware, and autonomous. And, if these were the only competencies, they would even enforce the highly individualistic world we are living in. The interesting other side of our Person 3.0 combines the individual competencies with binding, bridging behavior, aiming for co-creation, and connectedness. They are convinced that asynchronous reciprocity is the way in which to live your life. And, in fact, this set of personal values and competencies form the always-existing positive core in everyone. That is, in the eyes of the appreciative inquiry movement.

The question is, how to develop this positive core into daily behavior? Appreciative inquiry – the words say what to do: inquire appreciatively – was, in the end of last century, introduced by David Cooperrider as a change management practice, a method for constructive, effective organizational development. As a 'strength-based approach', it has become a strong competitor – often the better alternative – for old school change management building on new structures and top down communication (the word 'implementation' had to be re-invented because supposed changes didn't seem to work out, so they had to be 'implemented', which always asks for power relations). In an AI summit, the participants representing the whole system are invited to share their most powerful experiences, enabling them to discover the strengths that already have been proven, and to dream about the right circumstances in which these good practices multiply themselves.

The results of such a two-day event are at least two-sided: people have never experienced before such an inclusive and constructive meeting, in which every voice has been taken into account. At the same time, they co-created a set of change initiatives in which they feel co-ownership to realize them with all the energy they possess. This being already amazing, there's more to appreciative inquiry. It is firmly grounded in a manner of person-to-person conversation (the AI interview) that can be regarded as high-quality communication. Carried out properly – and this is a lifetime development – this practice is beyond skill and competence; it is conversational art. And, the more our citizens grow their conversational art into appreciative inquiry, the more Society 3.0 will flourish. The major challenge is that people already are communicating, and tend to think that they are already good at it.

In The Netherlands, more and more AI summits are being organized. We see them within organizations that want to include their employees in changes processes, and also in between organizations, where effective collaboration is needed. AI is not mainstreamed yet, of course. Corporate managers will have to accept less control of the content and outcome of the conversations. In return, by starting with the right question (the 'affirmative topic'), organizations will move faster, and with more fun. The outcomes are astonishing. The AI movement is growing. AI100.org has taken up the mission to bring appreciative inquiry into Dutch organizations. How? By presenting an action-learning program in which the participants develop in-depth AI behavior, and apply this in their carefully chosen organizational projects. And where people get constructively infected by AI interviews, they often try to bring the experience further. This is called the generative impact of appreciative inquiry. It keeps the conversation going. It ensures social behavior. It helps to make the world a better place.

The AI slogan says: 'it's our mind that creates this world', A beautiful building block for organizations in Society 3.0!

The tribe we belong

*Contradiction,
"me" or "we"*

Balance of nature

15
DOING BUSINESS IN SOCIETY 3.0: TRANSACTIONAL, SOCIAL OR BOTH, AN INTRODUCTION

Organizations in Society 3.0 have a drive and an urge to change because their stakeholders know that what is fine today is not probably fine tomorrow. New concepts, new movements, or new technologies are somewhere out there to disrupt you. During my presentations, I always alert the audience of the threat that lies around the corner –outside your familiar playing field – and, to be aware of disturbing, and even lethal, movements.

In fact, we all have learned this lesson because, in the 1990s, disruptive concepts arose quite frequently with the rise of the Internet, which put the establishment permanently behind. EasyJet and Ryanair have permanently changed the European airline industry, as did other low-cost carriers all over the world. Dell created disruption on the PC market: the consumer could customize their own computer online, which was then delivered to their home. This concept of mass customization was the deathblow for the PC division at IBM, which was sold out of pure destitution (to Lenovo from China).

Today, you have to be the catalyst of change. As an organization, you have to break through your own equilibrium because if someone else does it, it's too late. Every organization should engage in a practice of permanent evaluation of their business model because market disruption has become a goal in itself and a much-used tool to launch new products or services.

For outsiders, it is not always apparent how value is created with all those disruptive business models of successful companies. And if someone asks, 'What is your business model?' they actually want to know, 'how are you going to earn revenue, while you are (almost) giving everything away free of charge?' This question addresses an important quality of Organization 3.0: realizing a completely new business model, one that will help the organization transform from a link in the value chain to a change agent in the Social Economic Entities in the Mesh of value networks.

According to Switzerland's Alex Osterwalder, author of the much talked-about book, *Business Model Generation*, a business model is 'a description of the mechanism about how an organization creates, supplies and keeps value'.

I believe that 'business modeling' splits into a transactional and a social section. Although separating them both may already be old fashioned!

15.1
Social and transactional business, Concept 3.0

Organization 3.0 excels in renewal, in particular in its own organization. In order to (continuously) generate new value, they employ business models with exotic names, like peer-production, wikinomics, co-creation, co-branding, and brand detachment. I will explain these terms in later on. Obviously, this list is not restrictive. Today, people are working in Society 3.0 toward the business model of tomorrow.

Naturally, in the value networks of The Mesh, we work differently than we are used to in the old value chains. It is the alliance with all stakeholders and the organization that enables us to solve problems, create new ideas, communicate one-on-one, and use new feedback loops, resulting in sustainable products and services in ways that have never been done before.

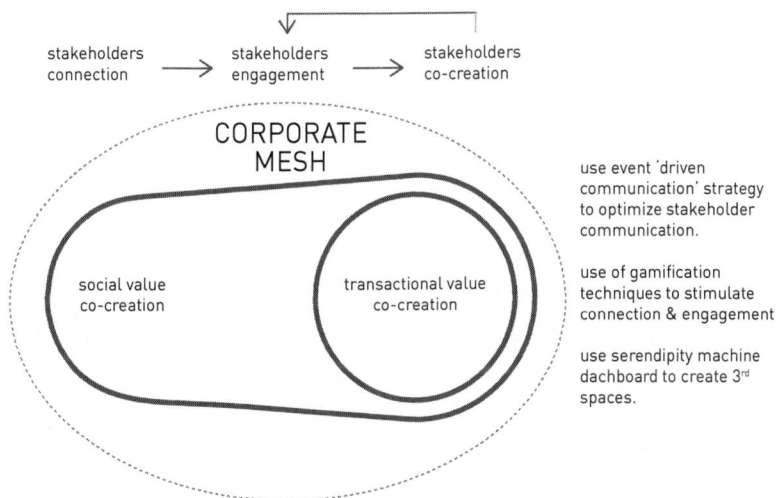

stakeholders connection → stakeholders engagement → stakeholders co-creation

CORPORATE MESH

social value co-creation

transactional value co-creation

use event 'driven communication' strategy to optimize stakeholder communication.

use of gamification techniques to stimulate connection & engagement

use serendipity machine dachboard to create 3rd spaces.

Let me reiterate: Organization 3.0 communicates with its stakeholders. Stakeholder engagement without mutual, two-way communication is impossible. The transactional business concepting of Organization 3.0 incorporates stakeholders in all aspects of the product and service development, using the social business concepting as the playground to achieve this. Every connection and every kind of collaboration is possible. Almost all communication has become reciprocal, and thus interactive, as the word 'communication' was once defined. Gamification is used to enhance stakeholder engagement. Solutions, like the real-time dashboard of our Serendipity Machine, can be extremely useful here as it creates an environment where the virtual world and reality blur, causing stakeholder knowledge to flow. Thus the social business design has become as important as the traditional transactional side of the business.

Using new business models, the old communication laws are becoming obsolete. We are no longer talking about the use of social media, but about 'becoming social'. 3.0 organizations professionally and officially, employ the use of new social media. They do not do this off the cuff; they do it based on their social business concept.

Having said that, it is about time that we forget also about the separation between social and transactional, but for the sake of clarity, I will discuss these topics one after the other.

16.1
Business models in historic perspective

A business model describes the rationale of how an organization creates, delivers and captures value.
— Alex Osterwalder, *Business Model Innovation*

In theory and practice, the term 'business model' is used for a broad range of informal and formal descriptions to represent core aspects of a business, including purpose, offerings, strategies, infrastructure, organizational structures, trading practices, and operational processes and policies.

Obviously, business models are the core of the right to existence of an organization. Business models consist of elements like assumptions, facts, figures, vision, and creativity.

Famous models of all ages.

Although it is more like a growth strategy, the (aged) Ansoff Matrix in still very popular. This model is a tool that helps businesses decide their product and market growth strategy.

ANSOFF MATRIX

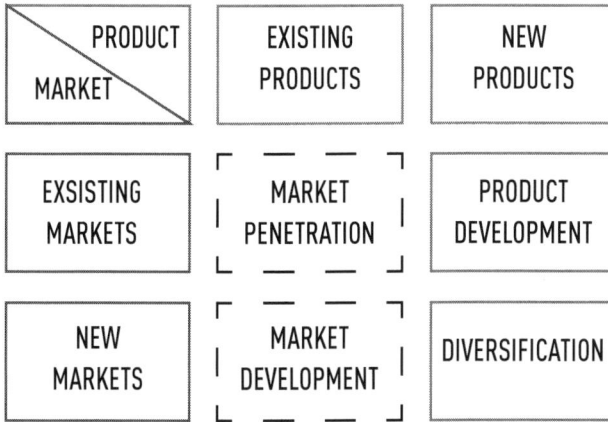

PRODUCT / MARKET	EXISTING PRODUCTS	NEW PRODUCTS
EXSISTING MARKETS	MARKET PENETRATION	PRODUCT DEVELOPMENT
NEW MARKETS	MARKET DEVELOPMENT	DIVERSIFICATION

The Five Force Model by Porter is a real classic. It is a framework for industry analysis and business strategy development. Porter's Five Forces include three forces from 'horizontal' competition: threat of substitute products, the threat of established rivals, and the threat of new entrants; and two forces from 'vertical' competition: the bargaining power of suppliers, and the bargaining power of customers.

FIVE FORCE MODEL

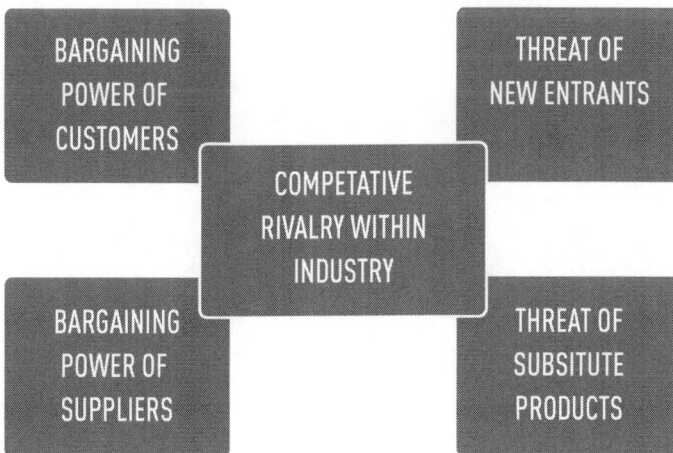

BARGAINING POWER OF CUSTOMERS		THREAT OF NEW ENTRANTS
	COMPETATIVE RIVALRY WITHIN INDUSTRY	
BARGAINING POWER OF SUPPLIERS		THREAT OF SUBSITUTE PRODUCTS

Porter

247

E-R-R-C GRID

ELIMINATE	RAISE
REDUCE	CREATE

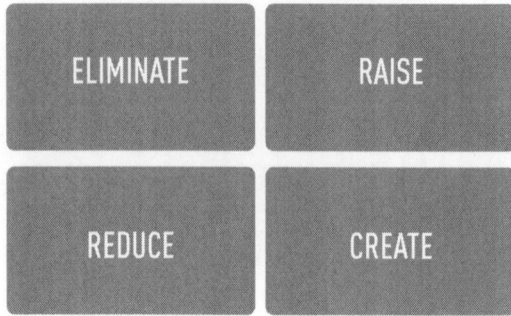

Kim & Mauborgne

Famous, and a bit more contemporary, is the Blue Ocean Strategy by Kim and Mauborgne. It is a strategy to create 'blue oceans' of uncontested market space (no competition), ripe for growth.

A blue ocean is created when a company achieves an innovation that creates value simultaneously for both the buyer and the company. The innovation (in product, service, or delivery) must raise and create value for the market, while simultaneously reducing or eliminating features or services that are less valued by the current or future market.

CO-CREATION VALUE: DART MODEL.

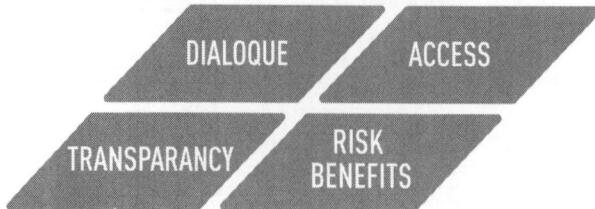

DIALOQUE	ACCESS
TRANSPARANCY	RISK BENEFITS

The market becomes a forum...
Prahalad & Ramaswamy

Prahalad and Ramaswamy's DART model contains the factors to achieve the ultimate co-creatiive success. Co-creation is vital to the shared value creation of the Organization 3.0 and its final goal: the transformation of all stakeholders.

The most recent model is the 'canvas', a technique/model developed by Alex Osterwalder in his book *Businesss Model Generation*. The model describes, through nine basic building blocks, the logic of how organizations make money.

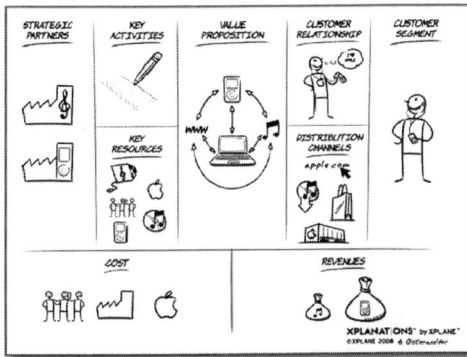

The nine blocks cover the four main areas of a business: customers, offerings, infrastructure, and financial viability. The model is a blueprint for a strategy to be implemented through organizational structures, processes, and systems.

Using the canvass technique, and, with the help of Alex Osterwalder and his Dutch counterpart Patrick van der Pijl, we had our own canvass drawn: the Seats2meet.com network model, facilitating the stage for our stakeholders to achieve their own transformations...

We are all human
Communication an art
Sunshine will be there

16
SOCIAL BUSINESS CONCEPTING

Traditional corporate communication no longer works. It makes no sense to pump the corporate website full of information, or to unilaterally bother the stakeholders with ads or other mass media. This is very 1.0. Everybody is sending, but who is still receiving? And stakeholders are simply making less of an effort to find you or your organization. It's the other way around; the organization needs to seek them out.

But where are these stakeholders? Well, most of the time, they can be found in their own social networks. Your organization plays a leading role in the stories that are being told here, and you may not even know it. These are stories about good customer service and about bad experiences. One thing is certain: these stories, reviews, endorsements, and complaints are more powerful than your ads or other manifestations as they express the authentic experience of the customer.

How do you, as an organization, gain control of this situation? From my own experience, I can tell you: you cannot control it other than by really slogging away at it.

Looking at collaborative consumption, you, as an organization, have to be aware that, as said many times before in this book, people often don't need you to get what they want. In these networks, there is a never-before-seen equality, and the borders between client and producer have completely disappeared. Or, the producer needs the network to make the market mechanics work, and the crowd needs the product or service which, in some cases, only the producer can make. So, you have to start connecting with potential clients, suppliers, staff members, and other producers you don't know yet, and they don't know you. You don't know where they are and how to get in touch with them. You get the picture, right?

The primary goal on your way to monetize your relations with your stakeholders is, obviously, to become part of a network of connected people. Can you create your Mesh? And, after creating this Mesh, can you engage stakeholders in such a way that co-creation becomes possible? Gamification plays a role here, but I will address that later.

Social media is not a magic wand. All too often, I see projects fail because the utilized tools are 'too complicated' or that the market is 'not yet ready' for it. These excuses mask the simple, yet sad, fact that organizations lack the knowledge of all the available new opportunities, have developed little vision in this area, put little effort into it, and flatly refuse to adapt the organization's structures and responsibilities to what needs to be done: optimally pay to attention to today's stakeholder and his/her individual wishes.

16.1
Paid or earned media?

As an organization, it is simply a must to know where the digital hangouts of your stakeholders are, 'hang out' with them there, and contribute information. You can, for example, make it easy for stakeholders to order through wizards, gadgets, or widgets as a part of other websites. Engage in discussions in these stakeholder hangouts – in other words, do not only talk, but also keep your eyes and ears open – because, especially on these network spots, a lot of information can be found that can contribute to the success of your organization.

In the marketing world, the following three-part division in media choice is made:
- Paid or bought media: sponsoring and advertising.
- Owned media: the own communication channels.
- Earned media: word of mouth by the target group.

According to Prahalad's formula, N=1, you can use this trio for your choices of media to attain a one-to-one form of communication with every stakeholder. Increasingly, lower costs and greater simplicity of digital media have made owned media much more accessible. The effect of earned media has increased exponentially. Paid media are losing popularity: every Euro spent on this is wasted money. In the near future, the average corporate website will be nothing more than a virtual business card. That same corporate website can also show a mix of all product and social information that is produced by your stakeholders. Maintaining such a website, containing lots of dynamic information, requires good organization.

The American e-commerce giant Amazon.com understands this concept extremely well, and is a prime example of it. The product specifications of every book that it sells is loaded with information, but only 10% of this is supplied by Amazon itself; the other 90% consists of social information from stakeholders. So it is facilitated, curated, and compiled by Amazon.com: book reports, book reviews, discussion groups about the book, book ratings, and much, much more. And because its stakeholders all love a particular book, they are peers, making sure other potential buyers perceive this 90% of the social information as authentic, and so, reliable.

It is superfluous to mention that the displayed social information is not only of importance to other stakeholders, but also for the organization, itself. In the past, this used to be called customer and market research, and it required the procurement and link of CRM and ERP systems and would cost a lot of money. If you use social tools smartly, that information will come to you automatically, and will be accessible to all of your employees!

16.2
Big Data on a corporate level

Since all this socially-produced information around your product or service will increase to considerable proportions, the need will arise to extract the relevant data. On top of that, there is also a staggering amount of data available, which is somehow related to your business.

Besides the enormous amount of data, the quantity of sources and the speed of data traffic are elements changing data into Big Data. Organizations have to collect, analyze, and understand data in order to use them in a meaningful way, and thus stakeholder transformations as the ultimate value creation for that organization: its right to existence in Society 3.0.

Big Data forces organizations to become real-time, meaning that the right data should be available to stakeholders at the right time, place, and format in order for them to act (if you re-act you are too late!). Stakeholders must therefore be empowered to undertake 'entrepreneurial activities'.

At Seats2meet.com locations, curated data, showing the available knowledge at that location, are displayed on dashboards and accessible to all stakeholders, thus enhancing the 3rd Space stakeholder experience: the unexpected meeting of relevant people (serendipity!), so our stakeholders experience a transformation.

Curating data is one thing. Data analysis is another. Our gamifier Horst Streck describes the beginning of this process as follows:
"To increase the profitability of using data, this data has to be translated to practical, open information. Working with data has to be a joint effort throughout the whole organization."

There is good software available, for sale but also free; basically everything can be measured. But then what? In my experience, there is too much data for smaller organizations and value networks, so look into your network for this particular data analysis knowledge. Start small and build it up. Funnily enough, old indicators don't mean anything anymore. We used to measure stuff like number of visitors, average check, cost percentages, etc. Now, there are data on your website visits, the number of views, popular pages, popular sequences, the way content is successfully organized on the site, and much, much more. Then, there is social info: who says what about your company and where. What is your social status, are the organization's tweets well read, and so on. I can make an endless list of data available to you. My solution is to divide the monitoring of data throughout the organization and not have a fixed department for that. Real-time data is for every stakeholder, who are too important not to work with in real time.

16.3
More social stuff...

Social business concepting is defined as the rendition, the customized arranging, and the timely opening of a broad data stream for the benefit of the value networks of the organization. The American Internet consultancy The Dachis Group uses the following definition of a so-called social business design: 'the intentional creation of a dynamic business culture that empowers all of its constituents to better exchange value'.

On the branch line of social business concept, you will find terms such as 'client-cloud model' – the data is, after all, up in the air and is accessible to all stakeholders via the Internet – or Social CRM (with this, it is emphasized that the old term, customer relationship management, should be supplemented with a social component). This all sounds rather technical, while I think that the personal touch is missing in many organizations. Stakeholders want to engage with people, not with an anonymous legal structure.

So, in a good social business concept (SBC), three aspects receive extra attention from the leaders of the organization. With 'attention', I do not mean management or organizing, but enabling the organization to inform itself and to organize itself in this area. It should create an (almost) informal and dynamically co-created and autonomous SBC system to stage stakeholder engagement.

- Corporate Story (-telling) and Branding:
  Which topic do we want to discuss with our stakeholders, what is our story, and what is the information that we would like to share? Which stories about our organization are being told?
- Engagement-gamification:
  How do we engage our stakeholders, and how de we create sufficient moments of contact to lay fertile ground for engagement?
- Social Media Strategy:
  What is the plan, how do we organize our communication streams, what do we want to achieve?

I can't emphasize this point enough: this is not specialized management literature. It is fuel for global citizens who want to advance in and with their organization to wholeheartedly enter the Interdependent Economy. There may still be a hint of a marketing department that can mark the boundaries of the SBC. But the realization of this communication policy is the responsibility of – unlike in the past – every member of the organization. One way or another, you, as a reader, belong to this, too. You contribute to the telling of the corporate story; you are a part of the social brand experience; you are an actor in presenting the social media around your organization. You are the global citizen who will help to further set up Organization 3.0, and, consequently, Society 3.0. I hope this will be your mindset when you read the last parts of this book.

16.4
Social media guidelines

The biggest fear of governments and companies listed on the stock exchange is that their employees consciously or subconsciously send out messages through social media that would be detrimental to the organization. We are talking about inside information, or messages about the Oval Office. Coca-Cola has made its employees very aware of these risks, and has therefore set up an 'Online Social Media Certification Program'. The program is structured around ten social media 'principles' regarding awareness and training:

1. Become certified in the Social Media Certification Program.
2. Follow our Code of Business Conduct and all other Company policies.
3. Be mindful that you are representing the Company.
4. Fully disclose your affiliation with the Company.
5. Keep records.
6. When in doubt, do not post.
7. Give credit where credit is due and don't violate others' rights.
8. Be responsible to your work.
9. Remember that your local posts can have global significance.
10. Know that the Internet is permanent.

We have written up 'Social Media Guidelines for Stakeholders of Seats2meet.com' as well. You can read them on the S2M website, and I encourage you to use it and spread them around in your own organization. Feel free to copy it!

Formmer CEO Jonathan Schwartz of Sun, one of the largest software companies in the world, left the company in 2010. He did not hold a press conference, but simply Tweeted a haiku and sidestepped the traditional public relations department of his former employer in the process:
financial crisis
stalled too many customers
CEO no more

16.5
Storytelling

Somewhere in la Mancha, in a place whose name I do not care to remember, a gentleman lived not long ago, one of those who has a lance and ancient shield on a shelf and keeps a skinny nag and a greyhound for racing.

– Miguel de Cervantes, Don Quixote (1605)

Storytelling is as old as history. Stories tell us who we are. They shape the landscape in which we find kindred spirits; the compass with which we try to navigate in networks of human connections. Since the dawn of time, we have been telling each other stories, sitting around a campfire, or in our cave. In the Middle Ages, the travelling minstrel acted as a singing newspaper or magazine. A good story has the power to entice you out off your linear thought process and to dream along. A well-told story is easy to remember and to pass on. When a story is passed on, the new narrator suddenly becomes the owner of the story, and the listener is on the verge of sharing that property. A sound story can deliver arguments, even evidence, and displays authenticity that shines on the storyteller. Stories always carry emotion. This gives the listener a sense of intimacy and a sense of security. He or she belongs to the community.

Corporate storytelling, or, to put it coarsely, the story of a company, network, or organization, is a powerful instrument with which to unite and engage stakeholders, include them in the organization, incite them to co-create, share knowledge, and inspire. The story ensures that stakeholders understand the identity of the company in such a way that they keep it in the back of their mind.

Besides reviews of services or products from stakeholders, I believe good corporate stories always contain elements or topics that refer to the vision, the culture, the leadership, and the conceptual and social business concept of a company or organization. These are, after all, the critical factors of success in Organization 3.0! What can an organization or company substantially 'talk' about? Basically about everything as long as commercial language is not used, and there is no self-glorification or other forms of introspection. As the former CEO of Coca-Cola once excellently articulated, "beware of the temptation to look in the mirror, while you should be looking out of the window."

The corporate stories – a term that has a broad definition, because it encompasses text, sound, and image – can be told in different places, both physically and virtually. They are entirely cross-media. Simultaneously, but also parallel or serial, sometimes entwined, sometimes independent of each other. They originate from different authors, producers, and suppliers. And, these are not always your preferred communication co-workers, because stories are not only told, but passed on. This is the crux of the situation. Obviously, the content of the stories has to be inextricably bound up with the total corporate (market) communication; otherwise the organization's credibility is at stake.

At the same time, the stakeholders are passing their stories back, usually via the same media. That is interesting. It is an illusion to think that you can control or correct a story-process these days. A wrong product is a wrong product. A slow call center is just slow. An unmotivated employee ruins the moment of truth. A good story can't fix that, and there is the snag. The dilemma is that it is not just a company or organization that tells stories about its products and/ or services. Customers, employees, and other stakeholders use the Internet to endlessly, really endlessly, tell each other stories about issues that they do or do not like. It happens in different places, and in places you did not even know existed: on blogs, forums, review sites, and other places, people gather to share their opinions of and experiences with you, your staff, and your products or services.

The consequences of this are well reported. On the website Wikileaks, you can find confidential information, such as 'secret' memos and reports, intentionally leaked by staff. There are infamous examples of organizations being demolished, and unfortunately, not always mistakenly. Dell Computers has to deal with the forums Dell Sucks and DellHell. On these forums, former employees and other stakeholders share their critical and funny stories about Dell. The classic blog *Dell Lies, Dell Sucks* by Jeff Jarvis forced the company to completely overhaul its customer service. Many other companies are given hell on a regular basis.

We can't escape the fact that like-minded people are more likely to believe each other than the company's story. This is an enormous challenge for organizations. There is a two-part remedy: continuously monitor your own reputation (risks), and continuously air your story. But you do have to have a good story to tell!

16.6
Branding

Your brand is no stronger than your reputation, and will increasingly depend on what comes up when you are Googled.

– Alan Jenkins)

There are many fascinating written works about branding (the promotion of a particular product or company by means of advertising and distinctive design). I believe there are three basic elements: brand experience, brand image, and brand engagement.

David Polinchock of the American Brand Experience Lab has come up with a great definition:

"It's simple. Everything you do is a part of your brand experience. From how you answer your phones, to how your employees look, to the physical experience of your environment, it all needs to play together into one cohesive narrative experience in order to win over the hearts of jaded consumers. Your brand experience should incorporate a 360° point of view."

The brand experience transforms into a brand image: a collection of observations and experiences concerning a service or product, composed in the mind of the consumer. The 'experience' and the 'image' should create brand engagement with stakeholders as a connection with your service or product. It is that engagement that makes your stakeholders willing to co-create with your organization.

In his book, *Personality Not Included*, Rohit Bhargava of Ogilvy even calls it the 'personality of the brand': "Personality is the unique, authentic, and talkable soul of your brand that people can get passionate about." The large advertising firm Saatchi & Saatchi has even traded in the term 'brand' in exchange for 'lovemark'.

In this context, the basic principles in this area are:
- I'm not the owner of my brand experience. The ownership of my brand experience lies exclusively with my stakeholders.
- My brand no longer covers just my product or service. It is about the whole process that a stakeholder experiences in all contacts with my organization.
- There are stories going around about my organization, our people, our products, our services, our customers, and these stories cannot be controlled.
- I can only attempt to influence the stories when I am in contact with my stakeholders.

So, it is good practice for organizations to optimize the moments of contact with their stakeholders (also known as touch points or moments of truth). Because it is only during a touch point that our organization is able to have the full attention (even if it is for a moment) of any stakeholder in question. Making some noise via mass media is no longer sufficient; people no longer listen to you. But the Internet is a completely different medium. In the past, it took a number of years to build a brand name, but on the information superhighway, it happens incredibly fast.

I have, therefore, defined branding as:
"The range of activities to create, facilitate, manage, and evaluate contact opportunities (touch points) and event-driven communications with stakeholders, resulting in unique and consistent stakeholder transformations, thus optimizing the process of the organization's stakeholders meeting, connecting, and engaging."

16.7
Personal branding
Your brand is what people say about you when you are not in the room
– Jeff Bezos

A person can be a brand too, or part of a brand. This is the result of personal branding. It is not unusual for self-employed professionals, but employees of an organization may apply personal branding too, and, with that, they enhance the brand experience of the organization as a whole. I promote the philosophy of our organization by posting on my blog, commenting on other blogs, being active on Twitter, LinkedIn, and Facebook, and by delivering lectures. I may be approached through the Web, and often work to connect people with each other. My business partner achieves this by making videos. Together, with all our stakeholders, we literally put a face on Seats2meet.com and our other companies.

By using RSS feeds, you can simply propagate your personal brand. Post a message or photo on the Internet, like on a blog, and let it appear on different sites all over the Web. The slide presentations of my lectures can not only be found on Slideshare, but also in my LinkedIn network and on my Web profile page. The same applies to my tweets.

In short, if you organize your personal branding well, you will be well-positioned on many Internet sites with little effort. The Dutch recruitment specialist Bas van de Haterd argues that, "companies should create more personal brands. People want to do business with like-minded people first and foremost and secondly with companies or organizations."

And, that certainly applies to working with or within the new value networks in the Mesh.

16.8
Stakeholder engagement by gamification.

Gamification is serious stuff. The Society 3.0 citizen has been playing computer games from childhood, from the Atari 2600 video game console (Atari, as a corporation, invented and published one of the first computer video games, Pong), to the Wii or X-box, or was introduced to serious gaming by throwing dice in your local pub for a drink. Or, by betting on football matches. The Romans had their 'Panem et Circensus' to engage the people and keep them occupied and happy.

Playing games has many benefits for our development and well-being:
- **Learning capability:** Gaming is done voluntarily. Games have mechanics to reward players, which causes a dopamine (neuron-transmitter) to create a sense of euphoria. In the long term, this strengthens our cognitive skills.
- **Self esteem:** Mistakes are common while playing a game. There is no severe penalty, and the player tries again. By doing so, the players become aware of learning effect of making mistakes.
- **Collaboration:** Multiplayer games, where players form teams and play together, teaches players to collaborate.
- **Creativity:** Sandbox games (games with much non designated-content and where the player can built anything freely) stimulate creativity.
- **Fun:** Gaming is fun and that is often not the case in organizations where people do their regular job. Having fun at the things you do generates energy.

Meet Horst. Horst is a gamifier, and, as a knowmad, connected to Seats2meet.com. Yes, a gamifier. A new profession, like other new professions and fields of expertise, with exciting titles like trust agent, data pilot, and cloud service broker. As gamifier, Horst is busy with gamification: the integration of game mechanics or game dynamics into a website, service, community, campaign, or application in order to drive participation and engagement.

But Horst's own straightforward definition that can be interpreted broadly and is easy to understand:
Gamification is to make things fun by adding game elements.

The main goal of gamification is stakeholder engagement. As we have seen before, you have to engage stakeholders in your Mesh to get them to start co-creating sustainable value with you and/or your organization.

Working with Horst, I learned a couple things. One is that the motivations and desires that exist in all of us for community, feedback, achievement, and reward are attained by using gaming techniques. So, when interacting with a group of people, whether it is a network or a more formal organization, gamification can improve learning, drive more sales, create a better collaboration, or obtain a deeper loyalty.

Secondly, using the event driven communication structure around the primary transaction processes utilizing the stakeholder's contact points, engagement can be done with little effort. So, even sending a thank you letter, combined with a new call to action, signed by the company's president after receiving an order, is already gamification.

People are motivated when playing to gain a higher status or by having access to stuff others don't have, and even by having more power than others and by getting something for free. A gamification strategy, therefore, is a meticulous planning process of challenges and achievements. A challenge is a known path the users move along consciously. So, he or she moves from one level to the next. An achievement is tracked in the background, and once reached, the reward may come as a surprise.

Software development is done in a different way than in the old days. In the past, software projects were huge, time consuming, and almost unpredictable in progress and cost. Today, you will see what are called 'agile development' approaches. A project is cut into small pieces, and every piece has a head, a tail, and is built rapidly. Also, instead of building the whole software product, a prototype is launched (quick and dirty) just to test the water. If it appeals to a community, the product is built to completion, with the help of the same community.

Our gamifier, Horst, calls it the Plus 4 method. This method contains four phases that lead to a complete gamification project. Every phase is a plus for the entity; hence the 'P' in Plus 4.

By now, we're seeing pre-packaged gamification software enter the market, so gamification has become an integrated part of any organization's structural development. At Seats2meet.com we operate a residents program where all the above mentioned gaming techniques are used to engage our stakeholders by making them better professionals.

16.9
Social media strategy

Social media strategy is not a marketing technique. It involves a completely new way of communicating for increasing engagement with all stakeholders.

Working with social media has to be ingrained in the company's DNA. It is all about creating moments of contact (attention) with stakeholders to secure the start of a next moment of contact, and to exchange as much information as possible. Stakeholders need to experience that they have one-to-one contact with other stakeholders.

Organizations can use existing social networks, or build one of their own. For the time being, the best choice seems to be a combination of both: specific and generic, inside out and outside in, linked to the brand and public. Perhaps social media strategies are too new; maybe they are too dynamic; it is a fact that the success of these strategies cannot always be predicted, and it can definitely not always be measured with the classic return on investment approach.

According to computer manufacturer Lenovo, the number of phone calls to their service centers has decreased by 20% since the implementation of social media as a communication and engagement tool. Blendtec, a once unknown producer of blenders and mixers, has become a classic example. The president of this company made a series of YouTube videos entitled 'Will it Blend?' In these videos, he throws various objects in his blender to demonstrate the quality of the product. The videos were a huge success and went viral, resulting in a 500% rise in sales .

At Seats2meet.com, the community has taken over our commercial communication process: stakeholders inform other stakeholders about our services and products. They have become our ambassadors, and since these fans are online 24/7, we can say that, "at Seats-2meet.com, we have the largest help desk in The Netherlands, consisting of more than 40,000 people, and we serve our stakeholders 24/7." They are not 'our' people, as in employees, but somehow they are our people. As a result, we no longer employ sales and marketing people, and we do not operate a help-desk ourselves. It simply works great!

As an organization that wants to built its own Mesh, the first step is to engage in a dialogue with your stakeholders in existing networks. Ask yourself the following questions:
- Where on the Web are our stakeholders active? On which social networks can they be found: LinkedIn, Baidu, Orkutt, or Facebook?
- What do your stakeholders do on these platforms? By answering this question, you can customize your approach, for example, by posting blogs or writing reviews.
- What kind of social information do you find? Are a lot of photos posted, or are books discussed?
- Who are the key players? Identify them and follow them closely.

Now that you have mapped out your social relationships, a follow-up answer is posed immediately: Who can do what for the organization? Do we set up centrally, or do we delegate? The same rule applies here as well: not or-or, but and-and! So, certain issues are set up centrally and other tasks are delegated to the people who are most visible in the organization, obviously facilitated by knowledge (the corporate story) and means (time and skills).

Do not try to plan everything beforehand, but experiment.

A summary of the practical points of interest in the social media strategy of Organization 3.0:

- The corporate website is the starting point of all communication activities, although in some cases it may be no bigger than a couple (landing) pages. We call this the hub. This is the place to show where you are active. The connections between the corporate website and the different social networks are the spokes.
- Illustrate for your organization how the hub and spokes are applied in your organization.
- De-centralize the flow of communication, and, by doing so, de-centralize your network.
- Ensure that your internal processes are up to standard. These processes also include actively maintaining a social media presence and assigning corresponding tasks and responsibilities to employees.
- Keep everything transparent, so you can stay abreast of the situation in your organization. Monitor this continuously.

No strings, peer to peer
Interlaced in harmony.
Cooperation

17
TRANSACTIONAL BUSINESS CONCEPTING

After creating its own Mesh in the form of an international fan base, the Royal Concertgebouw Orchestra in Amsterdam started to combine engagement with development of an additional money stream: the RCO Editions, a video magazine. As one can read on the website:

"With its RCO Editions the Royal Concertgebouw Orchestra is responding to current listening habits and using the capabilities of modern technology. If you only want to listen to music, you have access to RCO Radio with the free app. In addition, through the 360° video perspective the RCO Editions offer a total musical experience, a grab bag of interdisciplinary ideas. With second screen and parallax scrolling it is possible to alternate between levels in the app without interrupting the concert experience. Your television set at home becomes the stage for the orchestra with Apple TV, and the iPad can be used as a second screen for all the extras."

Looking back at the industrial era, doing transactions was the main purpose of the organization. It performed better in some particular transactions than others. Whole organizations, as we saw, had been organized around these dealings. A proper producer, achieving transactions (where money was exchanged for goods or services), had a competitive advantage. Not only in relation to the competition, but also to its clients. The end user could not make the product or service themselves, at least not in that level of quality/performance or for that price. Life was simpler then.

Today, we have seen many organizations lose their right for existence. In the previous part of this book, I demonstrated that communication with stakeholders has become a different ball game. After getting in touch with them, you have to engage them further in order to find out what each individual potential client really wants. A product or service has to offer more, even more than an experience, and has to achieve a transformation of the client by using the product or service.

Transactional business concepting is about your business model. This is a model where social capital and monetary capital maintain a healthy balance. One is strengthening the other, making your business model sustainable. Also some more traditional elements are part of the transactional concept too, especially if you have a larger number of stakeholders. You still need something like what we used to call a CRM system, but not only for clients. It is for all stakeholders, where you keep track of all transactions and the associated operational processes. On top of that, you need knowledge and experience of how to deal with the variable number of networks you are active in. Organizations may, in the future, be simultaneously involved in thousands of value creation networks such as pop-up project teams or Social Economic Entities,.

So, the unilateral focus on the business transaction from the past is simply not good enough anymore. I will limit myself in this chapter just to give you some inspirational examples of organizations creating value in a different way than we were used to. Then it is up to you: you will have to find your own solutions how to interact, engage, and co-create value with your stakeholders. You will have to see your own future. Yesterday's knowledge and insights are no longer sufficient.

17.1
Co-creation

Starbucks received over 70,000 tips and innovative suggestions in the first year after the launch of its website, My Starbucks Idea. According to Wikipedia, co-creation is:

"A form of marketing strategy or business strategy that emphasizes the generation and ongoing realization of mutual organization-stakeholder value. It views markets as forums for firms and active customers to share, combine and renew each other's resources and capabilities to create value through new forms of interaction, service and learning mechanisms."

Co-creation was first mentioned by the management thinkers Prahalad and Ramaswamy. Success factors are, according to these authors, captured in what they call the 'DART Model': dialogue, access, risks, benefits, and transparency.

Co-created value arises in the form of personalized, unique experiences for the customer and ongoing revenue, learning, and enhanced market performance drivers for the organization (loyalty, relationships, and customer word of mouth).

Collaborative customization is a word used to describe co-creation by many management thinkers such as Joseph Pine in his book, *Mass Customization*. Organizations talk to individual customers to determine the precise product offering that best serves the customer's needs (see personalized marketing and personal marketing orientation). This information is then used to specify and manufacture a product that suits that specific customer (e.g., some clothing companies will manufacture blue jeans to fit an individual customer and just rent the pants to the him or her). This development is also being taken into deeper customization via 3D printing with companies like Shapeways.

Classic example of co-creation is LEGO. LEGO is in continuous dialogue with six million fanatical little builders, who design LEGO models for, and on behalf of, LEGO. The new designs are displayed in the Club LEGO gallery, and visitors can vote for their favorites. The winning designs are taken into product production. And, as a member of the LEGO Club, you can order the model right away, so you can build the winning design at home. This intensive form of customer interaction saved the company after going through hard times. In an era when children are playing video games instead of building with toy bricks, survival was the ultimate challenge for LEGO. An additional advantage of this co-creation activity is that the company no longer needed to employ over 300 R&D staff as creative minds from all over the world were devoting their talents to the LEGO brand out of nothing but love for the brand. And so, LEGO got improved designs, lower development costs, and boosted sales.

The iPhone is a beautiful, cool smart phone. There are lots of handy tools for this device, called apps, which can be bought via the App Store. Some of them are free, and, for others, a modest fee needs to be paid. Apple allows external developers to create 'apps'. The strength of this setup is that the phone improves a bit with each app; it offers a few more options. The app developers are endlessly creative in this area. Apple earns its share from the sale of the apps along with the developers with a 30:70 profit split. Meanwhile, there are over 100,000 apps available, amounting to about 2 billion downloads annually. The revenue is great, of course, but it's the development cooperation that makes the iPhone stronger and stronger.

Co-creation does not always have to represent a conscious collaboration. The website geenfile.nl (No Traffic Jam) tries to detect traffic jams with help of cellular phone positions on freeways. In other words, they take positional data from cell phones and GPS systems. This data is then combined with a digital map, which can accurately display up-to-the-minute information on traffic jams. In this case, the motorist does not know that his data is used for services that others pay for. So, for me, this service touches on the boundaries of privacy.

Creating value through the co-creation of products and services is essential for creating the tailor-made stakeholder experience, the vital step in the process of stakeholder transformation – the ultimate goal in the progression of economic value. After all, the customer knows where the demand lies. Whether it's about developing a new product, implementing a marginal improvement, or going through an entire new experience, the stakeholders love to work on it as soon as they feel connected to the brand or organization. And, they do this free of charge. The condition for successful commercial co-creation can be found in a simple principle: the better the balance between the monetary value and social capital, the more sustainable and stronger the organization or the business model becomes.

17.2
Co-creation: Soccer and cars...

On the website *Myfootballclub*, English football fans co-created the exploitation of a football (soccer) club. Tens of thousands of donations amounted to a sizable pot of money, which was used to buy an actual football club: FC Ebbsfleet. These few thousand fans are involved with the daily dealings of the club, like any fan is, with the difference that they are also co-owners. This is, of course, a disaster for the old management thinker, because 6,000 opinions about the line up for Sunday seem to be unworkable. But the principle is that majority rules. This goes for all the important decisions, even financial ones. These decisions are not necessarily better or worse than when they are taken by big shots. What is great is that the club has an army of thousands of scouts at its disposal, who are on the lookout for talent all over the UK free of charge. A normal company could never afford so many scouts! The results are evident: slowly but surely, the club is climbing up from the lower regions of the leagues. On the website, I read: "In February 2008, the members purchased the football club for £600,000. Just three months later, Ebbsfleet United won the FA Trophy at Wembley – the club's greatest achievement in a history that dates back to 1890." So, they're definitely on the right track!

However, in the end, the Club management, embracing the input of money but not so much embracing the influence and social engagement of the fans, didn't commit itself really to this new form of running the show. Fans noticed and disappeared. "I think we failed to give many members the feeling of ownership and closeness to the club they had hoped for," admitted MyFC's founder, Will Brooks. So, it was a great experiment, but being authentic about 'sharing' ownership is easier said than done. In 2013, only about 1,000 fans out of the original 30,000 are left, and FC Ebbsfleet is back at square one.

Ford, however, had a co-creation campaign which was very successful:
In April 2009, Ford shipped 100 new Fiestas from Europe to the US, starting the campaign to introduce this model update to the American market. These cars were made available for free to a group of pre-

dominantly young motorists, selected for their affinity for social media, for a period of six months. Ford encouraged these test pilots, who were named agents, to share their driving experiences online. Ford cleverly approached this by giving the agents a mission every month. These assignments did not just relate to driving the car, but more to the lifestyle of these testers. There were missions like 'show your skills on a skateboard', or 'make a video with puppies'. The agents reported their mission progress on blogs, Twitter, and photo and video sharing websites. Within six months, this resulted in over 4.3 million YouTube views, over 540,000 photos of the car were viewed via Flickr, and there were over 3 million mentions on Twitter. To thank the agents for their work, a Fiesta Movement Celebration Event was held in Hollywood on December 1st. Via www.fiestamovement.com, people could vote for their favorite agent. This was, of course, a clever move, because these agents used their entire networks to win votes. Which resulted in more brand recognition for the Ford Fiesta. The promo website showed rankings, and every test driver had their own profile page with a link to their Twitter account, YouTube page, or (personal) blog. Furthermore, the website showed a live feed of all activities on different channels of the agents. The model was introduced to the market in the summer of 2010. Ford created 60% brand awareness for a product update that still had to be introduced, and that is, of course, an enormous success.

In an interview, Jim Farly, the Vice President of Global Marketing at Ford says: "If you would have told me that we would have 100 vehicles in the US and we would have 60% brand awareness in the segment, I would have said there is no possible way. To get 60% awareness in traditional media, it costs somewhere north of $50 million. The marketing world has changed dramatically both for Ford and for all major corporations in the past year. Online has become mass media. A Yahoo or Google page takeover actually gets more eyeballs than a network TV commercial now. That hasn't happened before. The importance of communicating through online social media platforms as well as through public relations has become far more important because of the evolution of technology."

Presently the website and community around the Fiesta is still active and used for campaigning around this model.

17.3
Peer production & mass collaboration: wikinomics

Open structures offer excellent conditions in which to create new value through open collaboration between global individuals. Don Tapscott calls this macro-wikinomics. He is referring to Wikipedia, the well-known digital encyclopedia that is authored by lots of different people. People like you and me, members of the crowd as new, global, non-state networks offer to create powerful, new solutions for cooperation, problem solving, and governance.

You can also use traditional experts to solve problems, collectively, like on the website Innocentive. Here, scientists are paid to utilize their knowledge. During the day, engineers will tackle problems with their bosses at Shell, Philips, and DSM; in the evening, they work for themselves, and share their knowledge freely.

You can let customers help you create something. Virtual Worlds, for example, offers its users a virtual infrastructure to create buildings and other objects. This is how the consumer becomes the producing consumer – a prosumer.

17.4
Good things come in small packages, or in big ones!

Co-creation on a small scale: Zeeuwier Jenever.

Co-creation can happen on a modest scale. Dutch Internet personality Petra De Boevere, aka 'Slijterijmeisje' (Liquor Store Girl), developed a new Dutch gin (jenever). Her Twitter followers helped her with the positioning, the design, and the brand name: Zeeuwier Jenever (Seeweed gin). Operating a local liquor store in the southern town of Breskens, De Boevere achieves a quarter of her sales through the Internet. By the way, Petra defines co-creation as 'thinking together, working together'. It is a nice definition, and contrasts with the ones usually lined with management slogans. In this context, it's good to know Petra's four P's of marketing: Passion, personal, profiling, and publicity. Petra may not be a big celebrity, but she is grand. She has proven that the Internet helps her to effortlessly hold her own amongst the greatest of the Earth.

Co-creation on a large scale: Amsterdam Open Innovation Festival.

It's the fall of 2009. A group of young civil servants of the City of Amsterdam organized an Open Innovation Festival, with the aim of introducing their 17,000 colleague officials to Web 2.0 and Government 2.0. Working optimally with new social media places new demands on an organization and its employees, and, since the Municipality of Amsterdam had to cut €400 million from its budget 400 over the next few years, recommendations on working smarter and differently are extremely relevant. For an entire week, dozens of sessions were organized daily around the theme of Web 2.0. Numerous speakers displayed their vision and knowledge for free; all the locations were available at no cost. Internet specialists set up a live stream, enabling people outside of Amsterdam to participate in the event as well. To sum up, a small group of people mobilized a mass of people, and this event reached much further than Amsterdam's city limits. By 2012, over 40 Dutch municipalities participated in this annual festival!

Co-creation on that scale is called crowdsourcing. Crowdsourcing can be turned into a service making the organization look good, make money, and deliver a better service:

In 2013, DHL/DeutschePost prototyped a new service in Stockholm called MyWays. When ordering a parcel via DHL, the package is delivered to a DHL service location. You can pick it up yourself, or crowdsource that task for a small fee to someone in the network who is passing the pick up location and lives nearby your home. A smart communication app establishes the contact, the drop-off, and the reviews of the behaviors of players involved.

So the Web enables this efficiently matching of supply and demand of small and simple tasks.

A platform by itself to crowdsource-outsource small household errands and skilled tasks is Taskrabbit. Even organizations use this platform to find people for tasks like data-entry and customer services.

17.5
More on brands: co-branding & brand detachment

Join forces. Coworking with third parties is one of the forces behind the vision-driven organization. In the case of co-branding, we are talking about working with another brand with the aim of launching a new (combined) product.

The Senseo coffee-making machine concept by Philips is a prime example. DE Masterblenders is responsible for the coffee. Combined, the Senseo coffee machine and the coffee pads provided a new and improved coffee experience. Both parties have their own turnover, but the branding of the two companies is done together.

Unilever makes Starbucks ice cream and transfers the license for brand use to Starbucks. Apple's iPod can be connected to Nike running shoes, making a personal running computer. This adds more value than just a running shoe or a digital audio player. Clothing retailer H&M co-brands as well. Every year, customers line up for the special H&M collection, designed by a prominent name in the fashion world, i.e.: Victor & Rolf, Roberto Cavalli, Karl Lagerfeld. Both H&M and the top fashion designer get increased exposure. What do we call this? It's a matter of looking past your own shadow.

Brand detachment is earned by saying goodbye to core processes. Initially, brand detachment meant that the consumer lost his or her interest in a brand. Lately, the term is also used when a manufacturer ceases its core activity and corresponding core processes, and only focuses on the brand. The brand has then become the proposition, and all underlying services have been outsourced to co-producers. It frequently makes us think – which is a good thing – about the core activities of our enterprise.

In the past, the core activity of an airline was flying planes. Now that Airbus or Boeing makes almost all commercial aircraft, there are few distinguishing features to be found in them. The airline could outsource the actual flights and focus on ticket sales and service. In due course, it may no longer be important if the right 'brand' is printed on the plane, as long as the right customer experience is created with and in the aircraft. This is a different field than owning and maintaining airplanes. Until now, airline companies have routinely outsourced catering, aircraft maintenance, call centers, and ground crews. The last two are involved with direct customer contact, so I would never subcontract these services. Who would outsource their customer 'moments of truth' to third parties?

Originally, Star Alliance was an alliance between traditional airline companies. By now, Star Alliance is increasingly presenting itself as an independent brand, while the member airlines are moving more to the background. It is then just a small next step to outsourcing flights to non-member airline companies.

Brand detachment can go so far that the proprietor of the brand is no longer the owner in the traditional sense. Take Upload Cinema, for example: a group of people that simply watches Internet videos in a cinema centered around a certain theme. The Upload Cinema website explains that they 'take movies out of the domestic setting to a place that is meant for a collective experience, the cinema'.

17.6
Transactional business connecting: conclusion.

This concludes the overview of new business models. These models have an optimal balance between 'doing business' and the 'social interaction' with stakeholders. Of course, we continue to monitor the information about our business with the customer, and, if applicable, his/her organization. However, this needs to be enriched with social information. This new way of doing business, in a nutshell, is done in the Interdependent Economy of Society 3.0 within the social value networks of the Mesh, using informal organizational structures, as a new form of co-operation.

At the moment you are reading this, undoubtedly other new versions are in development or are maybe even already active. The connecting factor of all these models is that they are 3.0, and that they assume the possibility to make connections with anyone or anything. And suddenly, there is an abundance of opportunities to surprise every customer with services that connect with all facets at the highest expectation, or even beyond that...

"The idea that you have 'your' clients is completely passé."
– Daniel Ropers, CEO, Bol.com

Many books have been written about how to become a better producer of stuff, how to be more efficient, how to organize your organization, how to motivate staff, or how to enhance your process quality. Or how to manage your cash flow, how to organize your database, and how to optimize your Customer Relation Management. I will not repeat those publications in this book. However we have to realize that we have to get used to the idea that traditional organizations are no longer required to create value. Learning does not have to be done in a school building, manufacturing does not have to be done in a factory, and working is no longer done exclusively in office buildings. Cars no longer need drivers. Moreover, we need fewer cars and other stuff as we swap, rent, lease, or share our goods. Building stuff doesn't need bricklayers, carpenters, administrators, or bookkeepers. Consumers and organizations no longer need banks, insurance companies, or other financial institutions. Everybody today can be a publisher, a manufacturer, a banker, and so on.

As I mentioned before, in my companies, we no longer employ sales-, marketing-, PR-, reservations- staff and managers. These jobs have been taken over in the form of roles done by the community. To make things work is not always easy, and it is often beyond your span of control. Still, we co-create great, meaningful value every day. We need less cash flow than traditional companies, and throughout our Mesh, less money circulates as we have found a new balance between social- and financial capital to operate.

Having said that, this chapter on the transactional business concepting is one of the shortest of this book. Transaction focus is something from the old days. There is much more going on around the value creation process than just making stuff in the most efficient way. I hope this much is clear. As a result of this, organizations have to learn to interact differently with their stakeholders. Remember: you don't own them, they are no longer 'your clients'. You don't have a market share. You don't own the communities around your organization. Rethink your relationship with your stakeholders, otherwise they will work around you. Knowing this, please read the chapters again in which I describe the Social Economic Entities or pop-up organizations. Please do yourself a favor and think in depth about co-creation in the Mesh, value networks, and stakeholder engagement.

A revolution
in transition:

A wrap up

18
MASTERING THE
GLOBAL TRANSITION:
A WRAP-UP

"INNOVATION KNOWS OPPONENTS, NARROW MINDED
AND NAIVE.
PEOPLE NOT REALIZING WHAT THEY WANT TO KEEP,
WAS ONCE UPON A TIME INNOVATIVE"
                                    – Ronald van den Hoff

It is time for a wrap-up of the story of Society 3.0. We have touched
and discussed many topics in this book, but remember, we are in a
transition period. What is new today is old tomorrow. People may
adore the new opportunities or may detest them. Some people see
the opportunities, while others are still in denial and assume that
sooner or later it will be business as usual again. Still, I don't think
we have a luxury of choice here. We have to change. We have to move.
We have to reinvent ourselves, society, and the way we create value.
The old is gone. Society 3.0 is imminent.

"In recent years, Western capitalism has done nothing more than
shift possessions from the poor to the rich, and it is aided by a complex monetary system that is holding us hostage. This form of modern capitalism does not only grind the faces of the poor, but also our
natural resources. Nothing is replenished or compensated for, and
everything is exploited and bled dry. This is no longer a sustainable
model. What we have come to understand as democracy is a poor
substitute for the essence of the words demos (people) and krateo
(rule). As a people, we have no say anymore. We have an immense
economic problem, but do not expect any solutions from our publishers, car manufacturers, housing contractors, or pharmaceutical

companies. The established companies are not going to solve this problem, and neither will our Western world political or administrative structures" (Van den Hoff, 2011).

The social market economy has ruled in Europe for decades. This system redistributed 65% or more of the national income, via the government, to all social groups. Traditional capitalism is predominantly focused on enriching the stockholders, and, in doing so, it is not only antisocial, but also far from being sustainable. We will not be able to keep the temperature on the planet stable, restore our supply of fossil fuels, and establish international banking control if we hold on to the redistribution policy of the Anglo Saxon (the capitalist macroeconomic model in which levels of regulation and taxes are low, and government provides relatively fewer services) and/or the Rhineland Economic Model (the capitalist macroeconomic counterpart which is founded on publicly-organized social security). All things considered, this way of redistributing wealth is an outdated concept. Why is our entire economic theory based on the scarcity of people, means, and time, resulting in having to make choices? Why do we have to give up one thing if we choose the other? Thinking in terms of limitations gets us deadlocked in an economic and social sense. We have seen many countries of the European Monetary Union build a larger budget deficit than others. In May 2010, the Euro almost collapsed because the collaboration and budget discipline was nowhere in sight. Obviously, an easy-going budget discipline is not desirable in normal times, but in times of crisis, it is deadly. We still reason from the viewpoint of limitations and boundaries, and we are building towering walls around our national interests, so the threat of a Euro collapse is still present.

This crisis will persist, and will be felt for a long time. Many countries within and outside Europe will have to put up with a great deal in the next few years. There is nothing but a lot of hot air, which will convert into financial disillusions. Just think of the enormous rise of the aging population in Europe, and the fragile situation of the welfare state, the pension system, and the connected level of spending of our municipalities, the rising costs of our health care, and the inevitable depletion of our natural reserves. We have yet to experience the effects of these developments. Hot air, after all, is intangible. And intangibility translates into financial depreciation. It is no wonder that there is polarization in our society. It seems as if it's time for a revolution, or innovation. What we really need is an Innovution!

(Note from the author: chapters 19, 19.1, 19.2, 19.3 and 19.4 , or parts from it, appeared in the book *Knowmad Society*, in which I wrote a chapter on the growing importance of knowmads and new value creation in Society 3.0).

18.1
Conclusion: the opportunity, the change

Fortunately, there is moss growing on the rocks, the convolvulus is creeping through the cracks, and the desert plants only need a few raindrops to bloom. A new order is presenting itself. It may still be an undercurrent, but maybe it is the best way to grow. A moorland fire, if you will. I see more and more people who have clearly chosen how they want to go about with themselves, their environment, and other people.

They are the people I call global citizens: people of the new world. These Society 3.0 citizens cannot, and will not, deal with the thinking of the establishment anymore. They want to add value in their work and life in a significantly different way, namely by creating value instead of growth. Most of all, the global citizen wants a sustainable society: the Society 3.0.

I think these global citizens – who are increasing in number daily – are the pillars which support Society 3.0, the society that really operates better!

Global Citizens, People of the World:
- Are open, transparent, and unbiased.
- See differences between people and cultures as a source of creativity.
- Want to learn with and from each other, and grow and work together.
- Are interested in other cultures and reflect on their own culture.
- See himself or herself as part of the world, and not specifically as a citizen of a nation or city.
- Act from transnational values and standards.

Hundreds of millions of people in the world move around without restraints, literally unbounded, across borders all over the planet. Sometimes they do this physically, but more often they do so digitally through the Internet: the World Wide Web. These people of the world are no longer bound to old organizations. They have organized themselves in virtual social networks. They have started to create value in a different way. They do not work according to a formal organizational structure. They guide themselves. They are themselves. Their social connections show great creative vitality and unleash an enormous amount of energy. From within their self-awareness they respect the individuality of anybody. People of the world are not after personal enrichment at the expense of others. They share, and they are prepared to do a lot for someone else, without expecting a monetary reward. I think it is both exciting and fun to be such a person, a knowmad of the world of Society 3.0.

We are ready for a new economic – and, with, that a new social and political model for the new Society 3.0. This economic model is called the Interdependent Economy, a social economic value system based on solidarity, sustainability, and reciprocity. Actually, it is a logical next step in the development of our society. History shows us a certain evolutionary order of ranking in different economic systems that had a limited shelf life. Every system was suitable for the specific circumstances of that period. Economic systems are transient, which is caused by changing environmental factors. So, at a certain point in time, these economic systems no longer connect to reality.

The real power within the Interdependent Economy of the Society 3.0 will shift to the consumer or the citizen. As it happens, these people organize themselves. They want to participate. They want to engage with suppliers. These engaged consumers or 'prosumers' (see esp. Toffler, 1980; Tapscott, 1995) want to co-create in order to develop customized products and services of impeccable quality. Transparency, accountability, and authenticity are the core values. The Internet makes these affairs transparent, making the prosumer more educated than ever about what's for sale at which price or about how your organization interprets its social role and responsibility. The prosumer has a whole range of alternative suppliers, provided by his or her social network, at its disposal. The prosumer wants to choose, can choose, and will choose. Hence, the Organization30 will have to seek an alliance with prosumers to ensure that consumers are participating at an early stage, and, in doing so, determine what is being produced and how. Call this social business, if you like. In this case, it is not about the product itself. More and more products are being packaged as a service. Many people want to have access to something, but do not necessarily have to own it. In their book *What's mine is yours*, the authors Botsman and Rodgers (2010) call this development collaborative consumption. I prefer to call it collaborative prosumption.

18.2
Conclusion: network value creation

Collaborative prosumption in the Sharing Economy means when we create economic value in the Interdependent Economy, we are moving automatically away from the traditional value chain toward value networks (Allee, 2008; Benkler, 2006).

There is no particular fixed connection between network members in a value network; the network is not always visible as a group. Generally, a value network has a few core members – including a potential client – complemented with 'occasional-collaborators' and some other people who contribute incidentally and/or if required (resonance). The core workers often do not know the marginal participants, while the source of knowledge is not always visible either; it is more of a cloud.

Value networks like this – I like to call these Social Economic Entities– almost exhibit Al Qaida-like structures and movements. Teamwork is a great concept, but working in a value network goes beyond the old team philosophy. It already starts with a different understanding of objectives. In traditional team-based organizations, the targeted goals are usually clearly defined, as is the road that reaches it, such as the allocation of tasks and responsibility. A value network is mainly characterized by shared points of view and a path of creation that is mutually discovered in a context of collective responsibility. In the collaboration as a Crowd Company with or within organizations, the community leader facilitates the process as much as possible, but you cannot call this managing. There is an open structure: for new knowledge and contacts, one can make an appeal to the entire outside world. The same goes for the capturing and making of the acquired knowledge by the value network available. The old 'team thinking' is disposed to keeping this within their walls, but value creation is, of course, best served by open connections.

For 'customers' it is therefore not always clear who bears the final responsibility for value creation, while it is not always clear to the network members how revenues will be shared or how copyright issues are dealt with. Within these entities, arrangements can provide insight for all stakeholders, including the final client. Whereas regular organizational teams or departments tend to mark their territories and build ivory towers, value networks have the ability to connect to each other. Individual members of value networks can organize themselves from one spot. In part, this increases the data portability between networks on a daily basis. This is how boundaries continue to dissolve: Value networks are extraordinarily dynamic and flow into each other. That is why it is so difficult for outsiders to understand: It is not always an obviously recognizable team or project group that is on the job. The work is also no longer done between four walls under a single roof, with the name of the organization on the façade of the building. The places where new value creation takes place are hard to identify... they can be found in what I like to call The Mesh, THE network of networks. Mesh networks can be described as a network system of nodes where each node must not only capture and disseminate its own data, but also serve as a relay for other nodes. That is, it must collaborate to propagate the data in the network ('Mesh networking,' n.d.).

Society 3.0 organizations are innovative, resilient network organizations within their own Mesh. They will grow towards so-called real time companies: network organizations with permanently connected stakeholders, where informal and formal relationships flourish. The Internet and other (mobile) technologies are optimally used to create value and are continuously working on facilitating the collaboration process. The network stakeholders are convinced of the fact that thinking in terms of relevancy and reliability can maximize interconnectivity. Organizations that are able to put this into practice can look forward to a successful right to exist, whereby working innovatively and creatively with, and in the interests of stakeholders, a meaningful product or service of actual value is created. This is what I like to call Organization 3.0: a sustainable organizational ecosystem where people can be proud of the stakeholder value that is being created. Obviously, this Organization 3.0 has a 'somewhat different design' than we have been used to. And, in building it, there is a big role for our knowmads.

Stakeholders of the Organization 3.0 want to be increasingly involved with the realization of services or products. This contributes to that 'special' user experience. Every experience from incidental co-creation to a full collaboration enhances the feeling that it is all about you, and, as an additional advantage, delivering a much more superior product or service. So much better, in fact, that the eventual sticker price, whether that be monetary or social capital, has become secondary as a selection criteria for doing business, procurement, and collaboration. In order to give the stakeholders that feeling of authenticity, and in order to co-create with them, the organization has to connect with them and start a dialogue. To gain access to a whole network of stakeholders, the modern decisive organization can do itself a favor by developing a solid social media strategy. The starting point is that all communication moments (so called touch points) are linked directly between a stakeholder and the person within the Organization 3.0 who is directly responsible for that part of the service or product. This requires dynamic and flexible internal processes and a large extent of operational freedom for the people involved.

Through the network of inter-human contact, a permanent connectivity comes into being between the organization, its people, and its other stakeholders. This social exchange of information and knowledge leads to collaboration and eventually results in 'doing business' with each other in value networks.

So, the most important value creation players in the Interdependent Economy, who are no longer large organizations, but increasingly small to medium sized networked enterprises, are complemented by an army of independent professionals – knowmads (Moravec, 2008). We're talking about a new generation of people who consider virtual social communication to be normal and find sharing generative for the common good; and, they find the use of the Internet common practice. The collapse or even the disappearance of large traditional organizational entities will accelerate this process.

The number of knowmads is growing fast. In 2002, in the United States alone, there were already over 33 million free agents, another term for knowmads, about one in four American workers (Pink, 2002).

In The Netherlands, we see the same picture: over one million traditional employees will retire in the coming 5 years, a process that started in 2010. They will be replaced by a staggering number of knowmads. In 2020, we estimate this Dutch group to be larger than 2.5 million people, representing 40% (!) of the total workforce.

The Organization 3.0 is forced to collaborate with knowmads in the process of survival by new value creation since there are not enough regular employees left.

18.3
Conclusion: the organization

If you want to claim your position in the clusters of new value networks as an organization en route to tomorrow in The Mesh, you will have to work with minimal standardization and a new informal corporate culture based on trust and open communication. Only then can you seriously make an appeal to autonomy and entrepreneurship in order to excel internally as well as externally around a dynamic organization. It is not a matter of 'being social on the side'. It requires a complete new vision on organizing. A vision to rethink the order of things. A vision that answers the question of how to challenge someone within the new value networks to feel, think, and operate with his or her entire capacity for the value of co-creation. A vison of how to supply the stakeholders of relevant information at the right time, so that they can operate independently and thus perform. And, a vision for a style of leadership to keep all of this on the right track.

People operate from within their social networks with the same objective, sharing goals. Knowledge is also being shared, resulting in new knowledge and thus creating new value. In Society 3.0, we are going to collaborate in a different way. And, we do that within open and flat organizations: Social network organizations that are in harmony with their environment, and are therefore sustainable. Individuals profile and organize themselves on the Web and connect with peers on platforms such as Facebook and LinkedIn. Their communication tools are called blogs, wikis, Tweets, Skype, or Google+. For their physical meet-ups, they use event software. Obviously, they communicate in various languages, but the Web translates for them. Groups of people can collaborate, grow organically, and fuse. Computers and software become a service. Many services are free, and content and data are abundant. Thus, access becomes more important than possession, and that becomes a leading vector for Society 3.0. The virtual social networks are the glue for this new value creation.

Sustainable value creation needs the connection between the old financial business models and the new social business models. When the Organization 3.0 collaborates with knowmads, the value creation process is organized through the Social Economic Entities. That means that the known social network groups like Facebook and LinkedIn are a mere starting point for this value creation. Only when traditional organizations start to realize this, they can start thinking in terms of value networks instead of traditional value chains.

18.4
Conclusion: Seats2meet.com as The Serendipity Machine.

These new value networks need virtual and physical locations in which to meet and collaborate. The office as we know it is gone. The traditional school, library, and meeting centers will follow.

We need new physical locations, located at new geographical spots, where people can meet, work, exchange information, and more. Organizations today have to rely on powerful, and above all, inspirational encounters around the workspace. This needs to occur not only with colleagues, but with everybody who is connected with the organization, itself. These encounters help us to create a sustainable value network around the organization, and that is what makes the Organization 3.0 future proof.

But, how do we find other relevant people within our organization, and how do we connect?

That is why Seats2meet.com invented 'The Serendipity Machine', a conscious contradiction. On top of any physical location, the transformational expierence is augmented by a branded real-time virtual dashboard, showing the people present, including their knowledge and expertise, and is enriched with social media buzz and local information. In this way, coworking and meeting other people at physical locations can become unexpectedly relevant, useful, and a new way to connect and form new ways of collaboration – serendipitously. Almost like a machine...

Seats2meet.com has a good reputation when it comes to connecting people. We operate a number of physical environments where people really experience, virtually triggered, serendipitous encounters, share knowledge, and form new ways to collaborate. Special transactional features, like capacity control and yield management, are, of course, incorporated in our systems, but we have also made sure that people get really engaged with organizations and each other. We use the techniques of gamification to trigger people to connect to new people. You can challenge each other on the leader boards, which really shows your participation in the network of your organization. Checking in on the Serendipity Machine can be done easily and quickly, simply with one of the existing social accounts.

Our formula offers venues for coworking, meetings, and collaboration between knowmads and traditional organizations on their way to Society 3.0. A super hub and spoke network of physical coworking, office, and meeting locations in which, besides dedicated venues, even individual coworking places in 3rd party office buildings (belonging to companies who believe it is an asset to welcome outsiders within their walls) are opening for participation.

Our meeting rooms and office spaces are booked by regular cooperate clients and knowmads who pay a fee per seat used (and not per room), where pricing is based on a sophisticated yield management system.

For knowmads who just want a place to work, meet, and connect with others, we offer coworking spaces, Wi-Fi, beverages, and even an occasional lunch, free of charge (in old monetary terms). 'Free' means, however 'no free lunch': upon reservation, the bookers/coworkers tell the system, thus the entire S2M network, what topics he/she is working on, where his/her interests lay, and more. This way, the booker commits him/herself to the network: he/she is available for unexpected meetings, and may be called upon by traditional clients in the meeting rooms to share their expertise and knowledge. Payment by knowmads is, therefore, done by means of social capital and this capital is visualized on the Serendipity Machine. As traditional organizations in transition are renting regular meeting rooms still pay per seat in traditional Euros, we have created a monetary system linking traditional and social capital.

On top of every physical Seats2meet.com location, there is more virtuality. When a physical meeting room is booked through the S2M online booking system, a virtual meeting space is generated automatically and linked to the group of people attending that meeting, training session, or conference. This service is offered in close cooperation with the Helsinki-based company, Meetin.gs. These virtual meeting rooms or classrooms are used to interconnect participants up front, to communicate with participants before and after the physical session, and to communicate organizational details around that meeting.

With these software systems, we enable our stakeholders to collaborate in real time within the Social Economic Entities of the world of Society 3.0. In blurring these virtual and physical products, services, and logistic components around our physical locations, we have created an organization in, what Pine & Korn name in their latest book, *Infinite Possibility* (2011) "The 3rd Space: The digital frontier, lying at the intersection of digital technology and offering innovation, beckons companies seeking to create new customer value by mining its rich veins of possibility... But by far the greatest value will come from those innovations that create third spaces that fuse the real and the virtual."

This 3rd Space enables us at Seats2meet.com to offer a unique, tailor-made experience, with a serendipitous educational element, to all our stakeholders. Experiences at Seats2meet.com locations become transformations, in line with Pine & Gilmore's theory of 'Progression of Economic Value' (*The Experience Economy*, 2011), where 'Transformations' are the subsequent drivers of value creation after the traditional experiences.

Research by the Rotterdam School of Management in the Seats-2meet.com Mesh supports that "many people at S2m actively engage in interaction with other coworkers and that the payoffs are manifold. Not only does working at S2M increase their social network, it helps also to develop people's skills and improves their products and services. These personal business outcomes are then followed by concrete business outcomes such as collaborating on a project or targeting prospects together. Even finding new jobs and assignments are not uncommon outcomes."

We, as an organization, get back a lot. The return is immense. Our stakeholders appreciate our products and services tremendously, and help us to position Seats2meet.com on the 'free agents' Mesh. They create an enormous flow of buzz on the web (we used to call that PR in the old days); they feed us with tips, reviews, knowledge, and their time (that used to be called marketing); and actively promote us to other knowmads and to corporate and governmental organizations (that used to be called sales). Whenever they have real business, they book their training and meeting rooms at Seats2meet.com locations without asking for a discount. So, at Seats2meet.com, we no longer have a PR, sales, or marketing and reservation department. How do you think that works out for our operational costs? And the still growing army of fans who do our commercial activities is staggering.

With (potential) coworking operators worldwide, we now share our coworking reservation and yield management system, the property management software, and operational knowledge (partially free) through a special program called Myowns2m.com. In The Netherlands alone, we have grown this way within 3 years, from 1 location to over 70 locations, while internationally, we are on the brink of making the same waves.

We are also selling, using the freemium business model, our software like The Serendipity Machine, the S2m Event Software, our Publishing Tool and our Coworking S2M location software are all available to 3rd parties, so we create nice additional money streams from our Mesh.

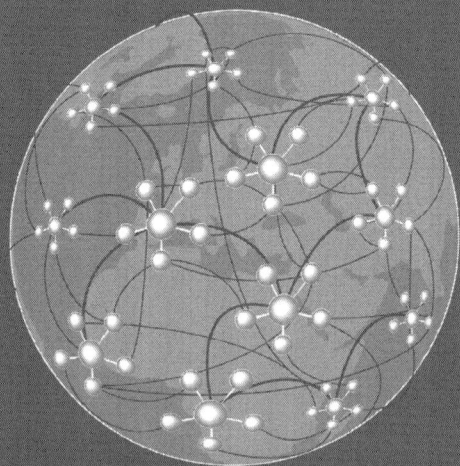

19
THE NOT-VERY-FAMOUS LAST WORDS: IT IS 2025, AND I AM AT 42,000 FEET...

...in the next five years, English on the Internet will no longer be the dominant language. Chinese will take over.
— Eric Schmidt, ex-CEO of Google

This is a quote by the former CEO of Google from 2009. I remember it well because I made a trip to China that year to research my first book. When I flew back to The Netherlands from China this week, I was reminded of this again. My first book was published in 2011 in The Netherlands, and in 2014 internationally. This book *Society 3.0* is still being read a lot in China, as well as in many other countries. That is why I like to travel there, to share our European experiences and thoughts with the Chinese knowmad community, if only to prevent them from leaving Europe behind in their still-speedy development. That would be disastrous for us.

All predictions that were made about China about ten years ago have come true, and some have exceeded the wildest expectations. I have been fascinated by China for years now. I find it an impressive country. In the past decade, its Gross National Product has risen phenomenally and Chinese banks have become the largest banks in the world after the demise of the American banking elite during the financial crisis ten years ago. On the tech front, some U.S. companies are still relatively dominant, although one could state that companies such as Microsoft-Cisco, Apple, and Google-Oracle have become more global companies than US companies. They have to share the global stage with the Sony/Samsung combination, and with relative newcomers, like Xiaomi and Huawei. All these tech corporations have absorbed the traditional broadcasting and publishing industry all right. Amazon.com is still the largest e-commerce shop in the world. E-commerce? That has become a traditional expression. Forgive me.

As a result of the hyperinflation in China, peaking in 2017, the resulting meltdown of the U.S. dollar in 2018, and the subsequent launch of the new U.S. dollar, the loyalty of China towards the U.S. dollar will dwindle. Combined with the global consciousness that the American national debt will never be paid off, China has made a definite choice to say goodbye to this New Dollar and has been setting the pace for years by dealing, in their currency, in bilateral trade with the other BRIC nations: Brazil, Russia and India. The Chinese economy is now the largest in the world. China has amassed quite an arsenal of unique raw materials (metals), which Western companies desperately need to produce, for example, catalytic converters, cruise missiles, windmills, cellphones, and flat screen televisions. Because they own 90% of the global supply of these materials, China is virtually a monopolist in this field. You can safely say that China is run more as a multinational than a nation, with a government acting as the Board of Directors. However, they have become more connectors, serving their 300 mega cities in their leading roles in the new world.

This is how China fundamentally differs from our familiar, stale, Western democratic model. Our view of China as a centrally run, planned economy is not always right. It is not the former East Germany or contemporary Russia. Chinese people respect the centrally-made decisions, and deal with them, in their own way, on a local level. The policy, launched in the beginning of this century, that forced Western companies to share their intellectual proprietary knowledge with local Chinese partners was very successful. That is how the government smartly made use of the Western capitalistic short-term thinking. In these times, the foreign multinationals were so afraid to lose a bit of sales growth in China, that they almost carelessly bargained their intellectual property away. For this, and other reasons, China has slowly moved to the global zenith of technological innovation. So, pretty soon, they will only need us as a market.

It is fascinating to see that video and Internet gaming is still big business in China. The modern Chinese love it. On one hand, because national TV is still very boring, and on the other hand, because, besides in the large cities, there is not much to do. Millions of Chinese play the game Legend in countless Internet cafés, a so-called 'serious' game that has been successful for 20 years. Legend once started out as a virtual world game, comparable to the then Western World of Warcraft, and has since evolved into a game where the virtual world is alternated with assignments in the real world. So, it is an alternate reality where forming teams and working together still forms the basis of the game. One of the companies I visited on my journey supplies a game management system to 170,000 Internet cafés. Cafés? You can hardly call establishments with 1,000 to 5,000 computer terminals cafés. And, computer terminals? These holographic humanity screens, filled to the brim with augmented reality, no longer look like screens we used to call computer terminals. There are screens almost everywhere. Also outside, as glasses, lenses, clothing, windows, and more. Alternate reality gaming, using the physical city itself as the playground, has become extremely popular, especially for tourists who, while playing their game, interconnect and meet local peers in real life. By offering the most spectacular local games, content and interaction, Airbnb, recently bought by Amazon.com, has become the largest tour operator in the world.

The super-Seats2meet.com locations with its Serendipity Machines in the mega cities have become more like urban meeting places of the new urban Society 3.0 citizen. These value creation locations replace old shopping malls, as the concept of a retail branch has almost disappeared under the influence of Web shopping. These hives are places to game, connect, and are always open to facilitate the process of meeting new people. Many urban people work, date, study, and sleep here regularly. Not only in the 300 mega-cities in China; it is a development in the world's largest cities. In that sense, the development of value creation within social networks, with both on-line and in-real-life meetings, has surpassed my wildest expectations.

Almost the largest part of what we used to call the Gross National Product is now realized from these global mega-cities via their value networks. Many have their own currency, although informal trust-based global money transfer systems, like the Indian/African/Arabic Hawala, are still in place, as this has proven to be a reliable and cheap way to move money from one city to another. The sharing economy is still roaring. And why not? The mega-cities, with populations ranging from 2 to 40 million inhabitants per city, form a living Mesh, a real-life cluster of physical people, as a much-desired counterpart of the virtual social networks. This is how society has found a much better balance than a decade ago. These city-dwellers on all continents are connected to each other as real global citizens. They have gained knowledge of each other's culture, and have developed a thinking and behavioral code of conduct that actually transcends the old national borders. The local and national governments gave up on any attempts to influence this a long time ago. Due to a lack of funds, the influences of the old governing institutes in society are waning. We see the new global citizens absorbing that local and national vacuum anyway. They realize that the physical living and working environment is just as important to them as the relationship with their virtual network. But it is because of this global connection that information and knowledge flows freely and local problems are solved globally!

This movement is much more important than we realized in 2011. That year, we were confronted unexpectedly with uprisings in Tunisia, Egypt, Yemen, Jordan, and Syria. In particular, the young generation in these countries were literally fighting for freedom and for a better future. At first, we thought it was a typical phenomenon in the Middle East. We did not yet realize that youth unemployment in these nations was just as high as in Europe: Yemen, 49%; Palestine, 38%; Morocco, 35%; Egypt, 33%; and Tunisia, 26%. It sounds staggering, but youth unemployment rates were then 20-40% across Europe. And in the USA, estimates ranged from 20-50%, "depending on how you count, and when," according to the famous Harvard blogger, Umair Haque, in his blog in 2011. This is how he argued that youth were paying the price for the global economic crisis, which is still the case today. This brings a new perspective on the revolt that arose in the Parisian suburbs at the start of this century. Today, there is regular turmoil in Rome, Berlin, and Rotterdam. We have to keep taking these signals seriously because the 1.0 approach of 2010 and 2011 employed by the former European leaders has, ultimately, not solved the problem. Europe as a state will never be able to offer a solution. I find it important to offer this group of young people more space to determine their own future. They are more than capable of achieving that.

The old forces still try to keep some form of control. The Halal Web is only being kept alive due to high funding form the Arab world, and countries like China, Vietnam, and others in that area could be called police states. However, that could be my subjective opinion, as I am still looking somewhat through my old fashioned 'Western' glasses. The Far East is the central theater of the world these days, the US is also still around due to its almost genetic entrepreneurial powers, Africa is still more like a promise due to its sociopolitical structure, and Europe? It is considered, by the rest of the world, to be an interesting market, where age is the dominant factor, but it is also seen as a huge museum, theater, touristic destination, and global juridical super-mediator/judge, with the International Court of Justice in The Hague as its center.

Technological developments are still moving forward at breakneck speed. Once the 2013 breakthrough by Austrian researchers using regenerative techniques to grow a miniature human brain in their lab still world news, but today almost everything can be reproduced artificially; almost in the same way as nature does it herself.

We are starting to realize that issues like the liquid and semantic Internet are providing us with things such as customized service and information that will help us assert ourselves better in this society, but the downside is giving up our privacy. We are still seeking a new balance as the price of customized information supply and service is transparency.

One of the results is a completely different type of crime, something that we are slowly starting to understand. Whereas the Europeans were ripped off between 2000-2010 through well-designed brochures and television programs selling investments that promised huge returns, like the Golden Sun Resorts in Turkey; or Palminvest selling real estate in Dubai; or Partrust promising to plant trees in Costa Rica, thanks to the Internet, the place where swindlers operate has changed. These hackers are leaving the consumer more and more alone, but they are regularly hacking the evermore poorly secured trading companies and deal in millions of digitally stolen emission rights certificates or hold the trade on the London Stock Exchange, where five quintillion Euros worth of stocks are traded daily, being held hostage like cyber terrorists.

Enough daydreaming. It is time to relax on board this Dragon Spaceflyer, as the newest Chinese built aircraft is called. Will I browse in the virtual library, where even the book *Feeling Logic* by Arnold Cornelis can be found, or will I have an old fashioned drink at the bar with a few entrepreneurs whose mental tag-cloud on the in-flight serendipity machine shows enough things in common to strike up a good conversation? According to my avatar-agent-butler, I have 45 minutes before I have to virtually attend the annual meeting of the Society 3.0 Foundation. There are some great actions in the pipeline, and a discussion about the fact of how we are dealing with Society 4.0, which, according to my colleague trendwatchers of the Dutch Trendrede Movement, is approaching a lot faster than I predicted in 2014. Georgina, as I have named my virtual butler, has already booked and tested my video channel, linking my plane flying over Mongolia with The Netherlands. An amazing world isn't it?

Life is still fun and meaningful: Cada Dia Es una Fiesta!

COLOPHON:

First edition in English
Published by Society 3.0 Foundation

Text:
Ronald van den Hoff / @rvandenhoff

Graphic design:
A10design
www.a10design.nl

Publishing advice and production:
Van Lindonk & De Bres
www.vldb.nl

ISBN
9781496007230

www.society30.com

Utrecht 2014

5801761R00169

Printed in Great Britain
by Amazon.co.uk, Ltd.,
Marston Gate.